CLEANSING THE COLONY

CLEANSING
THE
COLONY

TRANSPORTING CONVICTS
FROM
NEW ZEALAND
TO VAN DIEMEN'S LAND

Kristyn Harman

OTAGO

*For Rosie and for Nick, my wonderful
travel companions in life, including to and fro
across the Tasman, and through time in
archives and libraries.*

Published by Otago University Press
Level 1, 398 Cumberland Street
Dunedin, New Zealand
university.press@otago.ac.nz
www.otago.ac.nz/press

First published 2017
Copyright © Kristyn Harman
The moral rights of the author have been asserted.

ISBN 978-1-98-853106-9

Editor: Gillian Tewsley
Maps: Allan J. Kynaston
Indexer: Diane Lowther

Cover: Port Arthur penal station, Tasmania, showing convict labourers in 1843.
Coloured lithograph signed 'R.N.N' (or 'K.N.N'), State Library of New South Wales, SV6B/Pr Arth/5

Printed in China by Asia Pacific Offset.

Contents

ACKNOWLEDGEMENTS

Researching and writing *Cleansing the Colony* has been a wonderful journey of discovery. Historical inquiry is often a solitary pursuit, yet inspiration and assistance flow from many sources along the way. In my formative years my parents fostered my love of learning, and Jim Graydon (my history teacher at Wairarapa College) inspired my fascination for history. At the outset of this project I had the good fortune to be a visiting scholar with the Centre for Research on Colonial Culture at the University of Otago. My work benefited at various stages from discussions with scholars including Tony Ballantyne, Angela Wanhalla, Lachy Paterson, Michael Stevens and Paerau Warbrick. In Wellington, I enjoyed stimulating conversations with Kate Hunter and David Haines. Auckland-based Hazel Petrie has always been a generous companion.

Perhaps unsurprisingly in view of its convict past, Tasmania is a veritable hive of activity when it comes to researching convicts. Over the years, I have benefited from scholarly exchanges with Hamish Maxwell-Stewart and those who attend his 'convict club' gatherings. Colette McAlpine has been wonderfully forthcoming whenever I've quizzed her about the particularities of female convicts' experiences. In 2016 we were fortunate to host in Hobart convict and legal history researchers from Australia and beyond as part of the *Digital Panopticon* conference. As always at such events there were engaging conversations with numerous people – especially Clare Anderson, Lisa Ford, Charlotte Macdonald, Babette Smith and Martin Gibbs; and I would also like to mention Mark Finnane and his *Prosecution Project* team, including Andy Kaladelfos.

Aspects of my research have been presented at events hosted by the Tasmanian Historical Research Association and the Professional Historians Association (Tasmania) Inc. I thank the organisers of these events and those who attended, particularly Fleur Kelleher and Merle Hunt, who travelled from interstate to attend one of my presentations and with whom I have had some delightful discussions. One of these events also put me in touch with another Kiwi living in Australia, Pauline Weeks, and we have since had some interesting discussions in Camden, Hobart and Sydney.

Research and teaching are often inextricably intertwined. Over the past few years I have communicated with several thousand students online as they have explored convict life and their own convict ancestry. I would like to thank them for the insights shared as part of our learning journey. My thanks go especially to the wonderful tutors who have assisted me in this work – Imogen Wegman, Lydia Nicholson, Melinda Standish, Robyn Greaves, Rebecca Read, Colette McAlpine and Evan Pitt.

Historical research would not be nearly as rewarding without the friendly and professional assistance of archivists and librarians; I especially thank those at Archives New Zealand, Hocken Collections, State Archives & Records New South Wales, and the Tasmanian Archive & Heritage Office. Digital repositories such as New Zealand Papers Past and its Australian equivalent, Trove, are worth their weight in gold. Other digital resources that I'd like to acknowledge include the New Zealand's Lost Cases project housed at the Victoria University of Wellington, and the extensive London-based Old Bailey online database. Some documents are particularly difficult to locate; the University of Tasmania's intrepid document delivery staff are superb at finding and requisitioning source material. Thank you.

Obviously a manuscript requires a publisher to oversee its production as a book and to send the finished product out into the wider world. I have been very fortunate to work with Otago University Press and am grateful to publisher Rachel Scott, production manager Fiona Moffat and marketing and publicity coordinator Victor Billot. Editor Gillian Tewsley has been superb to work with throughout the transition from draft manuscript to finished book.

A special vote of thanks is reserved for those who continually encouraged me throughout the writing process, particularly Julie Henderson and Nick Brodie. Nick also generously read an earlier draft of my work, for which I'm tremendously grateful. Finally, my daughter Rosie has patiently coexisted with my historic obsessions over the years. I appreciate her forbearance, and her gentle reminders to return to life in the twenty-first century from time to time.

An extraordinary
discovery

Spectacular archival discoveries are something that happen perhaps just a few times in a historian's career. For me, one such moment dates to a midwinter's day in Wellington in 2013. Sitting in the reading room at Archives New Zealand waiting for my next order of documents, I filled in time by doing a few tangential online searches. Having relocated from New Zealand to Tasmania, I tapped into the archive's search engine 'Van Diemen's Land', the name by which this island at the bottom of Australia was known until the middle of the nineteenth century. Imagine my astonishment when one of the results referred to a register of indents for convicts transported from New Zealand to Van Diemen's Land!

From my earlier research I knew that a few Māori warriors were transported to Van Diemen's Land but, like most New Zealanders, I had no idea that this was a more widespread phenomenon.[1] We grew up with stories about men, women and children being transported to the Australian penal colonies from Britain, but not from New Zealand.

Just to be sure, I placed an order to see the register of indents. I am very familiar with this type of documentation. I have spent many, many hours poring over convict indents and related records held in the archives at Hobart in Tasmania. This remarkable set of convict records is so special that in 2007 it was inscribed on the *Memory of the World* international register endorsed by the United Nations Educational, Scientific and Cultural Organization, UNESCO. Its very preciousness meant that until recently the records could be viewed only on rolls of microfilm, although most have now been digitised. It was a particular pleasure when, in Wellington, the register itself was delivered to me in the reading room.

The large, slightly battered and rather weighty light-brown leather-bound volume opened to reveal a skilfully marbled grey, blue and white page on which a bookplate announced the register as the property of the 'Archives, Dominion of New Zealand'. Its full description reads 'Register of indents for convicts transported to Van Diemen's Land, 25 Nov 1847–22 Feb 1853'. Page after page of this register revealed neatly penned letters from Lieutenant-Governor Edward John Eyre to his Vandemonian counterpart with accompanying lists detailing each convict's name, age, marital status, trade or profession, offence, where and when tried, sentence, detailed physical description and other pertinent remarks. These indents were the legal documents transferring the custody and, importantly, the labour of prisoners convicted in New Zealand to the penal colony of Van Diemen's Land where their punishment to transportation was to be carried out.

As comprehensive as this register is, it tells only part of the story. Further research revealed that the transportation of prisoners from New Zealand did not commence in 1847, the year in which the register began to be kept: it dated back to an earlier period. In fact, the first person in the colony to be sentenced to transportation was hauled before a judge in 1841, the year after the Treaty of Waitangi was signed between the British and more than 500 Māori, and just months after New Zealand ceased to be administered from New South Wales.[2] After a necessary legal nicety and a few shenanigans that first convict was eventually shipped to Van Diemen's Land in 1843 along with 12 other prisoners who had, by then, likewise been sentenced to transportation.

As the register indicates, convicts were transported right up until Van Diemen's Land stopped receiving them in 1853. Even then, judges continued to impose sentences to transportation on the colonially convicted. Throughout the decade in which the colony was shipping its convicts across the Tasman Sea, at least 110 people underwent this journey into captivity.[3] This ethnically diverse cohort included 51 currently serving or discharged British soldiers, six Māori warriors, one Sandwich Islander

(Hawaiian) and a man from Cartagena, Spain, who was brought up in North America and was described as having copper-coloured skin, black woolly hair and whiskers, a broad visage and hazel eyes.[4] The rest – including one female – were from among the civilian population, including some who were emancipated convicts who fled the Australian penal colonies to seek refuge, anonymity and a fresh start in New Zealand but instead ended up being transported again. It is remarkable that the stories of these people have remained largely untold.

Very few writers have published any material about convicts being transported from New Zealand to Van Diemen's Land. The earliest account was an occasional paper in criminology by Robert Burnett. His 66-page report, published in 1978, comprised four chapters organised along chronological lines, dealing with cases heard before the general and quarter sessions, the county court and the Supreme Court, and a final chapter that summarised what transpired in New Zealand after Van Diemen's Land stopped receiving convicts.[5] This was followed by the publication in 1997 of a 13-page conference paper delivered by Verna Mossong. Building on Burnett's work, Mossong provided some details about what happened after several of the convicts transported from New Zealand arrived in Van Diemen's Land. She organised her case studies into five categories: male civilians with prior records, British soldiers, male civilians with previously unblemished records, Māori, and one woman.[6] The third and final author to have written on this topic is Heidi Huglin, whose five-page journal article, published in 2009, included a range of interesting, brief case studies, categorised in a similar way to Mossong's paper and likewise dealing with the convicts in both New Zealand and Van Diemen's Land. From records in New Zealand, including court cases, correspondence and newspaper reports, Huglin identified at least 125 people as having been sentenced to transportation.[7]

Ultimately, not all of the sentences to transportation handed down in New Zealand were carried into effect. In some instances, people successfully petitioned to have their sentences commuted to gaol time instead. In other cases, after transportation to Van Diemen's Land ceased, there was nowhere convenient to which prisoners so sentenced could be transported. And sometimes prisoners simply subverted the system. For example, Thomas Larkins was sentenced by Justice Chapman on 2 December 1848 to transportation for seven years for 'stealing on the 24th November, two sheets, a towel, a table cloth, three aprons, and other articles of wearing apparel, from the house of Charles Lewer, on the Porirua road'. However, as he was being returned to prison, Larkins escaped from police custody and was never seen again.[8]

Cleansing the Colony builds on Burnett, Mossong and Huglin's earlier work with extensive research in archives in New Zealand, Tasmania and New South Wales, and provides a broader and more detailed picture of convict transportation from New Zealand. As the following chapters reveal, transportation was a widespread global practice, spanning at least half a millennium, and in this big story New Zealand played a unique role. Rather than transportation being imposed as a punishment by British mandate or external forces, there was an impetus from within New Zealand to cleanse and purify these islands. *Cleansing the Colony* reveals the stories of the convicts exiled from New Zealand to Van Diemen's Land and the historical context to advance our understanding of the fraught processes and practicalities of colony formation and nation building – including crucial revelations about the development of a distinctively New Zealand legal system.

Opening with an exploration of the early life of William Phelps Pickering, the first person sentenced to transportation from New Zealand to Van Diemen's Land, *Cleansing the Colony* situates New Zealand within a broader colonial context, while also revealing the aspirations, social mobility (both upwards and downwards) and lived experiences of young Britons who travelled out to the Australasian colonies. As Pickering's life unfolds over several chapters, his encounters serve to reveal the backgrounds and crimes of the men who joined him as part of the first shipment of convicts between the colonies. The official scrutiny and processes to which they were subjected in Van Diemen's Land, the regulated and segregated lives they lived as convicts, and the aftermath of their punishments emphasise the interconnectedness of empire.

Later chapters explore other elements of New Zealand's convict experience, including its controversial role as a destination for former Parkhurst boys from a juvenile prison on the Isle of Wight. Some of these young men were later transported to Van Diemen's Land, connecting the phenomenon of transportation yet more broadly to global flows of prisoners by illustrating the circuitous journeys they undertook into captivity in Britain's southernmost penal colony. Another element of New Zealand's colonial 'cleansing' concerns the transportation of British soldiers across the Tasman: this further demonstrates the connectedness of imperialism and colonialism. The conviction of Māori warriors during a time of war and their experience as prisoners also illustrates the complexities of frontier New Zealand. The trial and transportation of the only woman sent from New Zealand to serve time in Van Diemen's Land reveals the gendering of colonial crime and punishment, and highlights how ambiguities can arise from considering criminal cases reconstructed from incomplete records.

By engaging with New Zealand's role in transporting convicts to Van Diemen's Land, *Cleansing the Colony* situates New Zealand's history within global histories of race; class; gender; law; punishment; social, geographic and economic mobility; colonial economies and forced labour – all through the largely forgotten story of New Zealand's own brand of convictism.

CHAPTER 1

Gentlemen
and gaol houses

C olonialism profoundly shaped New Zealand and Van Diemen's Land in the nineteenth century. People from all over the globe, particularly from England, Ireland and Scotland, travelled around the world to start new lives in the antipodes. Some travelled by choice, others were forced through circumstance to do so. These new arrivals and their ideas and trade goods had an enormous effect on the lives and, over time, the world views and wellbeing of the original inhabitants of the lands to which they were transplanted. Complex conflicts and collaborations were played out against a backdrop of rapidly changing socioeconomic and cultural environments. Natural landscapes changed irrevocably as convict, working-class and some indigenous labour, funded by government money, private capital and trade, transformed pathways into highways and huts into increasingly elaborate houses. Towns and, later, cities emerged where small villages once stood. New forms of government were imposed and evolved. Nascent colonial societies cohered around principles derived mainly from English laws.

These changes were observed by young men such as William Phelps Pickering, who experienced at first hand the global reach of Britain's criminal justice system. Originally from Herefordshire, Pickering was just 20 years old when he boarded the *Majestic* at Liverpool on 19 March 1837. People and goods flowed through the busy Lancashire port which, since 1830, had been connected by rail to the commercial hub of Manchester. Steam trains hauled raw materials from the port to the inland mills, returning with finished products to be loaded onto vessels like the *Majestic* and shipped to far-flung ports such as Hobart in Van Diemen's Land. Pickering, too, was bound for the Australian colonies. He was the only son in a family blessed with five daughters, but this had not hindered his keen spirit of adventure. He left his homeland a free man, drawn by the opportunities that were said to abound in the colonies.[1] Many of his compatriots – around 162,000 men, women and children – were shipped under sentence of transportation to New South Wales, Van Diemen's Land and later Western Australia as these places were gazetted by the British as penal sites.

Under Captain Martin, the 340-ton *Majestic* was at sea for close on four months before docking in Hobart on 12 July to discharge its general cargo and passengers.[2] Among Pickering's sailing companions were nine men who were also sailing unaccompanied. In addition there were two married couples, a young single woman, and a married woman and her child.[3] The gender imbalance in the party mirrored the colonial population they had come to join: male colonists substantially outnumbered their female counterparts in the late 1830s. This imbalance contributed to conflict across Australia's colonial frontiers.

As colonists gradually spread out across the Australian continent, taking more than a century and a half to move from the southeastern corner to the far north, frontier society was characterised by the expropriation of Aboriginal land, armed conflict with Aboriginal peoples and the acquisition by the colonists of Aboriginal women. Some colonial men and Aboriginal women formed lasting relationships, but many encounters were brief and some were forced. Others, as Henry Reynolds has explained, were arranged by Aboriginal men who hoped to bind the newcomers into socioeconomic relationships of reciprocity. Reynolds has observed how 'the courage of the men who went forward to meet the Europeans ... was probably surpassed by that of the young women who were frequently dispatched by their male relatives to appease the sexual appetites of the strange and threatening white men.'[4] But the colonists failed to appreciate the complexities of Aboriginal kinship systems, and they frequently did not meet the obligations imposed on them as a result of these sexual encounters. Their failure to act in the ways anticipated by their Aboriginal hosts escalated tensions and contributed to hostilities.

In Van Diemen's Land many Aboriginal women and girls from the north and east coasts of the island were abducted by sealers plying their trade in Bass Strait (the body of water that lies between Tasmania and mainland Australia) and beyond. Nicholas Clements estimated that 'several hundred' women met such a fate between 1810 and 1832, becoming incorporated into what he called 'a brutal system of female slavery'.[5] Penelope Edmonds observed how 'a strong thread of undeniable brutality and violence ... run[s] through these [sealing] histories'; she noted how slavery rhetoric characterised the sealing trade in Bass Strait since at least 1815, when travellers to the area used loaded words such as 'slaves' and 'Negroes' to refer to Aboriginal women taken from their homes by the sealers.[6] The use of such terminology to discuss the Tasmanian past has become more contentious in the twenty-first century, yet rightly or wrongly it has persisted for more than two centuries as historians continue to debate the role and extent of brutality and coercion in relationships between sealers and Tasmanian Aboriginal women.

During the 1820s, in parallel with an influx of colonists and cloven-hoofed animals, conflict between the newcomers and Aboriginal inhabitants of the island escalated. By the middle of that decade, armed conflict – known for well over a century as the Black War, but now increasingly referred to as the Vandemonian War – broke out in earnest. As Nick Brodie demonstrates, Colonel George Arthur, who as both lieutenant governor and colonel commanding held the top civil and military posts in the colony, orchestrated a series of bloody military campaigns to remove Aboriginal people from what were designated 'settled districts'. British soldiers, armed field police and other paramilitary parties comprised of settlers, convicts and Aboriginal auxiliaries scoured the countryside, deliberately using terror as a war strategy.[7] Aboriginal people were chased off, captured and killed, and a few hundred survivors were sent into exile. This war resulted in the deaths of more than 200 colonists and countless numbers of Aboriginal people; the original population of around 4000–6000 Aboriginal people was reduced to just a few hundred by the early 1830s. In comparing this conflict with New Zealand, Clements has suggested that the Tasmanian Aboriginal guerrilla fighters were sufficiently effective for these warriors to be seen as having been 'in a similar league to the Māori'.[8] His claim was based on the ratio of colonial deaths to Aboriginal and was designed to challenge persisting stereotypes of Aboriginal people in the colonial period as having been passive, offering little resistance to those who expropriated their land. Clements's referencing Māori as a comparative population is also interesting in the way that this challenges yet also reinforces colonial stereotyping. Tasmanian colonists regularly referred to Māori as being more warrior-like and altogether superior to the local Aboriginal population. For example, colonial newspapers used phrases such as 'extremely good tempered and industrious race' and 'in war they are terrific' when discussing Māori, whereas when they referred to Tasmanian Aboriginal people they often used derogatory language, describing them as a 'strange band' with a 'grotesque appearance'.[9] Clements's assertion that Tasmanian Aboriginal warriors were as successful as Māori in fighting against British colonists is therefore a particularly useful comparison to draw on in aiming to better understand and rethink colonial discourse about Tasmanian Aboriginal people. On the other hand, such uncritical use of this comparison perpetuates the problematic notion of Māori as 'natural born fighters' – a characterisation that has 'continued for more than two centuries'.[10]

When Pickering arrived in Hobart in the winter of 1837 it is unlikely that he saw many Aboriginal people. Less than three years earlier, in August 1834, the final 'friendly mission' among Tasmanian Aboriginal people had been completed by the oddly dressed government-contracted Conciliator of Aborigines George Augustus Robinson and his entourage of settlers, convict servants and Aboriginal emissaries. Drawing inspiration from the armed capture parties of soldiers, convicts, colonists and Aboriginal guides who pursued Aboriginal peoples across the island, Robinson and his companions spent months at a time roaming across Van Diemen's Land between 1830 and 1834. Their mission was to contact and capture Tasmanian Aboriginal survivors during and following the Vandemonian War. Once found, these few hundred people were shipped to Flinders Island in Bass Strait.[11] Most died there, but a few dozen survivors were repatriated to the main island of Tasmania in 1847 to a disused convict station at Oyster Cove, south of Hobart. At the year's end, most of the very few remaining children were sent to the Orphan School where several died. Those Aboriginal women abducted in earlier decades by sealers had in the meantime borne children who still lived on islands in Bass Strait. With a couple of notable exceptions – Dalrymple Briggs, who avoided being sent to Flinders Island, and Fanny Cochrane Smith, who was born there and survived incarceration at Oyster Cove – it is the Bass Strait islanders who are the forebears of Tasmania's present-day Aboriginal population; despite colonial claims and some residual belief to the contrary, they did not suffer extinction in the nineteenth century.[12] Sending Tasmanian Aboriginal people into exile effectively ended the Vandemonian War and paved the way for enterprising young men like Pickering who arrived free in the colony, and for those convicts who had served out their sentences but who were prohibited by law and/or unable to meet the costs of returning home, to exploit the resources and opportunities available to them. As he walked the streets of the island's capital, Pickering could not have failed to notice the redcoats who continued to maintain security, and the convicts whose labour contributed enormously to the construction and expansion of the colony.

At the time of Pickering's arrival, Van Diemen's Land utilised convict labour through a system of assignment that had been introduced into the colony in 1804 when it was still part of New South Wales.[13] Those who arrived in the colony under sentence were questioned closely about their skills and background then sent to a penal station or road gang, or assigned to a colonial family for whom they laboured as a servant in exchange for their keep. The prisoners were kept under close surveillance and many received brutal punishment for transgressions; men were flogged, for example, and women sent into solitary confinement and sometimes restricted to a diet of bread and water. Some of the male convicts wore the parti-coloured suits later made famous by filmmakers, but not all were dressed so distinctively. Nevertheless, groups of men labouring on the streets within view of their overseers and sometimes shackled in leg irons, or shabbily dressed servants accompanying their more finely attired master or mistress, were visible reminders of the socioeconomic divide evident in the colony.

The assignment system might on the surface appear to have been a useful and expedient means of matching convict labourers with the labour market's requirements, but ultimately it was viewed as 'ineffective either for reform or deterrence, and having about it altogether too much of the whiff of slavery'.[14] It was a system open to abuse. For example, punishment rates for convicts who were sent to rural locations varied in line with the seasonal demand for their labour. Busy farmers did not want to send their convict servants to the magistrate's bench to be sentenced to further punishments when they were needed in the fields. Other convicts were sometimes assigned to their free spouse who had followed them out to the colony, often with children in tow. Word had filtered back to England about excesses of largesse and, at the other end of the spectrum, punishment. At the same time, the crime rate in England was rising. Evidently transportation in its current form was not a sufficient deterrent.

As the *Majestic* sailed to Hobart, a select committee was sitting in London, chaired by Sir William Molesworth, to inquire into transportation. Members heard how 'in Van Diemen's Land, between 1833 and 1836, nearly three-quarters of the prisoners were brought before the courts each year' charged with additional offences such as disobedience, negligence, or drunk and disorderly conduct. A fifth of those who had become free by servitude were appearing before the Supreme Court or at the quarter sessions accused of serious offences. This and similar scenarios in New South Wales sparked moral outrage in London, and led to the establishment of what was known as the 'Molesworth committee'.[15] Out of this crucible a new policy emerged, posited by the newly appointed lieutenant governor of Van Diemen's Land, Sir John Franklin.[16]

Pickering seems not to have been particularly interested in labouring for others in the colonies. He was much more intent on becoming a self-made man. Although he maintained links with Hobart, his port of disembarkation, he became a businessman of sorts, a broker who travelled between the Australian colonies wheeling and dealing and working as a middleman. In this he was not altogether dissimilar to Captain Martin of the *Majestic*, with whom he had sailed out from England. The seaman plied his trade within the Australian colonies as well as between the centre of the British Empire and its colonial peripheries: by November 1837, four months after its arrival from Liverpool, the *Majestic* was back in Hobart with a cargo of 1500 sheep from Newcastle in New South Wales.[17]

Rather than Newcastle or Sydney, it was the newly established settlement at Melbourne that attracted Pickering's attention. In November 1837 he sailed across Bass Strait to the Port Phillip District of New South Wales (now the state of Victoria). Just two years earlier, in 1835, the region was 'opened up' for settlement without government sanction by a trickle of enterprising colonists from Van Diemen's Land that soon became a veritable flood. The influx of squatters in search of fresh pastures was so extraordinary that James Boyce has described the founding of Melbourne as opening 'the floodgates ... to the continent's vast pastures'.[18]

Pickering presumably arrived in Melbourne independently from his future business partner Frederick Pittman. Pittman had already tried his luck at the Swan River Colony (now part of Western Australia), but left there in 1834 to pursue other opportunities in the Port Phillip District.[19] By June 1838 Pickering and Pittman dissolved their Melbourne enterprise 'by mutual consent'.[20] Pickering soon seized a new business opportunity: by 20 July 1838 he was the agent for the *Hobart Town Courier* at Port Phillip (Melbourne).[21] At the time, Sydney (established in 1788) and Hobart (dating back to 1804) were still the two largest settlements in the Australian colonies; and news from these colonial centres was of interest to those newly arrived in Melbourne and its outskirts. Pickering's stay in Melbourne was relatively short-lived, however. By 1839 he was trying to re-establish himself in Launceston, the main town in the north of Van Diemen's Land. But good fortune continued to elude him. He was working as a commission agent but was unable to settle an account with William Couzens, a 'chemist, tea merchant and grocer' in St Johns Street; Pickering later blamed Couzens for his insolvency.[22] He was confined for debt in Her Majesty's gaol in Launceston.[23]

Built in 1827 in Patterson Street, Launceston gaol was a group of bleak buildings surrounded by high stone walls that housed adult prisoners as well as children as young as eight or nine.[24] The prisoners' quarters were cramped: there were complaints registered in 1830 that as many as 70 prisoners were confined within two rooms at the gaol, while 'the Gaoler has no less than four rooms, besides a kitchen, a fowl-house, a stable, a cow-shed, and piggery'; in other words, the gaoler had more space for himself than that provided for all of the debtors and criminals together. Debtors such as Pickering were confined to a third room that measured 16ft by 14ft with 12ft-high walls – and sometimes found themselves with felons as cellmates. Because of a lack of suitably segregated accommodation, the few women who were confined to the gaol were often housed in the cells for the condemned to keep them separate from the male prisoners. The local newspaper conjectured that a 'miserable and parsimonious spirit' had kept the building confined to one storey; but the newspaper's call for a new gaol would not gain traction until 90 years after the inadequate building's construction.[25] Launceston gaol was not shut down until 1917.

Throughout the 1830s there was mounting pressure for something to be done about the plight of debtors confined to Launceston gaol. In 1834 a group of debtors wrote to the lieutenant-governor asking that their 'dreadful distress' be relieved. The debtors pointed out how they had contravened the civil rather than the criminal code, and begged for some chance of being liberated. Debtors who were confined to the gaol at Hobart Town in the south of the island could apply to the court for arrangements to be made to satisfy their creditors, but those in the north had no means of redress other than to await the next sitting of the Supreme Court in Launceston. In the meantime they remained behind bars, worrying about what would become of their wives and 'orphaned families' during their enforced absence. *The Colonist* printed a copy of the debtors' letter to the lieutenant-governor, and the editor commented: 'this is manfully taking the bull by the horns and if this does not move His Excellency nothing will'.[26]

Distressed debtors continued to lobby for relief. In 1835 a debtor confined to Launceston gaol wrote, 'I must have starved, was it not for the kindness of my fellow inmates, giving me a small portion of victuals'. The prisoner had waited five days for someone to take their affidavit, and another 12 days had passed since it was lodged. The *Cornwall Chronicle* published the debtor's account of their plight. The editor was 'convinced that Mr Mulgrave [the chief police magistrate] would not wantonly permit a fellow-creature to starve'; he supposed that the prisoner's state of affairs must surely have slipped from Mulgrave's memory.[27]

The following year the *Launceston Advertiser* published a letter from another debtor that drew attention to the 'extreme hardship to which the Debtors in Launceston are subjected in consequence of the Government refusing to appoint a Commissioner to dispose of cases of insolvency on this side of the Island'. Legislation providing for such an appointment was passed on 1 November 1835, yet no one had been appointed to the position. This was, the letter writer alleged, because of 'a squabble between the Judge and the Governor, each claiming the right of patronage'. In the interim, debtors still had to wait for the arrival of the Supreme Court on its circuit, or go to the considerable expense of travelling to Hobart to have their matter heard, using funds, the debtor argued, that ought to be going to their creditors. Meanwhile their families were left to starve.[28]

As a result of the debtors' political lobbying and the Launceston newspaper editors' willingness to print their petitions, Mulgrave was appointed as the northern commissioner to deal with cases of insolvency. Pickering's incarceration was therefore not as bad as it could have been: he was able to present his petition to Mulgrave in March 1839, shortly after he was taken into custody.[29] Over the months that followed, creditors' meetings were called, adjourned several times then reconvened. Pickering's case was heard two months later, in May 1839, at the courthouse in Launceston by William Gardner Sams Esq. Sams, like Mulgrave, was a commissioner appointed under 'An Act for the Further Amendment of the Law of Debtor and Creditor'. Another hearing was scheduled for 12 June to consider Pickering's application for an order of discharge, and this in turn was rescheduled to be heard on 11 September 1839.[30] Pickering later claimed that a 'want of means' prevented him from standing trial. He was eventually released after spending more than six months in Launceston gaol.

In September 1839 Pickering made his way south to Hobart where he spent a few weeks, during which he 'formed an arrangement' with Ken Alexander to go to Launceston as a clerk. The job fell through, so after remaining in Launceston for six weeks he sailed to Melbourne in November 1839. Over the coming months he took part in four trading voyages between the Port Phillip district and Hobart. He then sailed on the *Ferguson* from Melbourne to Sydney where, on 18 March 1841, he boarded the 150-ton barque *Earl of Lonsdale* and sailed with Captain Piele to the Bay of Islands in the far north of New Zealand. Pickering was one of 29 passengers, including two families, a doctor, a single woman and 18 other unaccompanied men. The barque also carried a cargo of 'sundries'.[31]

By the time Pickering arrived in the Bay of Islands, Christian missionaries had lived there among Māori for a generation already. Samuel Marsden, the Sydney-based 'flogging parson', had accompanied the first four Church Missionary Society families to Rangihoua in 1814. The newcomers were housed in a large raupō (*Typha orientalis* or bulrush) structure built by the locals. Each family had a separate room, but the structure had none of the fixtures and fittings they would have been used to – such as floorboards, windows and chimneys.[32] As Tony Ballantyne demonstrated, although the missionaries were heavily dependent on Māori tolerance, patronage, protection and hospitality for their very lives and livelihoods throughout the early years of their ministry in New Zealand, gradually the balance of power shifted as more Europeans arrived. At the same time, the missionary presence among Māori brought about spiritual, behavioural and linguistic shifts – both overt and more subtle – among the local population.[33]

Missionaries were not the only Europeans who made homes for themselves in New Zealand during the early decades of the nineteenth century. Others such as timber fellers, convicts who had escaped from the Australian penal colonies, sealers and whalers and traders established themselves temporarily or in some cases permanently in New Zealand. Like the first missionaries, many of these newcomers were dependent on Māori for food, shelter and permission to live within or near their communities. Without such patronage they would not have survived. The newcomers had something to offer in return, though: the musket. This was a trade item that Māori were increasingly interested in acquiring.

The introduction of muskets into New Zealand together with new types of food such as the potato provided the means through which Māori could undertake lengthier and more effective expeditions against their enemies. The ensuing musket wars were fought over several decades across most of New Zealand; Ron Crosby has dated the wars from 1806 to 1845, but most of the action was over by the early 1830s.[34] As well as muskets, Māori also made extensive use of artillery including cannon, carronades and swivel guns: Trevor Bentley has identified at least 165 pieces that were in use. Around 120 rangatira (chiefs) possessed artillery during the musket wars; they acquired the pieces through trade, plunder and from shipwrecks.[35] These inter-iwi wars had a devastating impact on Māori population numbers: tens of thousands died as a result of around 3000 clashes. Thousands more were displaced, effectively redrawing tribal boundaries across the land in the decades leading up to the signing of the Treaty of Waitangi, the formal instrument considered to be the founding document of the modern nation.[36]

As the debtors in Launceston gaol lobbied for more humane treatment, top-ranked officials in the Australian colonies were musing over what action ought to be taken to curtail the more negative impacts of the growing

European population across the Tasman. In May 1833 the Scotsman James Busby arrived in the Bay of Islands from New South Wales to take up the newly created position of British Resident. Governor Richard Bourke instructed Busby to protect the European population, to prevent them from attacking Māori and to apprehend escaped convicts who sought refuge there. He did not, however, provide Busby with any means by which he might enforce his authority; he was left to rely on his skills as a mediator, which were apparently somewhat lacking. Busby is remembered for having convened a meeting of Māori leaders at Waitangi on 20 March 1834 at which a national flag was chosen; and for encouraging 52 chiefs to sign a Declaration of the Independence of New Zealand in 1835 – in part to forestall the self-styled 'Baron' Charles de Thierry from establishing an independent state in Hokianga. The signatories were seeking protection from the British crown from possible incursions by other European powers; and they were also aiming to manage their relationship with the British.

Life did not run smoothly for Busby: ongoing local conflicts made his position untenable, or so he claimed. Captain William Hobson, an Irishman, was sent to New Zealand in 1837 to assess and report on the situation. Two years later, in 1839, Hobson accepted an appointment to negotiate a treaty with Māori. He went on to become the colony's first lieutenant-governor.[37]

When Pickering stepped ashore in New Zealand for the first time, a little over a year had passed since Hobson had stood in the Church Missionary Society church at Kororāreka (Russell) and publicly read his commission as lieutenant-governor and gathered Māori signatures on the Treaty of Waitangi. When these formalities were over, Hobson concluded a transaction with Ngāti Whātua to obtain 3000 acres of land. Hobson named the site 'Auckland' after his patron Lord Auckland, the viceroy of India, and declared the nascent settlement the capital of the new colony.

For the first few weeks after Pickering arrived in New Zealand, though, the colony was still formally part of New South Wales. It did not become a separate colony in its own right until 3 May 1841, the date on which Hobson swore his oath as governor and commander in chief. Hobson was joined in Auckland soon afterwards by the beginnings of New Zealand's legal fraternity: William Swainson, who became attorney-general from October 1841; and William Martin, the colony's first supreme court judge, who took up his position in January 1842.[38]

Pickering did not linger in the Bay of Islands but travelled south to the growing township of Auckland. Around half of the town's several hundred new inhabitants – including government officials, soldiers and merchants – had, like Pickering, arrived there via the Australian colonies. Their first dwellings were built of raupō, and Māori built numerous public buildings such as courthouses, churches, schools and public houses for the colonists from locally sourced materials. Even the first government house at Official Bay in Auckland was constructed from raupō after the ship from London that was carrying the prefabricated wooden structure for the building foundered on a reef.

As the name implies, many of the government officials lived at Official Bay. The tradespeople resided in the adjacent Mechanics Bay, and the downtown area was known as Commercial Bay. The main street, Queen Street, was renowned for being particularly muddy and at times unpassable on foot, as the Waihorotiu Stream flowed down it towards the sea. Early Aucklanders sometimes resorted to rowboats to navigate the town centre.[39] During the winter of 1841 the *Auckland Herald* described the roads about the town as 'an accumulation of water, mud and mire'.[40]

The rawness of the newly established urban centre may well have evoked memories of Melbourne for Pickering – but it was surely to Launceston that his thoughts turned when he found himself once again in gaol. During that muddy season, on 4 May 1841 Pickering dishonestly tried to pass himself off as a full-time agent for the Sydney Banking Corporation, instead of just a commission agent. His deception was discovered after he tried to trick Israel Joseph into providing him with £62 10s. He was charged with 'obtaining a valuable security under false pretences'.[41]

Joseph, like Pickering, had arrived in the Australian penal colonies as a free man. He worked initially as an auctioneer. In July 1836 he opened a shop, 'Israel Joseph's Sydney Store', at Maitland in inland New South Wales. He later returned to London, then sailed back out to Britain's antipodean colonies. This time, he established business interests at Port Nicholson (Wellington), Auckland and Kororāreka.[42] Joseph, who was also an attorney, entered into a business partnership with David Nathan. The men were merchants and general commission agents who sold goods including alcohol, household furniture and effects and raw hides in Auckland and in the New Zealand Company settlement of Nelson in the South Island in the early 1840s. Joseph eventually ended his partnership with the man who would later become renowned as the founder of Auckland firm L.D. Nathan & Company. He travelled back to London, then returned south to re-establish himself in New South Wales, this time setting up a business in the colony's capital, Sydney.[43] Given Joseph's business acumen and legal mind as well as his familiarity with New South Wales, he was well placed to discover that Pickering was not what he was representing himself to be to residents of Auckland.

The law that Pickering contravened was part of a bundle of English-derived colonial laws, adapted in New South Wales and initially adopted in New Zealand. Earlier that same year, on 24 May 1841, New Zealand's legislative council sat for the first time. The council was chaired by Hobson, who opened the first session. Other luminaries who attended the proceedings included Colonial Secretary Willoughby Shortland, Attorney-General Francis Fisher, Colonial Treasurer George Cooper and Justice Edmund Halswell – one of the colony's three senior judges. After they had sworn the required oath and taken their seats, James Coates took his oath as the newly appointed clerk of the council.

Hobson put before the legislative council an ordinance to adopt the laws of New South Wales under which New Zealand had operated before it became a separate colony; substituting a word here and there – such as replacing 'South Wales' with 'Zealand' – would serve the new colony's immediate purposes well. It was not, Hobson explained, his intention to adopt the laws of New South Wales over the longer term but instead to use the recess 'to prepare for your consideration, such laws as will best provide for the administration of justice, and the contingencies of social life, which may be expected to arise in New Zaaland [sic]'. It was expedient to utilise the body of law imported from across the Tasman Sea to fill a hiatus in the interim.[44]

At the inaugural sitting of the Legislative Council of New Zealand, Hobson indicated that he intended to assume powers as governor that were equivalent to those exercised by his New South Wales counterpart: to collect revenue for Her Majesty's customs; to prohibit distillation; and to establish courts of quarter sessions and courts of requests. He spoke eloquently on the British colonists' 'solemn and important duty' to improve 'the condition' and elevate 'the character of the Aboriginal inhabitants'.

After tabling an indemnity bill to ensure the laws, acts and ordinances of New South Wales would continue to apply in New Zealand as an interim measure, the legislative council adjourned until 27 May.[45] Pickering was to appear before the court of general quarter sessions – a short-lived measure that was replaced the following year by a system of county courts.[46] In the meantime, he was confined to Auckland gaol.

In 1841 the Department of Public Works and Buildings was allocated £500 to construct a police lock-up and temporary cells at Auckland gaol, and £390 was set aside for the construction of the courthouse that had already been ordered, and an additional £600 to complete the building.[47] Despite the expense involved in constructing the first of Auckland's gaols, the building attracted notoriety; the concerns raised were similar to those that were aired so publicly in relation to its Launceston equivalent. The Queen Street gaol was a wooden building with cells that were between 11 and 13ft square and often overcrowded. It was said to be 'low in the ceiling and worse than badly ventilated'. A little over a decade after Pickering spent time there, a Taranaki newspaper described the Queen Street gaol as an 'inhuman kennel', the state of which was 'absolutely revolting to humanity' and 'even worse than our own wretched place of imprisonment'. The newspaper observed how 'in its very best condition it was but a confined and ill-contrived wooden structure' that had, by 1853, deteriorated to become 'a rotten and ruinous hovel overrun with rats, and only fit to be used as a place of torture'. The Taranaki Herald urged the chief justice to act to remedy the situation; and it pointed out how the wholly inadequate accommodation provided by the crown had been drawn to the governor's attention on multiple occasions.[48]

Pickering's initial court appearance was on 6 October 1841, just the second day on which the Court of General Quarter Sessions sat in Auckland. The chairman was Francis Fisher, formerly the crown solicitor of New South Wales and the acting attorney-general of New Zealand. Fisher was effectively demoted when he became the chairman of the quarter sessions at Auckland with a salary of £300 per annum;[49] he had previously been earning £730 per annum. Fisher was sufficiently disenchanted with his new circumstances to resign and return to Sydney. Before this, however, he chaired the inaugural Court of General Quarter Sessions in Auckland from 5 to 7 October 1841. On 5 October a large crowd of 'jurors, witnesses, and spectators' gathered to watch the proceedings held in the schoolhouse that served as a temporary court while the new courthouse was being built. The weather was showery, and this led to newspaper speculation about how his honour the chief justice and other officials would be able to access the nearly completed building in a decent manner, given the often muddy nature of the surrounding streets.

Pickering's initial appearance before Fisher was brief; the jury acquitted him after deliberating for only 10 minutes. A second charge was then brought against him, supported by almost exactly the same evidence. In this case the jury found Pickering guilty, but recommended mercy. Fisher ignored their plea for clemency, however.[50] Auckland and Wellington newspapers reported that 'at the Court of General Quarter Sessions, Mr Pickering was tried on a charge of fraud and misrepresentation, and, being found guilty, was sentenced to transportation for seven years'.[51]

Pickering was the first person residing in New Zealand to be sentenced to transportation. His crime was unusual; most of his fellow prisoners were committed for drunkenness, assault, or deserting ship.[52] The sentence handed down to Pickering can be understood within the broader context of Britain's long-standing use of transportation as a punishment and its adoption within the Australian penal colonies to punish free settlers, so-called secondary offenders (convicts who reoffended) and Aboriginal prisoners – as well as in light of New Zealand's early adherence to, and subsequent adoption and adaptation of Australian colonial law.[53]

It was one thing for New Zealand courts to sentence a prisoner to transportation, but quite another, when Pickering's sentence was handed down, to be able to carry that into effect. Nothing had yet been done about gazetting a penal colony where prisoners could be sent. New South Wales was no longer accepting prisoners transported from beyond its own borders; Norfolk Island was available to be used as a penal station only for prisoners transported from Britain; and Western Australia was not yet available as a penal colony. Van Diemen's Land was the obvious choice. Accordingly, on 4 November 1841 Governor Hobson and his executive council decided that authority devolved to them from a British 1825 order in council to enable them to stipulate Van Diemen's Land as the site to which convicts would be transported from New Zealand. A proclamation to this effect was signed by

Colonial Secretary Willoughby Shortland and published on 10 November 1841 in the *New Zealand Government Gazette*.[54] The sheriff (who was in charge of the gaol) was now in a position to arrange for Pickering to be conveyed there. This involved getting quotes from the masters of various small intercolonial trading vessels until they reached an agreed price for transporting the prisoner to the penal colony. The sheriff successfully sought approval from the colonial secretary for the schooner *Sisters* to convey Pickering to Van Diemen's Land at 'the rate of seven pounds and ten shillings sterling'.[55] As the harbourmaster informed the colonial secretary, Pickering could be taken out to the vessel on the afternoon of Tuesday 21 December 1841 before the vessel set sail the following day for Hobart.[56]

Aucklanders interpreted the spectacle of Pickering being marched in irons down Queen Street to the waterfront to be taken out to the *Sisters* as a 'judicial display of cruelty'. The *New Zealand Herald and Auckland Gazette* bemoaned the heavy sentence handed down to him: Pickering was, after all, a gentleman and a merchant. Until the moment of his impending departure, he had apparently been locked up only at night; during the daytime he had enjoyed the relative liberty of being able to pace up and down outside the gaol.[57] A British convict called Barber, who was transported for forging wills, described the physical pain of being put in leg irons: 'the operation of riveting on the irons is a painful one, and is performed with as much rudeness and with as little feeling as it could have been done five centuries since – each stroke of the riveting hammer causing a sensation of pain something like toothdrawing'.[58] There was also the mental anguish and the emotional pain to be taken into account. As he was marched down Queen Street, the reality of his situation may well have weighed as heavily on Pickering as his leg irons. After all, he had already seen for himself what the convict system in Van Diemen's Land had in store for him.

Pickering was so determined to avoid serving time in Van Diemen's Land that he absconded when the *Sisters* stopped at the Bay of Islands to load firewood for its galley.[59] He later recalled how he 'escaped in the ship's dingy [sic]' with the help of 'a single accomplice'. As Pickering later told the authorities in Hobart, 'my irons were taken off by the Constable. His name I think was Peter. I think the Constable was told by the Sheriff to take them off. I was four or five weeks at large until apprehended by some constables Peter not among them.'[60] As it happened, Pickering did not roam far from the small settlement at Te Puna, which meant that he was quite readily recaptured. The constable who caught him received a £5 reward plus a £2 reimbursement for expenses.[61] In the meantime, the *Sisters* had long since sailed for Hobart where it arrived with Pickering's indent but no prisoner on board. The Vandemonian colonial secretary wrote on 10 March 1842 to inform his New Zealand counterpart of this.[62] Meanwhile in New Zealand Pickering underwent a health inspection by medical doctor John Johnson on 4 March at the gaol in Auckland. Johnson certified that Pickering was 'free from any putrid or infectious Distemper and fit to be Transported'.[63] He remained in Auckland gaol until May 1843, at which point he was put on board the brig *Portenia* bound for Van Diemen's Land.[64]

CHAPTER 2

English laws
and the *Portenia*'s cargo

As the colony of New Zealand expanded and the new settlement at Port Nicholson (Wellington) began to grow, rivalry fomented between Auckland, the government town, and the New Zealand Company settlement.[1] Despite their differences, many of the new colonists envisioned a colony free of convicts. They wanted a place where respectable and industrious people could get ahead in life. However, this dream was a departure from reality. Urban growth seemed to foster an increase in crime; policing the growing towns was proving difficult; and makeshift courthouses and flimsy gaols did little to increase respect for the rule of law or to facilitate the imprisonment of those who were flouting its precepts. While there was certainly a place in New Zealand society for the industrious poor, those who were visibly poverty-stricken and apparently unmotivated to improve their circumstances seemed to quickly fall foul of the law. All too often such incorrigible rogues appeared before law courts that were themselves evolving to better serve the colonists.

As the cases of the men transported on the *Portenia* amply demonstrate, the vast majority of those sentenced to transportation from New Zealand to Van Diemen's Land were working class or unemployed men. It is evident from remarks made by the judiciary that class perceptions influenced sentencing decisions: those who were viewed as wastrels were far more likely to end up in Van Diemen's Land than in a local gaol. Nevertheless, throughout the decade during which sentences to transportation were imposed in New Zealand, several 'white-collar criminals', including William Phelps Pickering, committed crimes of sufficient seriousness to earn them a passage to the penal colony.

When Pickering was taken on board the *Portenia* at Auckland in May 1843 he joined 12 other prisoners on the brig. His fellow passengers had been tried at Wellington in the preceding months and sentenced to transportation to Van Diemen's Land for periods ranging from seven to 10 years. They ranged in age from 19 to 56, and four of them claimed to be married. Pickering was 28. Four of the men had acted alone; the rest had offended jointly with others. Eight of the men's cases had been heard before the newly established Supreme Court in Wellington, and the others were determined by the county court. Those sentenced in Wellington were transferred to Auckland, where they had spent a month in Queen Street gaol alongside Pickering before the *Portenia* set sail for Van Diemen's Land.[2]

Unlike Auckland, which was a government town, Wellington was a New Zealand Company settlement. The Company aimed to facilitate the colonisation of parts of New Zealand in accordance with the theories of Edward Gibbon Wakefield. As Miles Fairburn has explained, at the core of Wakefield's colonisation theory was the notion of a 'sufficient price'. Rather than giving away crown land, Wakefield proposed that these so-called 'waste lands' should be sold at a price that was sufficient to slow the rate at which colonial wage earners could become landowners. Proceeds from land sales would facilitate the transfer of as many labourers as possible from Britain to new colonies like New Zealand. These measures were designed to ensure that sufficient labourers would be available to support the growth of the colony and meet the needs of the wealthier, landowning classes. A growing colonial economy would in turn increase local demand for goods imported from Britain. In the New Zealand context, a small parcel of land equating to one-tenth of the land the New Zealand Company acquired would be set aside for the use of local Māori. In their practical application however, Wakefield's theories extended well beyond the shores of New Zealand, influencing crown policy in New South Wales, South Australia and Canada.[3] In New Zealand, the ideal society envisaged by the New Zealand Company failed to materialise, but settlers held on to their dream of an antipodean utopia. This led to tensions between Wellington, the Company town in the lower North Island, and Auckland in the north.

As early as 6 February 1841, the *New Zealand Gazette and Wellington Spectator* published a lengthy diatribe against Hobson, claiming that he had sent a vessel to Wellington to transfer skilled labourers to Auckland. 'The supply of labour now at Port Nicholson,' railed the newspaper, 'has been paid for by the capitalists and purchasers of land.' Rather than follow the same model as the New Zealand Company, the new government settlement at Auckland found it more expedient and 'cheaper to cheat'. The tactics that Auckland was resorting to in order to entice mechanics to migrate north included the chief constable at Wellington (who took his instructions from Auckland) offering free passage to those who agreed to go; and soldiers who were stationed in Wellington but were soon to depart were allegedly 'spread[ing] all sorts of lying reports about attacks from the natives, the cheapness of bread at Auckland &c'. The newspaper article fostered a perception that skilled labourers were flowing from south to north.[4]

Either way, such labour mobility did not stem the growth of Wellington. In January 1842, as Wellington celebrated its second anniversary, 'beautiful weather' enticed Wellingtonians to attend the Second Anniversary Fête. At Te Aro Flat, Mr Ludlam constructed a temporary stand in his gardens from which ladies and gentlemen could view horse races. Other events included hurdles and boat races in which 'a large body of natives' from nearby Petone proved victorious against a crew of their colonial counterparts. In addition to sporting feats and entertainment the 'First Exhibition of the Wellington Horticultural Society' took place at the Exchange. The size and quality of the produce on display attracted considerable acclaim, in particular the 'remarkably fine' carrots, potatoes and cabbages grown in the Hutt Valley, near Wellington. The colonists admired Baron Alzdorf's exhibit of wheat and barley, and the displays of a wide variety of colourful flowers that, like the vegetables and grains, were reminders of their now far distant homelands.

The same edition of the *New Zealand Gazette and Wellington Spectator* also reported how Governor Hobson had assented to several ordinances that were introduced during the second session of the new legislative council. These included ordinances for establishing a supreme court, to regulate the constitution of juries and to establish county courts for civil and criminal jurisdiction.[5] Edmund Storr Halswell, who arrived from England in March

1841 to take up the position of Protector of Aborigines in the New Zealand Company settlements, was appointed judge of the County Court for the Southern District of New Ulster, the part of the North Island north of the Patea River. Halswell was expected to sit at Wellington on the third Tuesday of every month to hear criminal and civil matters.[6] The court's jurisdiction also extended 'over the two Southern Islands' (the South Island and Stewart Island).[7]

The magistrates and lawyers of the Wellington district treated Halswell to a gentlemen's dinner at the Southern Cross Hotel on Monday 18 April 1842 to mark the opening of the first county court the following day. On Tuesday Halswell's chaplain, the Reverend McFarlane, opened the first session of the court with a prayer. The judge's clerk read the formal pronouncements: the ordinance for establishing the court, the governor's proclamation for holding it and the patent appointing Halswell as judge. This was followed by the commission for swearing in justices of the peace, the magistrates of the district, the crown prosecutor and the coroner. A jury list was read and 12 of the 24 men were selected. Finally, the proclamation against vice and immorality was read and Halswell explained to those assembled how the court was constituted and delineated its jurisdiction.[8]

The first matter brought before the court was hardly a landmark case. John Bryce and John Barker faced a charge of killing a pig whose owner was unknown. They were acquitted after the sole witness could not recall any of the evidence he had deposed two months earlier. The suspect witness was then reprimanded by the judge and detained in custody. Despite this odd start, the local newspaper applauded Halswell, whose 'familiarity with the procedure in the English Courts of Justice, as well as a professional knowledge of the law' ensured that he had been 'enabled to put his court at once on the footing of an old established tribunal'.[9] It was a new court, but administering venerable law.

Four months later the court handed down a sentence to transportation. The first of Pickering's fellow passengers was a Protestant in his mid-thirties called James Beckett; he was 5ft 2in. tall, with light brown hair and grey eyes. He appeared before Halswell in August 1842.[10] Beckett's trial was heralded by a government notice dated 5 August that appeared in the local newspaper on 16 August 1842, the day the court was scheduled to sit. Issued by Clerk of the Peace Robert Strang, it announced that the

county court of civil and criminal judicature 'will be holden at Barrett's
Hotel, at Wellington aforesaid, on Tuesday, the 16th instant, at 10 o'clock
in the forenoon precisely'. All those who had been summoned to appear as
prosecutors, witnesses or defendants or to transact relevant business before
the court were 'desired to give their attendance'.[11] In the intervening months
between the county court's opening and Beckett's trial, a more salubrious
edifice had been found to house it than the 'tumble-down old Maori barn'
in which it originally sat. The barn, which had also served as a church, post
office, police office and district court to the newly arrived colonists, was
temporarily replaced by the original Barrett's Hotel on Lambton Quay while
a new fit-for-purpose building was constructed.[12] Named after Richard
'Dicky' Barrett, the hotel at Wellington's waterfront was as legendary as its
proprietor.

Barrett and his business partner Jacky Love forged trading relationships
with Māori; they brought European-style clothing and blankets as well
as weapons, alcohol, tobacco and food from Sydney to Kororāreka, Port
Nicholson, and to Queen Charlotte Sound at the top of the South Island in
a schooner known as the *Adventure*. In return they obtained pigs, potatoes
and flax from Māori, for which they found a ready market in Sydney.
Barrett was fluent in te reo Māori and had forged a strong relationship with
Te Atiawa people; in 1828 he married Wakaiwa Rawinia who was a niece of
Te Atiawa rangitira Te Puni and sister to Te Wharepōuri. Barrett later built
a whaling station at Queen Charlotte Sound. He became an interpreter for
the New Zealand Company when the first of its ships, the *Tory*, arrived in
New Zealand in August 1839 with Captain William Wakefield on board.
After assisting in negotiations between the colonists and local Māori,
Barrett provided the land and timber for the courthouse to be constructed
in Wellington.[13]

In his opening remarks to those gathered at Barrett's Hotel in August
1842 to participate in the county court proceedings, Halswell expressed his
regret that the 'nature of the Calendar laid before him … contained a list of
so grave a character as had not come before him in this Colony'. Crime was
on the rise. All of the cases before Halswell were property crimes of one sort
or another. Beckett stood indicted 'for stealing from the stores of Henry
Martineau, a variety of cloth, wearing apparel, &c., the property of Thomas
Bryson, George Wynter Blaithwaite, and Henry Martineau, respectively'. Mr

Hanson acted for the crown; Dr Evans for the defendant. Eight witnesses were called, including the store owner Martineau, his storekeeper Bryson, two policemen, the Wellington gaoler, a local maltster and brewer, a butcher and one of Beckett's neighbours.[14]

A tale of intrigue and deep yet largely unsubstantiated suspicion emerged. A Jewish man with Wellington connections called Charles Cohen, who was visiting town, had shown considerable interest in a wide range of goods in Martineau's store. He was keen to take the goods on three months' credit but these terms were not acceptable to the store owner. Not long after, on a June morning a couple of months before Beckett's trial, a large quantity of goods was stolen from the store. Much of the stolen property, which ranged from shawls, shoes and hose to a black vest, shirts, breeches, pins and needles, matches, cotton wicks, cotton cloth and buckskin, had been of interest to Cohen. Suspicion fell on the man, who was about to leave Wellington for the Bay of Islands on board the *Kate* or *Catherine*. A search of the vessel failed to turn up any of the missing property, meaning there was no tangible evidence against him.[15]

Some of the stolen items were distinctive or even unique in the colony. One piece, for example, was a blue jacket 'lined with flannel and bound with blue ribbon' that was Bryson the storekeeper's personal property. The missing cotton wick was the only stuff of its type available in the colony; while the hose bore a particular 'private mark' to indicate the price. Several items, including some blue cloth, were located in the small tent that Beckett the local sausage-seller shared with his wife at the beach – which, in the 1840s, was adjacent to Lambton Quay. Beckett told several stories about the origins of the goods found in his possession: he claimed variously that he had bought them from the Bay of Islands, or had found them on the street near Barrett's Hotel. Evidence emerged, though, that despite having enjoyed a good reputation locally up until this point, Beckett had allegedly stowed a box containing a number of items identifiable as those taken from Martineau's store at Thomas Pascoe's house across the road from the beach. Pascoe the maltster and brewer had been in the colony only six weeks or so and was keen to distance himself from the affair: he claimed he had never looked inside the box.[16]

John Turner, the tailor located on nearby Willis Street, said that Beckett had approached him under cover of darkness and tried to sell him some blue cloth and some buckskin. The man had declined the offer, and said he recognised the fabric from Martineau's store. The butcher Alexander Lyall, whose shop was on Lambton Quay, claimed not to know Beckett's occupation but said he had worked previously at a hotel. A man named Brewer, a barrister to the high court, said he knew Beckett well and had seen him at Coromandel harbour 10 months earlier where he was employed as an outdoor servant by Messrs Abercrombie and Webster, rather well-to-do gentlemen. Brewer had 'never heard anything against his character'. Despite attestations as to Beckett's previously unblemished character and a strong lingering suspicion that Cohen was somehow involved in the burglary at Martineau's store, Beckett was found guilty and was sentenced to 'be transported for the term of seven years, to such part of Her Majesty's dominions, as His Excellency with the advice of the Legislative Council, should think fit'.[17] Seven years was the maximum sentence to transportation a judge of the county court could impose. Beckett was to be sent to Van Diemen's Land – although by the time the *Portenia* set sail he had spent almost a full year in Wellington gaol.

By 1843 the colonial population of Wellington was estimated at 852 householders and 63 building proprietors. There was no estimate in the early censuses of the number of Māori resident in the town. Their influence was apparent, nevertheless, in one of the town's recorded statistics: of the 877 houses that had been built in Wellington by 1843, 491 were 'built on Native plan' and 386 were constructed according to European designs and building practices. In addition there were 24 warehouses and shops, eight forges and workshops, and three mills driven by wind, water or steam. The young settlement was administered at a local level by those occupying offices within the 10 public buildings erected to date – men who had become newly answerable to their Auckland-based superiors.[18] The 'present straggling nature' of newly erected buildings and 'consequent scattered state of the population', however, had a downside. It made the growing town difficult to police effectively on the budget that was available. The local Police Office was therefore gratified to be able to report in January 1843 that Wellington's leading merchants had private watchmen in their employ. At the same time, the Police Office congratulated the colonists on 'a good riddance of bad rubbish' after 'some 15 or 20 rogues and vagabonds' were expelled from 'their old haunts'. The police viewed these destitute people as having little means of support and 'as little disposition to acquire them honestly'.[19]

As the case involving the next of Pickering's fellow passengers on the *Portenia* illustrates, however, not all of those transported to Van Diemen's Land were among the town's apparently needy and desperate characters. Barrett's Hotel, as well as continuing to provide temporary accommodation for the county court as and when required, was a hub of social activity for Wellingtonians. On 17 January 1843, for example, James Stuart Freeman placed an advertisement in the local *New Zealand Colonist and Port Nicholson Advertiser* newspaper to advise local gentlemen that the governor would be holding a levee at Barrett's Hotel on Friday 19 January.[20] Freeman worked for Governor Robert FitzRoy, who had replaced William Hobson in September 1842.[21] In the same column of advertisements, an expensive new book titled *New Zealand As It Is* was advertised as 'preparing for the press' by its author George Delvin Nugent, who held a Bachelor of Medicine from Trinity College, Dublin. Nugent's book was illustrated by Robert Wigmore and the asking price was £2 2s. Publication would proceed as soon as a sufficient number of subscribers expressed interest. Within days Nugent promised a more modestly priced pamphlet, 'Englishmen in New Zealand', to his reading public at five shillings a piece.[22]

Several days later Wellingtonians could read the list of 82 gentlemen who were presented to His Excellency in his suite at Barrett's Hotel. It read like a veritable who's who of early colonial Wellington, with local luminaries such as the mayor, the land commissioner William Spain and Halswell in attendance alongside Sheriff Henry St Hill, Colonel William Wakefield, various men of the cloth, at least one land surveyor and several 'Native Chiefs', including Pomare of the Chatham Islands and his son. Five doctors were also among the guests.[23] According to naturalist and painter George French Angas, who stayed at Barrett's Hotel while he was visiting Wellington, 'liquors and champagne circulate rather too freely [at the hotel] for a new colony'. He described how 'the state of "society" may be inferred, from the not unusual circumstance of the most fashionable of these "gentlemen" being trundled home in wheelbarrows from a ball, at the late hour of ten in the morning' – a spectacle Angas observed on two subsequent days.[24]

Despite his social standing in the colony, Nugent's name was not listed among the gentlemen invited to attend the governor's levee in

January 1843.[25] Despite having arrived in Wellington on 6 March 1842 from London on the *New York Packet* along with the colonial treasurer Alexander Shepherd and his wife and five children and a small group of other cabin passengers, the surgeon, who seemed to have all the right social connections and credentials to be part of the company gathered at Barrett's Hotel, was unavoidably absent.[26] Nugent had instead taken centre stage at Barrett's Hotel earlier that week, on Wednesday, where for a full day the county court had deliberated over his 'extraordinary [criminal] conduct' in the days leading up to the governor's grand event.[27]

The surgeon would have cut a tragic figure when he was brought before the judge in the county court at Barrett's Hotel. A Roman Catholic born in County Westmeath in Ireland, Nugent was a married man in his late thirties, 5ft 5½in. tall with black hair, dark brown eyes and a sallow complexion.[28] Earlier that same year, in January 1843, he claimed to have been robbed of various private letters and manuscripts that were 'supposed to be stolen from Barrett's Hotel'; a £10 reward was offered for any information leading to his identifying the thief.[29] Now as he appeared before the county court, a burn on Nugent's chest detailed in surviving description records was probably hidden underneath his clothing. He was also described as being 'paralysed in the lower extremities'.[30] Nugent was charged with stealing 'sundry articles' from Barrett's Hotel, 'the property of various gentlemen living there'. The stolen goods included shirts and some pistols that belonged to a Mr Rollo O'Farrell. The missing pistols were found in Nugent's portmanteau. The local newspaper facetiously observed that the surgeon's misconduct might only be accounted for 'by supposing that he was anxious to make an extensive collection of materials for his forthcoming book'. Instead of becoming a published author the disgraced surgeon was sentenced to transportation for a period of seven years.[31]

Halswell used the opportunity of the court's opening to draw attention to an increase in both the volume and seriousness of the cases before him. The previous month he had tried only nine prisoners. Now, in February 1843, there were 17 prisoners waiting to be brought before him. The judge also observed that those awaiting trial before the Supreme Court were accused of a number of serious offences. As a consequence, the woefully inadequate 'miserable Maori hut' that served as Wellington's gaol was overcrowded, and the behaviour of those confined within breached gaol regulations.

Halswell provided a graphic example of this. 'Two of the female prisoners,' he told the County Court, 'had been engaged with the men and a fiddler in getting up a dance.' In advocating for a separate system where prisoners were housed according to their classification rather than indiscriminately, Halswell described the 51 x 27ft gaol as the town's 'hot bed of vice and crime'. The only solace the judge took in the February proceedings lay in the fact that the prisoners 'were all strangers'. 'None of them,' he said, 'could be properly called emigrants, or even settlers.'[32] They may well have been in the colony, but they did not belong there.

The judge heard several other cases – involving a man charged with embezzling from his master, nine sailors charged with stealing ale and other articles from their ship's master, and a man who had stolen from the till of the Ship Inn. The next case involved William Clarke, an illiterate seaman, 5ft 6½in. tall with dark brown hair and a ruddy complexion; and James Clarke, a labourer with dark brown hair, hazel eyes, a long nose and a fresh complexion, who could read and write and who stood as tall as his co-accused.[33] These men, it was reported, had been 'engaged to come here from Van Diemens Land, in a cattle ship under the names of Black'. Why the men had used a surname different from their own remained unexplained at the time of their trial for 'robbing the house of Rowland Davies, of sundry articles of wearing apparel' – which turned out to be women's clothing. Both men were found guilty and sentenced to transportation for seven years.[34]

Additional charges against the two Clarkes – of breaking out of Wellington's raupō gaol – were dropped, probably because of the deplorable state of the facility. The materials of which it was built were 'slight' and prisoners could only be contained on the ground floor of the flimsy building.[35] As William later explained, 'we escaped from gaol with our irons on by breaking through the gates. The constables offered no resistance. We were apprehended by the natives.' James described how he had 'locked the constables up'.[36] When Floyd the gaoler set off on Wednesday 19 April 1843 with two prisoners to have their irons adjusted, six prisoners – the Clarkes and four other men sentenced to transportation – seized the opportunity to escape. In the gaoler's absence they stole some muskets and other weapons from a chest and used these to usher the constables and other prisoners into cells, where they locked them up. As they rushed through the prison gate, the absconders 'knocked down Mr Macdonogh, the Chief Police Magistrate', whose attention had been drawn by the yells of the incarcerated constables. Despite Macdonogh's presence shortly afterwards on nearby Thorndon beach, and that of Captain Richards of the government brig *Victoria*, which was waiting to transfer the prisoners to Auckland, the men in irons managed to commandeer a whaleboat with just two oars and rowed off into the distance. Sheriff Henry St Hill gave chase but the absconders had too great a head start and were halfway across the bay before the sheriff's boat was launched. In response to the debacle, 14 special constables were immediately sworn in by the mayor.[37]

The escapades of the Clarkes and their companions outraged local colonists, who were vocal in their condemnation of 'the miserable building which in this place is the only substitute for a gaol'. Once again the issue of failing to separate the convicted from unconvicted prisoners, felon from debtor and 'the hardened offender from the tyro [beginner] in crime' was publicly aired in the *New Zealand Colonist and Port Nicholson Advertiser*. The newspaper was quick to point out that while the dilapidated state of the gaol may not have mattered in Wellington's early days, a more secure arrangement for detaining convicted felons was now demonstrably required. Over the past 12 to 18 months Wellington had been 'visited by men of desperate character and irreclaimably criminal habits'. The newspaper observed that none of the men were free immigrants. The fact of their escape, the newspaper wryly observed, was less surprising than their having remained for as long as they had within the confines of the notoriously inadequate prison.[38]

Four days after the prisoners' escape the presses were stopped so that a short news item could be included in the Saturday newspaper to announce that the men had been 'captured by the Natives yesterday afternoon and brought into town the same evening'.[39] The Wairarapa Māori who had captured the absconders in the vicinity of Cape Palliser each received £5 reward for returning the men to the colonial authorities in Wellington.[40] This was a handsome reward compared to later rewards where the authorities promised to pay just £1 for the return of escaped prisoners, regardless of the size of the capture party, and 1s 6d per day reimbursement for food given to the captive, and up to £2 or even £3 for men whom the authorities had a strong interest in recapturing. Advertisements offering rewards for the capture of absconders and deserters were published in *Te Karere o Nui Tireni* (printed in te reo Māori) in the 1840s. Usually these gave the name and a brief physical descriptions of the wanted man and his clothing, although several advertisements appeared in this newspaper in late 1843 that repeated the offer of a '£1 reward and 1/6 per day reimbursement for food for the return of any escaped prisoners'.[41] The colonists' desire to involve Māori in retaking absconders can be read as both practical and symbolic. Māori were, at the time, far more numerous than the colonists, and familiar with the terrain: they were much more likely to discover those who were fleeing from the authorities. Encouraging Māori to be captors inexorably drew them into socioeconomic relationships with the colonists through payments of monetary rewards and exposure to the mechanisations of the English justice systems that were developing in New Zealand.

The four prisoners who escaped with the Clarkes had all been sentenced to transportation in the Supreme Court at Wellington on Tuesday 18 April 1843, the day before their breakout from gaol. In fact, all eight of the remaining prisoners who later joined Pickering on the *Portenia* were sentenced to transportation at the Supreme Court on that same day. New Zealand's Supreme Court was ostensibly created under ordinance 5 Victoria, AD 1841–2 which was sent to England for the Queen's approval.[42] The ordinance provided for a chief justice to be appointed who was expected to sit in Auckland for eight months of the year, allowing only four months for him to undertake the 'long and hazardous journeys' to Wellington and Nelson to hear the more serious cases that arose there. This inconvenienced the chief justice and those beyond Auckland. It also meant that those charged with crimes whose punishment might exceed transportation for seven years had to spend months in gaol awaiting trial. At law, these prisoners were presumed innocent until they were proven guilty.[43]

William Martin, born in Birmingham, went to Cambridge then became a student at Lincoln's Inn in 1832. He was called to the bar in November 1836 and just five years later, in 1841, was appointed as the first chief justice of New Zealand. Four days before he set sail for New Zealand he married Mary Ann Parker, the daughter of a London rector. He then departed alone for New Zealand. His young bride followed eight months later, by which time Martin was established in Auckland.[44]

The first session of the Supreme Court opened on 28 February 1842. During that session, Ngāpuhi rangatira Ruhe's son Wiremu Kīngi Maketū, sometimes known as Maketū Wharetotara, from the Bay of Islands, was tried for the murder of Ngāpuhi leader Rewa's granddaughter. Maketū had been working as a farm labourer for the widow Elizabeth Roberton in 1841 in the Bay of Islands. Her extended household included a servant, Thomas Bull, who mistreated the young Māori labourer. This led to a violent altercation between the two when Bull apparently kicked Maketū during a disagreement over money. Two days later Maketū killed his adversary by splitting his head open with an axe. He then killed Mrs Roberton and two girls on the property – the Robertons' infant daughter and Isabella Brind, Rewa's granddaughter. Maketū chased and caught the Robertons' eight-year-old son Gordon and threw him over a cliff to his death.

After these dramatic events, Maketū retreated to his father's village where many Māori began to congregate. This alarmed local European officials, who were loath to intervene. However, the murder of Rewa's granddaughter was an incendiary act. Rather than inflame intra-iwi conflict, Ruhe, with strong encouragement from missionary Henry Williams, surrendered his son to the colonists. In doing so, the chief demonstrated a willingness on the part of some Māori to utilise the colonial courts strategically.[45]

When Maketū appeared before Martin at the Supreme Court in Auckland on 1 March 1842, the chief justice asserted that as a British subject Maketū fell under the Supreme Court's jurisdiction and was expected to comply with the newly introduced British-derived colonial laws, even though he was not familiar with them. Maketū was found guilty and sentenced to death.

As well as being Martin's first major trial, the case set legal precedents in the relationship between Māori and colonial law. The judgment was translated into te reo Māori as Martin handed it down and word of the outcome spread far and wide. Just two years after the signing of the Treaty of Waitangi, Martin was reinforcing the notion that Māori had become British subjects and were answerable for their actions under English-derived colonial laws, despite the fact that many Māori believed they had not yielded their sovereignty. Māori and Pākehā were now considered equal in the eyes of the colonial law courts and could and would be dealt with severely if they were found to have contravened any of the recently introduced laws.[46] This caused some consternation among Māori, who were growing increasingly 'concerned about the power the British had assumed over rangatira' as demonstrated through Maketū's public execution at Auckland.[47]

The second session of the Supreme Court was held in Wellington on 18 April 1843. The first case involved Edward Young, who was found guilty of breaking and entering into John Sutton's premises and stealing bottles and other goods. In sentencing Young, Martin told him he was taking into account recommendations from the jury regarding his 'higher position in society, and better education' as well as his 'previous good life'. Young's social position in the colony stood him in good stead: he avoided being sentenced to transportation and was instead given six months' imprisonment with hard labour. The next prisoner to be brought before the chief justice was Thomas Britannicus Pilcher, who had tried to set fire to William Lye's house with intent to injure and defraud Lye. Again the jury strongly recommended mercy, this time on the grounds that Pilcher's family was in a 'distressed state'. After condemning the 'very heinous nature' of Pilcher's crime, Martin acknowledged that his actions, while wrong, had been motivated in part by having 'to look upon the misery of those near and dear to him'. He handed down the same sentence as he had imposed on Young: six months' imprisonment with hard labour.[48]

No such recommendations for mercy were forthcoming from the jury in regard to the remaining cases on the court's calendar for that day. Next to appear were four men: Patrick Mullins, Denis (also known as Francis or Daniel) McCarthy and two brothers, William and Joseph Root. Mullins, tall with brown hair and grey eyes, was one of the prisoners who had broken out of Wellington gaol with the Clarkes.[49] So, too, had the 23-year-old thinly whiskered and ruddy-complexioned Joseph Root and his younger brother William, a 19-year-old clean-shaven groom and coachman with dark brown hair and grey eyes;[50] McCarthy, a 24-year-old pit sawyer and bushman with blue eyes, greying hair and a small narrow chin and who went by at least three different first names, had remained in the cells.[51]

William Root was not exactly a stranger to court process in Wellington; his first appearance, albeit as a witness, had been at the third session of the county court in June the preceding year. On 29 June 1842, the *New Zealand Gazette and Wellington Spectator* reported a case heard by Halswell that involved allegations against two Māori, Te Kopo and E Pokai, of having stolen two pieces of pork from the butcher Henry Brown in Mulgrave Street, Thorndon. Māori were heavily represented among the spectators crowding the court, and a chief from Kaiwharawhara, known to the colonists as 'Turingha Kuri' (Taringa Kuri/Te Kaeaea), sat at the bench with the judge. Māori involvement in helping to dispense colonial justice in New Zealand had a long lineage dating back to a proclamation of 9 November 1814 in which the governor of New South Wales, Lachlan Macquarie, 'being equally solicitous to protect the natives of New Zealand and the Bay of Islands, in all their just rights and privileges, as those of every other dependency of the territory of New South Wales', appointed the missionary Thomas Kendall as 'resident magistrate at the Bay of Islands' and also named 'Duaterra [Ruatara], Shunghi [Hongi Hika] and Korra-korra [Korokoro] magistrates' in New Zealand.[52]

Richard Davis, missionary, interpreted the evidence literally to the accused as Brown the butcher told the court how he had seen Te Kopo look cautiously around his shop before picking up half a leg of pork and hiding it under his blanket. E Pokai, Brown alleged, had likewise picked up some pork and hidden it on his person before running off with his companion towards the schoolhouse. After Brown's cross-examination, William Root was questioned as a witness to the crime allegedly committed against his master, Brown. Root recalled seeing the butcher chasing and catching Te Kopo, who then dropped the pork he had taken. Root pursued the other fleeing man, E Pokai, and saw him throw some pork into the bushes. Root caught E Pokai and took him to gaol where, he claimed, E Pokai said Te Kopo had given him the pork.[53]

Te Kopo told the court that he was from Whanganui and had gone into Brown's butchery to buy some pork that was to be paid for by his father. A dispute had broken out, he said, between himself and the butcher, whose prices he considered to be too high. He claimed to have paid Brown for the pork he had taken. E Pokai said he had witnessed the exchange between Te Kopo and the butcher. He saw his companion pay Brown half a crown and a shilling for some pork, after which Brown had demanded sixpence more from Te Kopo. According to E Pokai, the butcher 'took him [Te Kopo] by the neck, and Te Kopo said what have I stolen; Brown said you make a thief'. E Pokai denied having run from the scene of the altercation.

Taringa Kuri was now given an opportunity to speak. He vouched for the men, whom he had known for two years; and he told the jury, 'if they did not steal the pigs, let them go; if they stole the pigs, keep them in prison; give the property back to Brown if they are guilty, and let them give him payment besides for the wrong'. After Halswell's summing up the jury retired for 15 minutes before returning to the court to announce their 'guilty' verdict and to recommend mercy. The judge sentenced both men to be confined in Wellington gaol for one month with hard labour. He explained to Taringa Kuri that he would not be able to provide 'payment for the prisoners according to the native custom'. Instead, Te Kopo and E Pokai would have to serve their sentences.[54] Under the Native Exemption Ordinance 1844, Māori who stole property could avoid a custodial sentence by paying four times the amount of the goods taken. This provision was included in recognition of utu – a Māori concept of reciprocity and balance – and also applied to matters involving Māori seeking compensation from Pākehā offenders.[55] It is not clear why Halswell did not allow Te Kopo and E Pokai to make restitution on this occasion, rather than be imprisoned.

When William Root appeared before the Supreme Court the following year with his brother and two companions, it was to face a charge of having 'burglariously broken and entered the dwelling-house of William Lyon, and having stolen certain goods therein'.[56] Lyon was one of the town's gentlemen; he had sat on the committee to raise funds for victims of the ferocious fire on Lambton Quay in November 1842, and he was a vice president of the local mechanics institute.[57] He was also one of the organisers of the Wellington assemblies held at Barrett's Hotel, where 'the dancing was kept up with great spirits until the first beams of "Phoebus" warned the fair disciples of Terpsichore that it was time for them to retire'.[58] Perhaps it was at a social occasion such as this that Lyon was introduced to the Scotsman William Barr's second daughter, Margaret, whom he married on 5 January 1843.[59] Or maybe the Barrs were customers at Lyon's shop, where he stocked a wide range of goods, from fowling pieces, rifles, razors, carpenters' and joiners' tools to stationery, household cutlery, aprons and fancy printed handkerchiefs.[60]

When the Root brothers, Mullins and McCarthy broke into the Lyons' home they stole prints, ribbon and cloth.[61] After the jury found them guilty, Martin informed the four that he saw them as 'men, not driven to crime by the slow pressure of long endured poverty; nor stung to a deed of violence by sudden provocation'; instead they had embarked on a 'deliberate war against the peace of society'. These were evildoers, Martin pronounced, who deserved to feel the full impact of the righteousness of the law. That being the case, he sentenced them all 'to be transported beyond the seas, to such place as His Excellency the officer administering the Government, with the advice of the Executive Council, shall appoint for the term of ten years'.[62] There was to be no mercy for any of them for, in the eyes of the chief justice, they had no redeeming features.

Next to appear were Charles Rowley, John Coglan (Coughlan) and Henry Rogers. Rowley and Coughlan had already appeared before Halswell in December the previous year to face a charge of having stolen blankets from James Taylor, a baker whose business was located on Lambton Quay. The baker used the blankets to cover his dough while it rose; he identified the stolen blankets as his from pieces of dough still attached to them. Constable James Futter told the court how he had found Rowley standing near the fireplace at Mrs Mary Barker's house at Bolton Street near the cemetery, and had located the stolen blankets on a nearby bedstead. Futter handed over Rowley and the blankets to Floyd the gaoler, and he also handed over Coughlan after he had apprehended him about an hour later. John Lloyd, another Lambton Quay baker for whom Rowley worked intermittently, told the court the prisoner was 'a very honest man [but] he will drink'. Lloyd found that whenever he sent Rowley out to sell bread the man returned to him with the correct amount of money earned. On the night Rowley allegedly robbed Taylor of the blankets, Lloyd had seen Rowley looking 'very tipsy'. Drunkenness did not, however, work in Rowley's favour as a defence. Coughlan was found not guilty on this occasion, but Rowley was sentenced to two months' imprisonment with hard labour.[63]

Rowley's confinement in Wellington gaol did nothing to reform his behaviour: he was barely out of prison before he was once again arrested, this time with Rogers as well as Coughlan. The three were charged with having broken into the house of John Lloyd, Rowley's erstwhile employer, where they allegedly stole £5. Rowley turned Queen's evidence but this did not prevent his also being found guilty: Martin sentenced all three men to transportation for 10 years.[64]

The last to appear before the chief justice was William Jackson, a 56-year-old tailor from London with blue eyes, dark brown hair that had started greying, a small chin and a sallow complexion. He had been found asleep in 'Wheelers [William Villier's] house' from which some goods had been stolen. Jackson was charged with stealing the missing 'wearing apparel'.[65] He was found guilty and sentenced to transportation for 10 years.[66]

On Saturday 22 April, the day after the six prisoners who had broken out of Wellington gaol were returned, all 12 of the prisoners being sent to Van Diemen's Land were loaded onto the government brig *Victoria* to be taken to Auckland. Because of the escape, 'a force of constables' accompanied the prisoners north.[67] The men were lodged in Auckland gaol alongside Pickering, who was also bound for Van Diemen's Land.

In the meantime, the 222-ton brig *Portenia*, captained by a man named Frasier, had docked.[68] The Shortland Crescent storekeeper S.A. Wood happily informed the ladies and gentlemen of Auckland of a vast range of stock newly arrived on the *Portenia* from Sydney, including black silk velvet, artificial flowers and wreaths, needles, Mousseline de Laine dresses, flannel and moleskin jackets, Blucher boots and much more.[69] Besides all the finery imported to satisfy the tastes of Auckland's gentlefolk, Wood also had stock on hand to appeal to pastoralists. He placed a separate newspaper advertisement on the same day addressed to 'Agriculturalists', informing them of the availability of working bullocks, horses and sheep recently offloaded from the *Portenia*, which he was making available at 'low prices'. The imported beasts could be viewed at Epsom.[70]

The *Portenia*'s return cargo included the first 13 convicts to be transported from New Zealand to Van Diemen's Land. The men were loaded onto the brig at Auckland on 27 May 1843. The negotiations entered into by the *Portenia*'s agents, Waitt and Tyser, set the rate for conveying prisoners from Auckland to Van Diemen's Land at £7 per prisoner provided the government supplied guards to accompany them, rising to between £10 and £12 per prisoner if the vessel was left to procure the necessary guards. In comparison, the sea passage between Auckland and Hobart usually cost around £8 for a passenger in steerage. As Robert Burnett has pointed out, when convicts later started to be transported directly from Wellington to Hobart, the authorities at the southern settlement found that they could not procure passage for their prisoners at such a favourable rate: they were faced with bills ranging from £13 up to £20 for an unaccompanied prisoner.[71]

In January 1844, the year after the first 13 convicts were shipped out, the New Zealand authorities found out that the ordinance under which the Supreme Court had been established had been disallowed by the British government when the necessary paperwork reached England.[72] This necessitated the rapid preparation and passage of a new bill, passed on 13 January 1844, which legally constituted the first Supreme Court of New Zealand. Modelled closely on the English system, New Zealand's Supreme Court enjoyed the same jurisdiction as Her Majesty's Courts of Queen's Bench, Common Pleas and Exchequer at Westminster. It was also to have, in New Zealand, 'all such equitable jurisdiction as the Lord High Chancellor hath in Great Britain'. Its jurisdiction extended to all matters generally heard by the ecclesiastical courts in England with regard to deceased estates, and it was also to function as an instance court of vice-admiralty. The ordinance set out provisions pertaining to the personnel and practices of the Supreme Court and allowed for cases that had commenced under the now disallowed ordinance but were 'pending and incomplete' to continue under the new ordinance.[73]

When the 1844 ordinance was passed into law, Supreme Court cases that had already been heard were conveniently ignored. In essence, such cases had been brought before a court with no legal standing and whose findings were therefore open to being legally challenged and potentially overturned. By the time this became apparent to New Zealanders, the Root brothers, Mullins, McCarthy, Rowley, Coughlan, Rogers and Jackson had served the first six months of their sentences in Van Diemen's Land. The men were likely oblivious to the legal loophole that could possibly have seen them released from penal servitude.

CHAPTER 3

Lives
inscribed

Throughout the first half of the nineteenth century Van Diemen's Land received convicts transported from across the British Empire. Chinese, Scottish, Khoisan, Italian, Australian Aboriginal, Canadian and African-American convicts joined the better known English and Irish convicts in the Australian penal colonies.[1] Some were former slaves. Van Diemen's Land also absorbed free migrants and hosted temporary visitors. Early Māori traders and whaling and sealing gangs frequented the islands in Bass Strait and also operated around New Zealand's coastlines and further afield.[2] Colonial traders plied their wares between Wellington, Auckland, Sydney and Hobart – and transported convicts and other passengers between these colonial ports. In the context of this unprecedented mobility of people and labour in the nineteenth century, the colonial authorities in Van Diemen's Land developed systems – and a very good eye – for discerning where people who arrived on their shores came from.

On their disembarkation in Van Diemen's Land convicts underwent a medical inspection and were closely questioned about their background. Those from Auckland were interrogated about how they came to be in New Zealand in the first place. Sometimes the tales told by these men did not match the meticulous written records kept by the Convict Department, which contained alternative narratives of the men's presence in the region.

The men's bodies sometimes contradicted or confirmed their stories about themselves. Tattooed inscriptions could testify to a life at sea through images such as anchors and mermaids.[3] Bodily markings on former convicts were often of a bloodier kind: scars from earlier floggings, if they were not earned at sea, might well be a sign of an escaped convict. Regardless of their past, each convict was questioned about their profession or trade to determine how their labour might best be used to the penal colony's advantage. Such intense questioning was just the start of the lengthy period of surveillance that each man, woman and child was subjected to while under sentence in Van Diemen's Land.

The *Portenia* took 25 days to sail from Auckland to Sydney.[4] Three days later, on 23 June 1843, it arrived in Hobart to unload Pickering and his 12 fellow prisoners, as well as general cargo likely taken on in Sydney.[5] The *Portenia* was in port only a matter of hours and departed the same day 'in ballast' for Port Albert in Victoria under the command of a man named Harrison.[6]

Since Pickering had first set foot in Hobart in 1837, the convict system had changed considerably. The old assignment system was replaced by a system of probation. London-based secretary of state for the Home Office, Lord John Russell, hoped the new system would prove more efficacious in reforming prisoners of the crown. Key elements of the probationary system were an emphasis on a 'separate system' that required convicts to be kept in individual cells during the first stage of probation, and the introduction of successive stages of punishment.[7]

When they arrived in Van Diemen's Land convicts were ordered to serve an initial period of labour at a probation station located well away from the main town centres. There they were sorted into gangs with new arrivals being classified as third-class prisoners. Their character could be assessed daily, and credits and debits added to their conduct record, which operated like a bank account of sorts, recording their perceived behaviour. Misdemeanours, punishments, good deeds and rewards filled the pages of their conduct record as their every act was scrutinised. Convicts could gradually improve their lot by being reclassified as second-class then first-class prisoners. Each class of prisoners could be distinguished by different living arrangements, and a differentiated scale of rewards and punishments. Those in the lowest class were typically made to do the least favoured and heaviest work.

As men moved into the second stage of probation they joined work gangs of several hundred convict labourers who performed tasks such as clearing land for settlers. Each gang had an overseer and his subordinate officers as well as a clergyman and a visiting magistrate. On progressing to the third stage of probation, male convicts received a probation pass that allowed them to work as though they were free. Between employers, however, they were required to return to a probation station and to government service.[8]

After serving at least half of their sentence a convict reached the fourth stage, and became eligible to receive a ticket of leave. This was an indulgence – a reward rather than a right – and was valid only within the colony in which it was issued. The ticket holder was constrained to a specified district. Such a ticket could be rescinded if the ticket holder committed any further offence. When a convict reached the fifth stage of probation they became eligible to be considered for a conditional or absolute pardon. A conditional pardon bound the convict to stay within a prescribed region, often the Australian and New Zealand colonies. An absolute pardon meant they were free to travel wherever they desired, including back to their homeland.[9]

When convicts arrived in Hobart they were closely questioned by Convict Department officials. On large convict transports from Britain, this interrogation usually took place on board the vessel on which they arrived. In some instances quarantine was necessary if disease had broken out on board during the lengthy sea voyage. However, the 13 convicts who disembarked from the *Portenia* were probably marched off the wharf at Hunter's Island to the nearby Hobart penitentiary, where they were incarcerated temporarily. The penitentiary incorporated the prisoners' barracks and took up several blocks on the town side of Campbell Street. If the small group from New Zealand had not already been interrogated on board the *Portenia* they would have been mustered opposite the penitentiary at the government paddock for questioning. The paperwork sent from New Zealand with the men – indents that legally transferred their persons and labour to the lieutenant governor of Van Diemen's Land – was carefully inspected, and convicts were interrogated to ascertain to what extent their verbal stories tallied with the documented ones, thus testing their level of honesty and something of their character. No lists of questions have survived but they can be inferred from the men's responses. A letter confirming their arrival in Hobart was sent to New Zealand.

Convicts in the Australian penal colonies provide a wealth of evidence about working-class lives in the nineteenth century before conviction, but also during their term of punishment. Each prisoner was allocated a police number to track them within the convict system. Their indents were the first of numerous records kept throughout their sentences. Neatly ruled columns provided space for their police number, name, place and date of trial, height, age, term of sentence, religion, level of literacy, marital status and number of children. The convict's 'statement of offence' was noted in their own words, followed by a sergeant's report on their behaviour, their trade (valuable information when it came to allocating men and women to roles of servitude), their 'native place' (where they were born and brought up) and finally a wide column was reserved for 'remarks'. For those who arrived on the *Portenia*, information usually gathered and recorded about the convicts' closest relatives was supplemented with details about how these particular men had come to be residing in New Zealand. The Hobart officials saw their very presence across the Tasman Sea as cause for deep suspicion and gave particular attention to their histories. The men's responses to the authorities' questions were meticulously recorded on their Vandemonian indents, leaving a remarkably detailed set of records in Hobart about early New Zealand in the process.

The first of the police numbers allocated to the newly arrived men, number 214, was allocated to Pickering. He provided a lengthy account of how he had arrived in the Australian penal colonies a free man, his failed business dealings, time spent in Launceston gaol, his move to New Zealand, the reason behind his sentence to transportation and details of his sisters and uncles in England. Details emerge in his indent about how he worked as a schoolmaster, tutoring the other prisoners at Auckland gaol over the 16 months following his capture at the Bay of Islands before he was taken on board the *Portenia*. Pickering also claimed to have intervened in an altercation and saved an assistant gaoler's life. Despite extensive lobbying by the inmate and his friends, no material evidence existed of a pardon he claimed to have been promised by Governor William Hobson.[10] Unfortunately Hobson had died suddenly on 10 September 1842, leaving his intentions as to Pickering's fate unclear or at least unspecified.[11] Nonetheless, Pickering arrived in Van Diemen's Land with two written character references, one from the acting governor of New Zealand and the other from 'the Minister of Auckland' – patronage that no doubt helped his cause in Van Diemen's Land.[12]

Prisoner 215, the next interviewed, was James Beckett. The 35-year-old Protestant reported being able to read and write and was a married man. His wife, Beckett said, lived at the Port Phillip District. He had, however, 'not heard of any relations since leaving home' – which, in his case, was originally Manchester. Beckett claimed to be adept at lime burning, fence splitting and dairying. His passage 'down under' had been on the *Manlius*, a convict transport that disembarked Beckett in Sydney, after which he had worked as an assigned servant of the Australian Agricultural Company for four years and nine months.[13] This company relied on Aboriginal labour as well as the labour of convicts such as Beckett to carry out the multitude of tasks required to bring the land into English modes of production.[14] Beckett claimed never to have been punished in Australia, and this is supported by his having received a ticket of leave followed by a conditional pardon in January 1834.[15] Beckett said he went to New Zealand to work as a whaler at Cloudy Bay and later as 'a trader with the natives', although he had also taken up sausage selling at the beach by the time of his arrest.[16]

White-collar criminal George Delvin Nugent, police number 216, was then questioned. He painted himself as a medical man – a surgeon, an accoucheur (male midwife) and apothecary (preparer and seller of medicines). He was a married man and had two sisters: one lived in Watling Street, London; the other lived at Rathmines, Dublin, and according to Nugent 'never had patience with her sister'. He claimed to have arrived in New Zealand as a cabin passenger and free man on the *New York Packet* some 12 months earlier.[17]

Police numbers 217 and 218 were allocated to the Clarke 'brothers', William and James. Under each man's name in his Tasmanian indent was an annotation suggesting that he went under various aliases, including Blick or Black, and William was sometimes known as Joseph. William claimed to be a seaman from Manchester who arrived in New Zealand 14 or 18 months previously. He denied using any aliases and said that he 'never was in these [Australian penal] colonies'. William's indent was annotated with the statement that 'the man named [James] Clarke on board is not my brother'.[18]

As it turned out, the other 'Clarke' was a convict absconder from Van Diemen's Land. As James Thompson, he was originally transported to Van Diemen's Land on the *Lord Lyndoch* in 1840.[19] On 6 January 1840 he and his co-defendant John Jones had been tried in London's Central Criminal Court, the Old Bailey, for pickpocketing. The men were 'indicted for stealing, on the 23rd of December, 1 purse, value 2s.; 7 sovereigns, 5 half-sovereigns, 8 shillings, 2 sixpences, and 1 30*l*. note; the property of John Wells, from the person of Jane Wells', wife of a London pawnbroker. Thompson had picked the woman's pocket while they were on an omnibus somewhere between Hyde Park Corner and Knightsbridge. Thompson and Jones, aged 24 and 28 respectively, were caught, found guilty and sentenced to transportation for 10 years.[20] Thompson arrived in Van Diemen's Land on 5 February 1841. On 26 August he absconded from the prisoners' barracks, 'remaining illegally at large' until sent back from New Zealand in the brig *Portenia* under the name 'James Clarke', an escapade that saw two years added to his original sentence.[21] Thompson later described how a few days after his escape he stowed away in the hold of the *Clydeside*, the ship on which he first made the acquaintance of the seaman William Clarke, a man whom he claimed never to have seen before that. The men worked their passage to New Zealand.[22]

Patrick Mullins, a 27-year-old bricklayer from County Louth in Ireland, was allocated police number 219. He had been transported to New South Wales from Ireland for seven years after being found guilty of street robbery at the Lancaster Quarter Sessions on 13 April 1835. The then 20-year-old brown-haired, blue-eyed boy had been recorded as a 'tolerable' bricklayer on his arrival in Sydney on the *John Barry* in January 1836.[23] After labouring for four years within the convict system, during which time he received 50 lashes at Sydney 'for neglect of duty', Mullins received his ticket of leave. This indulgence enabled the recipient to work as a private employee while being required to remain within his allocated district. He said that he worked for Frank Mitchell before leaving for New Zealand at the expiration of his seven-year term. He was in New Zealand for about six months before his arrest.[24]

William and Joseph Root were allocated police numbers 220 and 221. They had arrived in New Zealand, around two and a half years before their arrest, on the *Catherine Stewart Forbes* as steerage passengers, along with their brother Samuel and his wife Mary Ann, who had given birth to an infant daughter while at sea. Of their three sisters only Sarah, a 16-year-old servant, came out to New Zealand with them. She had since 'married to the mate of a vessel' and moved to Manila. Like their erstwhile companions in Wellington, the brothers admitted to having broken out of gaol there. For some reason the older of the two, Joseph, was suspected of having run a brothel. William, who had been living with his brother, was adamant that his brother 'did not keep a house of ill fame' but instead 'kept a butcher shop'. Joseph admitted that he was 'reported to have kept a bad house', but claimed to be a pork butcher in addition to being a coach-spring maker who could use a hammer or a pick. He left behind in Wellington his wife Anna and their two children.[25]

Next interviewed was the pit sawyer and bushman known as Denis or Daniel McCarthy, whose record states his 'proper name' was Francis. Allocated police number 222, he stated he could use the plough – a useful skill to lay claim to in colonial Van Diemen's Land. He said he was from Brickfield Hills, an inner-city area in Sydney that has since been absorbed into Surry Hills. His brother Jonathon and sister Ellen remained in New South Wales – one at Bathurst and the other at Goulburn. McCarthy proffered no explanation for his presence in New Zealand; presumably he was not pressed in relation to this.[26] Perhaps having family in New South Wales was considered sufficient proof that the man was not a convict from elsewhere in the British Empire.

Police number 223 went to London tailor William Jackson. He was evasive when it came to making his 'confession'; he simply claimed to have been 'found asleep at Mr Wheeler's house' at a time during which some clothing had been stolen and consequently, he said, 'I was charged with it.' He listed his next of kin as two brothers, John and George, and explained his presence in the colonies in part by stating that he had been in New South Wales. This was probably an oblique reference to his having served time as a convict. A man of the same name and birth year, hair and eye colouring and occupation had arrived at Sydney on the *Ocean* on 30 January 1816 to serve a sentence of transportation for 14 years, handed down at Middlesex. This earlier Sydney-based convict received his ticket of leave and was likely the same man.[27] On his arrival at Hobart Jackson said he was on the frigate *Salsette* in 1813. Captain John Bowen had commanded the vessel and sailed it to Madras, accompanying some East India Company vessels, before serving at the Indian station until 1816. Bowen is remembered in Tasmania as a founding father who helped establish the first European settlement at Risdon Cove near present-day Hobart. The settlement, founded in 1803, was a small camp of 49 colonists, including 21 male convicts, three female convicts, members of the New South Wales Corps and some free settlers.[28] Jackson's reference to Bowen was probably his way of claiming association with a respected colonist of some fame.

Charles Rowley, police number 224, said he was a seaman from New Bedford in Massachusetts, America. He wore material evidence of this on his left arm, on which was inked 'the American flag, Liberty of America, [and an] Indian War Dance'. His body carried numerous other tattoos consistent with a life at sea, including a 'boat in pursuit of whales'.[29] Rowley, who had no known relations, said that he had arrived in Sydney in 1835 and worked for several masters there, including a man named Hassall. He had relocated to New Zealand on the *Magnet*, where he had been in trouble over some blankets and had been gaoled for one month.[30]

John Coghlan from Cork was then interrogated and received police number 225. He was also a seaman and told the authorities he had been involved in stealing blankets with Rowley but was discharged without conviction. He explained his presence in New Zealand by saying he had sailed from London as a whaler in 1832 'in the *Mary* to the South Seas'. After spending some time in the Pacific, Coghlan sailed home in the *Asia* from Sydney; the ship was carrying a cargo of wool, oil, hides and horns. He claimed to have spent some time at home in Ireland before sailing for New Zealand in 1839 via Sag Harbour, New York. His final two statements are telling: 'I never was flogged. I never was at Norfolk Island.'[31] Clearly, Coghlan was strongly suspected of having been one of numerous convict absconders: some had attained illicit freedom, some had died trying and others were recaptured, sometimes thousands of miles from the place from which they had escaped.

The last of the *Portenia* convicts questioned was Henry Rogers, police number 226. Originally from St James in London, he also claimed to have been a whaler – a trade he practised for around 16 or 17 years. Rogers said he had been whaling out of Sydney from 1831 and had later arrived in New Zealand on the *Susannah*. After being taken on by another whaling vessel he ended up becoming a castaway. Like Rowley and Coghlan, Rogers admitted to an earlier encounter with the law in Wellington where, he said, he had served 12 months' imprisonment for stealing £10 or £12.[32]

News of the men's arrival from New Zealand on the *Portenia* spread to the north of Van Diemen's Land, where it was incorrectly reported in the *Launceston Examiner* that they had all been 'convicted at Port Nicholson' – a statement that did not take into account Pickering's trial and conviction in Auckland. According to the newspaper, four of the men were 'bolters from New South Wales'.[33] Given that Beckett had received a conditional pardon, his presence in New Zealand was likely legitimate, provided the pardon allowed him to live in the Australian or New Zealand colonies. This did not, however, seem to prevent his being seen as a 'bolter' on his return to the Australian penal colonies. The two ticket-of-leave men, Mullins and Jackson, had both served out their original sentences but were required by law to remain within the districts to which these tickets confined them. Both said they could read and write, so they must have understood the terms of their indulgences.[34] The fourth of the so-called 'bolters' was probably Coghlan, the man who was adamant that he had never been flogged but whose body told a different story. On his conduct record, which commenced on his arrival in Van Diemen's Land from New Zealand, the space reserved for additional remarks about his physical description states that he bore '2 scars on Back, breast having marks of being flogged'.[35] 'Two have been detected by the authorities at the Prisoners' Barracks, as runaways from this colony', the *Launceston Examiner* reported, 'and despatched to Port Arthur.' The newspaper was less interested in sensationalising the fate of these men than it was in highlighting 'how complete is the surveillance of the convict system'. It emphasised 'the importance of printed descriptions of runaways being sent from one colony to another'.[36] Surveillance could transcend colonial borders, extend across the seas and heighten the possibility that no man or woman would go unnoticed if they fled a penal colony while under sentence. New Zealand justice enjoyed a global reach.

A convict's conduct record, as well as providing a running record of their misdemeanours, additional punishments and rewards or indulgences, repeated some of the information gleaned at interview and inscribed on the indent. The prisoner's police number, name, place and date of trial, sentence, dates of embarkation and disembarkation, religion, whether they could read and/or write and their confession taken down in their own words headed up their page in these large, leather-bound registers. Comments were often included about their conduct while in gaol and/or in transit to Van Diemen's Land. The next section of the record noted the prisoner's trade and provided intricate details about their physical characteristics. This information served a twofold purpose: it was valuable in helping the colonial authorities decide what type of labour the prisoner might best be suited to; and it served as a detailed description if the person later needed to be formally identified. This could be to confirm the identity of a deceased person, to advertise the details of a runaway convict or absconder, or to allow the authorities to disprove an assumed identity, such as that taken on by James Thompson when he adopted the alias Clarke. The physical description included details such as a convict's height, age, complexion, head size, hair colour, whiskers, visage, height of forehead, colours of eyebrows and eyes and details of their nose, mouth and chin. Their native place (place of origin) was also recorded, potentially so they could be identified by their accent. Below this detailed description an additional section was provided for remarks: this is where distinguishing features such as tattoos or the scars on a man's back – such as Coghlan's – were recorded.

In addition to providing as complete a picture as possible of a convicted man or woman, their conduct record pinpointed their whereabouts at any given moment in Van Diemen's Land and noted their transfers within the system. This very valuable information gives insights into what became of convicts once they were absorbed into the system – at least as they were viewed from the perspective of their overseers, local magistrates and so on. Despite the high levels of scrutiny these men and women were subjected to, there would also have been numerous acts, good or bad, that went unnoticed and therefore unrecorded. Beneath their detailed description, each convict's conduct record in the probation period contained space for recording their initial period of probation, and the location or 'station of gang' where that was to be served. A large portion of the page beneath was available for recording, over time, any further offences committed and sentences accrued, and the magistrate's initials and date were added to each of these.

A narrower column on the right-hand side of the page, headed 'Remarks', provided space for details such as the name of the master or mistress to whom a convict was assigned. Other information, such as letters or petitions received about their circumstances, were sometimes entered here too, along with miscellaneous notes. Usually written in a larger script centred across the bottom of the page, sometimes very neatly and at other times hastily scrawled, were details of any indulgences the convict eventually received, such as a ticket of leave or a pardon. The date granted was noted, as was the date rescinded if a ticket of leave was withdrawn. The type of pardon was also jotted down, if one had been granted. If circumstances led to the convict's death within the system, that event formed the final entry flowing across their page in the conduct register. Reference was often made to another record set that contained more details about the death, but these records no longer survive. Where there are no newspaper reports of inquests, the details of convicts' deaths while under sentence remain elusive.

These conduct registers reveal the diverging paths each man or woman's life took while under sentence. According to surviving records, there were at least 80 probation stations across the island to which convicts could be sent.[37] Not all of these were operational at the same time. Their use depended on market factors, including local demand for convict labour and the costs involved in the upkeep of the station. Factors that influenced the location of an initial term of probation included the professed skill or occupation of the prisoner and local demand for it, their propensity for escaping – those with a record of absconding would be sent to a station from which escape was considered more challenging – and whether the authorities wanted to separate them from others with whom they had formed 'bad' associations. Nevertheless, in many cases convicts who arrived on the same vessel from New Zealand tended initially to be sent to the same probation station or general area.

CHAPTER 4

A segregated society

S egregation was a core concept in mid-nineteenth-century British transportation. Convicts were spatially segregated from the society they had offended against, and they were also segregated within their place of punishment. The spatial configuration of Van Diemen's Land, with its urban population clustered around major centres in the north and south of the island and smaller townships scattered between the two, was well suited to penal reform. Just as the British colonists segregated Aboriginal people who survived Australia's frontier wars onto reserves located beyond white settlements to train them to fit better into colonial society, convicts were initially segregated to be assessed and reformed.[1]

Convict labour was used to build remote probation stations in the lightly forested hills and grassy regions of Van Diemen's Land. Ideally, the architecture of probation stations supported the tenets of nineteenth-century penology, which increasingly required convicts to be reformed not only through segregation from mainstream society but also by maintaining silence and sleeping in separate cells apart from other prisoners. In reality, an ongoing influx of convicts and a lack of adequate resources to support them meant such visions of separatism were only ever partially realised.[2]

Vandemonian convicts formed a highly mobile population. Some of this movement was seasonal, some was the result of punishments being meted out, and some was simply due to shifting demands for labour. Through their conduct registers, appropriation lists, musters and other related record sets, convicts' movements can be tracked between and beyond probation stations in minute detail.

Wherever convicts were sent, they were kept under a strict regime of discipline and surveillance. Misconduct was dealt with harshly. Common punishments included hard labour in chains, solitary confinement and flogging; their rations might be reduced to bread and water, or their sentence extended. Men and women emerged from the system reformed or broken; many an old lag took to the bottle to dull their physical and psychological pain. Some failed to emerge at all – they died while still under sentence. Others managed to escape and avoid recapture. The *Portenia* convicts were no different – they underwent this broad range of experiences and outcomes, although the white-collar convicts among them seemed more adept at reinventing themselves after their sentences expired, with their character not smeared by the dreaded 'convict stain', the stigma attached to people or places formerly associated with convicts.

Convict probation stations stretched across the length of Van Diemen's Land from north to south. However, it was to the east of Hobart, to various sites on the hilly, bush-clad and isolated Tasman Peninsula, that the *Portenia* convicts were sent to serve their initial period of probation. The Tasman Peninsula was a key site of convict management in colonial Van Diemen's Land. Barely connected to Forestier Peninsula and from there to the rest of the island by a narrow isthmus at Eaglehawk Neck, Tasman Peninsula was used solely by the Convict Department. A garrison stationed at the neck, with large dogs chained together across this narrow strip of land, further deterred any convicts who might have considered absconding overland. The peninsula housed 12 main convict sites that served a range of purposes, including a transfer station at Norfolk Bay, the Coal Mines located at Sloping Main, an invalid station at Impression Bay, a probation station at Cascades (Koonya), an agricultural station at Saltwater River and probation stations at Slopen Island and Wedge Bay. The penal station at Port Arthur and its adjacent juvenile counterpart, Point Puer, also operated throughout the probationary period.[3]

Fine-grained details about key probation stations across Van Diemen's Land were recorded in a report sent to London-based Secretary of State for the Colonies Earl Grey. This lengthy document was produced by Charles La Trobe while he was the administrator of Van Diemen's Land for four months in 1847, after the dismissal of Lieutenant-Governor Eardley Wilmot and pending the arrival of Sir Thomas Denison. La Trobe's report is a key source of information about the natural and built environments, resourcing, staffing allocations and the number of convicts at 37 sites across Van Diemen's Land and Norfolk Island at the time. Such observations are useful for measuring the extent to which the built environments at these sites reflected the evolution of a distinctly nineteenth-century model of prisons.

Imprisonment was rarely used as punishment in Britain before the eighteenth century. Its rise in use throughout the empire in the nineteenth century was partly inspired by a shift away from earlier forms of punishment such as public hangings. Yet the increased use of imprisonment also encouraged various reforms. High-profile reformers such as the well-connected Quaker Elizabeth Fry (cousin to Edward Gibbon Wakefield, whose theory of systematic colonisation underpinned the New Zealand Company) campaigned successfully for practical improvements to the disgraceful conditions in many prisons, such as housing female prisoners separately from males, and organising prisoners into various classes. Prisoners were clothed in distinctive garb and were expected to perform labour. These practical changes had strong moral overtones.

Refashioning the physical structures of confinement to reflect penal thought at the time was an important change. Social reformer Jeremy Bentham's panopticon – a model prison with a central tower that gave guards an unrelenting view of every prisoner in their cell – became an important conceptual model. Bentham wanted prisoners to know they were under constant surveillance; at the same time, they were unable to see the guards or their fellow prisoners. An increasing emphasis on enforced silence exacerbated the physical separation of prisoners from each other. Pentonville Prison, which opened in London in 1842, became a model for this 'separate system', even though it did not implement all of Bentham's ideas.[4] Arguably, however, it was Port Arthur in Van Diemen's Land that eventually conformed more closely to Bentham's vision.

La Trobe described Port Arthur as 'the principal Penal Station of the Colony with the exception of Norfolk Island'. In the 1840s its buildings were mostly wooden, although vast sandstone structures now dominate the remaining ruins. It troubled the visiting administrator to discover how many of the 1185 convicts there were housed in huts that accommodated between 16 and 30 men; only a few were kept segregated from other convicts, in separate single apartments and solitary cells in a wooden building that was 'divided into ten passages, each containing fourteen cells'. La Trobe noted disapprovingly that the construction of this building did not prevent the prisoners from communicating freely with each other. But he could see signs of segregation at work: soldiers were housed in military barracks, separate from the convicts; and sick boys from nearby Point Puer were kept apart from adult male convict patients when they were brought to the hospital in the Port Arthur complex.[5]

La Trobe noted that Port Arthur provided a 'good house' for its commandant, inferior accommodation for his underlings, an 'excellent' brick cookhouse, a 'very fine' ordnance store (also brick), a large clothing store, a 'large, handsome and excellent' church, a school room and the hospital. The convicts cultivated some 80 acres (32ha) of land and produced most of the vegetables required at the station. They also laboured at the site's mill and, in various workshops, they produced goods such as locks, brass and iron castings, bells, taps, lathes, anvils and beams. They also manufactured leather boots – about 250 pairs a week – that were sent to Hobart. Seventeen convicts manned boats that ferried goods to and from the station, and 54 convicts hauled freight-laden carts along a tramway that extended across the peninsula.[6] It was the ultimate end of transportation: segregated from society and segregated within itself. It was also a long way from New Zealand and an impossible distance from England.

The 'bolters' who were sent to Port Arthur shortly after their arrival in Hobart in June 1843 were James Beckett and Patrick Mullins. Beckett, the erstwhile sausage seller and jack-of-all-trades, was recorded by the Convict Department as a brick maker. A slight man with grey eyes, a ruddy complexion, light brown hair and 'small' whiskers, Beckett bore 'marks of the King's evil' on his neck – in other words, he had suffered from tuberculous cervical lymphadenitis, or scrofula. His period of probation was set at 16 months at the penal station. However, a little over a year later, on 11

August 1844 Beckett was sent back to the Hobart prisoners' barracks, and he was admitted to hospital two months later. By 20 October 1844 he was 'released from the first stage of probation' and was ordered to complete the remainder of his sentence at the Royal Engineer's Department in Hobart. However, Beckett's conduct record reveals that between August 1848 and June 1849 he was assigned to labour for a rural settler at Prosser Plains (the area around present-day Buckland to the northeast of Hobart) and, later, to settlers in Liverpool Street, Hobart. His assignments were interrupted by a brief period of freedom between 2 March 1847 and 12 September 1848; his ticket of leave was revoked when he was found guilty of 'larceny under £5'. On 16 August 1849 he finally received his certificate of freedom.[7] Yet it seems that Beckett may not have been an entirely reformed character, as a little over five years later a man of the same name was accused of regularly stealing small bags of flour from the Andersons' bakery in Argyle Street, Hobart, where he purchased his rolls every morning. He was found guilty and sentenced to three months' imprisonment with hard labour.[8]

Mullins' initial period of probation was longer than Beckett's: it was set at two and a half years. He served the first 10 months at Port Arthur, where he was punished with 10 days in solitary confinement for gambling, and six weeks in chains for spoiling work. In April 1846 Mullins assaulted another convict and was sentenced to 12 months of hard labour in chains. By May 1847 he had been transferred to Tasmania's midlands – initially to Oatlands, then to Bothwell, where he was assigned to several different settlers over the next 18 months. His conduct record depicts a broken man who regularly frequented the pub without his master's leave and sought solace in drink. For these transgressions, Mullins was sentenced to more hard labour and more time in solitary confinement. On 4 September 1849 the Irishman received his ticket of leave, only to have it revoked several times for offences relating to drunkenness and disturbing the peace. He was ordered to do two months of hard labour at Impression Bay for 'being in a public house'.[9]

On 5 November 1851 while still under sentence, Mullins applied for permission to marry. His status as an absconder was scrawled against his name in the register of applicants.[10] His intended bride was Margaret Mannion, a petite, freckle-faced young woman with dark brown hair and hazel eyes who had arrived in Hobart a little over a year earlier in October

1850, aged 16, with her older sister Bridget. The two young women were convicts on the *Duke of Cornwall*. Both were servants from Clifton (Clifden) in County Galway, Ireland, where, in October 1849, they were found guilty of stealing three cows and were sentenced to seven years' transportation.[11] The marriage register notes that Mullins and Mannion were married on 18 November 1851: only their names and the transports on which they had arrived were recorded in the scribe's sloping cursive script.[12] Mullins' certificate of freedom was issued on 28 April 1853.[13]

It seems that Mullins may have left Mannion widowed shortly thereafter, as on 1 November 1854 Thomas Larkin, a convict transported on the *Blenheim* from Galway for 10 years for killing a heifer, was given permission to marry Margaret Mannion: the two were wed on 27 November.[14] This marriage may not have lasted either: offences ranging from being a 'common prostitute' and 'vagrancy' to 'larceny', committed in the north of the island at Launceston and Campbell Town throughout the 1860s and as late as 1879, are scrawled across Mannion's conduct record.[15] Interestingly, at times she reverted to her former married name of Mullins, under which she was also charged with a number of offences against public order, including disturbing the peace.[16]

James Thompson, after he had been identified as the convict absconder rather than 'Clarke', had his sentence extended by two years. He was sent to Port Arthur to perform a year's hard labour, after which he was to be sent to a probation station for two and a half years. On Christmas Eve 1846 he was transferred to Brown's River hiring depot, seven miles south of Hobart – previously used as a probation station.[17] When La Trobe visited the hiring depot the following year he remarked on the improvements to the buildings which had formerly been 'of a most miserable description'. At the time of his inspection in 1847 the site boasted two-tiered separate apartments that 'were considered to be the best built of any in the Island'. However, these were not occupied at the time as the number of convicts at the site was well below its capacity of 420.[18] Thompson was charged with only one offence while under sentence: on 14 February 1848 he received seven days in solitary confinement for having been 'in a public house for the purpose of tippling'. From March 1848 he was hired out as an assigned convict servant, initially to a Mr Storey at the Eastern Marshes, to the east of the midlands town of Oatlands, and then to other settlers. The final annotation on his conduct record is a short note written on 4 September 1848 that simply states 'abs?' – implying that Thompson had absconded.[19] The lack of any further annotation on his conduct record seems to indicate that, this time, Thompson successfully managed to evade recapture – at least under this name.

La Trobe described Impression Bay, where Mullins performed two months' hard labour in 1851, as being situated in 'a depression of the Coast of Norfolk Bay, Tasman's Peninsula'.[20] Poor choices had been made in relation to building materials on the site – specifically the bricks – and this had led to insecure foundations. La Trobe approved of the superintendent's quarters but declared the rest of the staff accommodation inadequate. At the time of his visit there were 445 convicts accommodated at Impression Bay. They were organised into classes, with first-class prisoners having the use of three mess rooms. All those on site were fed via a cookhouse and a bakehouse equipped with two ovens. Three stores met the clothing and ordnance needs of the convicts. In addition to a school room and workshops for carpenters and blacksmiths, there was a hospital that could accommodate up to 100 convicts under the care of a resident medical officer. Some of the invalids performed light duties such as vegetable gardening or cultivating hops, but the poor quality of the soil meant that such activities could not fruitfully be undertaken on anything approaching a commercial scale. The invalids were, according to La Trobe, 'a difficult class to manage in every respect'.[21]

The grey-haired, grey-whiskered and grey-eyed whaler Henry Rogers from the *Portenia* gradually became ill while labouring within the convict system. He was sent to Impression Bay to serve a probationary period of two and a half years.[22] Over the decade that followed he was assigned as a servant to masters at locations ranging from Veterans Row in North Hobart up into St Patrick's Plains in the central highlands. He was returned to the prisoners' barracks four times between assignments and accrued three stays in hospital. Ill health may have been the reason he was charged with only two additional offences while under sentence: escaping from his work gang on 20 December 1845, and being 'found drunk' on 21 June 1852 for which he got 14 days in solitary confinement. On 13 April 1853 Rogers received his certificate of freedom. After 10 years in the convict system he was an elderly pauper in poor health, and spent a large part of the next decade in and out of the general hospital in Hobart, the hospital at Port Arthur and the invalid depot at Impression Bay. He died, aged about 69, at Port Arthur on 30 December 1862.

Rogers' story does not quite end there, though. Beneath the inked annotation recording his death, a 'surcharge made by Colonial Government for maintenance in hospital' provides an itemised account of costs involved in caring for Rogers, totalling £141/10/3. Noted by the Convict Department as 'Claim No. 8', it was rationalised on the basis that the man had 'contracted disease before free'.[23] This additional cost was levied against the Vandemonian government, which would have anticipated the costs involved in maintaining the prisoner for the duration of his sentence – outside of periods of assignment during which his master was financially liable for his upkeep – but generally not thereafter.

John Coghlan, like Rogers, was required to serve an initial period of two and a half years at Impression Bay. The black-haired and brown-eyed Irishman's conduct record is crammed full of numerous additional offences committed while under sentence. On 27 occasions he was found guilty of misconduct – mostly relating to drunkenness, but also 'being absent without leave', 'resisting a constable in the execution of his duty' and 'representing himself to be free'. Habitual drunkenness was not at the time understood to constitute a disease (alcoholism), in Coghlan's situation likely exacerbated by a desire to escape his difficult circumstances. Punishment – ranging from hard labour to fines – failed to curb his behaviour. In 1846 he served several months at Port Arthur, then found himself back at Impression Bay before being returned to the prisoners' barracks in Hobart in May of that year. He was assigned to George Stokell at Richmond, an inland settlement to the northeast of Hobart, and then to various settlers in the far north of the island and, later, inland to the west of Hobart at Ouse. On 25 July 1851 Coghlan was sent to work at the Marine Department. He eventually gained his ticket of leave on 28 September 1852 (although this was rescinded several times for drunkenness), followed by his certificate of freedom on 27 April 1853.[24]

Joseph Root was the third and final *Portenia* convict ordered to serve his initial period of probation at Impression Bay and was also sent there for two and a half years. His life course was remarkably similar to Coghlan's:

his conduct record was peppered with offences relating to drunkenness and associated infractions such as 'disturbing the peace' and 'falsely representing himself as being free'. While he was under sentence he was punished for his misdemeanours with solitary confinement or hard labour. By October 1848 Root may have reached breaking point, as he absconded. When captured, he was ordered to perform hard labour for six months with a road gang at Spring Hill in the midlands. He absconded again within days, was caught again and was sent back down the Tasman Peninsula to Cascades.[25]

Cascades was a punishment station located east of Impression Bay. It had carpenters and blacksmiths, and had 70 acres (28ha) of land producing vegetable crops. The station included separate apartments and solitary cells, and more were being constructed when La Trobe visited. It had its own hospital, school and chapel in addition to mess rooms, a cookhouse, bakehouse, provisions store and officers' quarters. It housed 403 prisoners, some of whom were boys; La Trobe was quick to emphasise that the youths were 'entirely apart from the rest of the gang'.[26] From February 1849 until 28 May 1850 when Root received his ticket of leave, he was assigned as a servant to several different settlers around Hobart and also did a stint labouring on public works. As a ticket-of-leave man Root was once again found drunk. He was also charged with resisting arrest and was fined. His certificate of freedom was eventually awarded on 11 April 1853.[27]

The sawyer, bushman and ploughman Denis McCarthy (also known as Daniel or Francis) was sent to Cascades for an initial probationary period of two and a half years. Afterwards he was assigned to a number of different settlers in the midlands and in the north of Van Diemen's Land. While under sentence McCarthy was charged with seven other offences, mostly relating to behaviour that was not sufficiently submissive: he was considered insolent and was punished for making use of threatening and obscene language. On one occasion he was also charged 'as a watchman [with] procuring provisions etc. for prisoners under sentence', for which he was sentenced to three months in prison with hard labour. Towards the end of his sentence he was sent to prison for a further three months with hard labour for 'refusing a service at a reasonable rate of wages' and was later reprimanded for 'idleness'.[28]

In November 1849 McCarthy received a ticket of leave, but in February the following year he was punished for 'idling about town' and was gaoled for three months with hard labour, after which he was required 'to reside in the interior' of the island. A year later he was charged with having absconded and 'being on board the *Shamrock* with intent to escape from the colony'. His ticket of leave was revoked and McCarthy was sent to Port Arthur. After a similar escapade the following year, the Marine Board charged him with misconduct for being on a vessel after hours. He was sentenced to hard labour in chains for nine months, with the additional imposts of being 'kept separate' from other prisoners outside of working hours and being required to serve a further probationary period of nine months after his sentence expired. McCarthy finally received his certificate of freedom on 9 April 1853.[29]

Several of the *Portenia* convicts – William Clarke, William Jackson and Charles Rowley – were sent to the Coal Mines to serve their probation. Built in 1833 as a punishment station, by 1843 the Coal Mines had become a probation station. When La Trobe visited in 1847 he described it as capable of housing more than 600 men. However, at the time of the administrator's visit only 403 prisoners were housed there. Here, too, the infrastructure reflected the latest penal theories of the time, with sleeping huts for the wardens situated near the front walls of the station 'so as to command a view of all that is passing'. The Coal Mines had 108 'good' separate apartments constructed from stone and brick as well as 100 wooden ones that were due to be pulled down. Keeping the men apart at night was considered an important strategy in preventing homosexual relations. There were also a small number of solitary cells on site to house men undergoing additional punishment. The rundown hospital was barely serviceable. La Trobe found the chapel 'roomy', and noted that a hospital ward had been set aside for use by Roman Catholics. The absence of a school room and schoolmaster was problematic, as it meant there was no provision for children of soldiers stationed at the site to be educated. Progress on the building projects at the Coal Mines was delayed because the site relied on timber from the nearby Cascades, which had been very slow in arriving.

Convicts labouring at the Coal Mines extracted about 300 tons of coal each week;[30] they ended up filthy and exhausted. Former convict William Derrincourt said that men working at the bottom of the deep mineshafts were nicknamed 'Devon donkeys'. They were harnessed to trucks of water and made to haul them: 'because of the lowness of the drive, [the men were] almost on all fours, holding on and dragging with their hands on the rail'. Some of these convicts had boots; others had none. 'They were puffing and blowing,' Derrincourt said, 'and reeking and steaming from their exertions.' The men worked in threes and were under pressure to complete their shift within a certain timeframe. Those who finished last were left down the shaft to wait without any food while the others were hauled to the surface before them.[31]

William Clarke (also known as Joseph Blick or Black) was sent to the Coal Mines to serve an initial period of probation for two years. Unsurprisingly, given the harsh conditions, he absconded within months. Unfortunately for him he was recaptured and, on 24 November 1843, was sentenced to 75 'stripes' (lashes of the whip). On the same day he was also found guilty of 'larceny under £5' and sentenced to hard labour for three months, with 30 days in solitary confinement. Perhaps he had hoped the stolen items would assist his flight. On 17 January 1844 Clarke was again found guilty of 'larceny under £5'; he may have been stockpiling goods for another escape attempt. This time he was punished more severely with hard labour in chains for a year, with 60 days' solitary confinement to be served at intervals throughout his sentence. On 16 February he was relocated to the nearby probation station at tiny Slopen Island off the tip of Tasman Peninsula, where fewer than 200 men laboured. Less than a fortnight later Clarke was dead. An inquest found that he 'was supposed to be drowned in endeavouring to effect his escape' in the rough waters typical of this region.[32]

Many a man drowned trying to escape the peninsula by sea – including Richard Whithous, who was sentenced at the Wellington Supreme Court on 8 June 1849 to seven years' transportation for piracy. Whithous was a boatbuilder and mariner, born in Nantucket in the United States but brought up in England. He was found guilty of making away with the schooner *Comfort*, despite claiming to be the master of the vessel and proclaiming his innocence. He drowned at Lagoon Bay on 10 February 1853.[33]

One other convict was transported from New Zealand to Van Diemen's Land for piracy: the seaman William Ellis, also born in Nantucket. Ellis and the crew seized the schooner *Hannah* and put the master onshore at the Chatham Islands. Ellis also shot and wounded a seaman and forced him ashore. Ellis and the crew dumped the cargo and sailed the *Hannah* to

New Zealand. While the pirated ship lay at anchor in the Mercury Islands the colonial authorities became aware it had been seized, and a schooner carrying soldiers from the 80th Regiment retook the vessel.[34] Ellis claimed in court that he was not on board the *Hannah* when it was 'lying at the Chatham Islands'; he said the mate and several men had approached him later, and he had agreed to sail the *Hannah* to New Zealand. However, the mate had turned Queen's evidence and Ellis's story was not believed. He was found guilty and sentenced on 11 March 1844 to transportation for seven years for piracy. Ellis eventually received his conditional pardon on 16 April 1850.[35]

The tailor William Jackson was also sent to the Coal Mines. His initial period of probation was for two and a half years. His first offence while under sentence was recorded on 25 November 1847 when he was found to have been 'drunk, overstaying his pass & having a pair of tweed trousers and two cloth waistcoats in his possession', crimes for which he was put into solitary confinement for a week. In January the following year he served 10 more days in solitary confinement after being found 'under the influence of liquor'. He had a couple of stints in hospital that year, indicating that his health was beginning to fail. He then spent a month at Impression Bay in the autumn of 1850 before he was transferred to nearby Saltwater River. On 7 May 1850 Jackson received a ticket of leave. This was, however, rescinded in 1851 when he was absent from a muster that all convicts were required to attend. While he was a ticket-of-leave holder, Jackson was reprimanded twice – once in February 1852 for being drunk and again in April the same year for using profane language and being insolent. By July 1852 he had absconded but he must have been caught because, on 11 March 1859, his ticket of leave was once again rescinded when he failed to attend the muster.[36]

Charles Rowley, a baker and a seaman, joined Clarke and Jackson at the Coal Mines to serve an initial period of probation set at two and a half years. Like his fellow *Portenia* convicts Rowley racked up a number of other offences. He was 'admonished' on 26 October 1843 for 'misconduct in concealing some meat in the Bakehouse or conniving to do the same'. This was followed by two more offences: being in possession of tobacco and money, and being insolent.[37] The money was possibly Rowley's own, as records show that, after he arrived on the *Portenia*, the sum of 10 shillings in his possession had been banked on his behalf into the Convict Savings Bank and was later paid out to him while he was at the Coal Mines.[38]

The Convict Savings Bank was set up by Lieutenant-Governor George Arthur in 1828 on instructions from England. It was a further demonstration of the focus on segregation, which extended even to money and property being confiscated from convicts on their arrival in Van Diemen's Land. Money was supposed to be 'deposited under regulations for their ultimate use'. Convicts who received a ticket of leave and were able to earn their own income were encouraged to add voluntarily to their savings, and received 10 per cent interest.[39] Thrift was taken as a sign that a man or woman was on the pathway to becoming a truly reformed character.

In early December 1845 Rowley was relocated to nearby Saltwater River probation station. The station was principally set up to grow wheat. La Trobe noted that the buildings were mostly of brick, but in some instances the bars on the prisoners' windows were made of wood; presumably a determined man would be able to cut his way to freedom with relative ease. La Trobe found the store that housed provisions and clothes rather insecure. The cells, on the other hand, were strongly built but poorly ventilated. The men dined in mess rooms according to their class of probation. The largest (first-class) mess room also doubled as a chapel and school room. Roman Catholics were relegated to the third-class mess room for Mass, and the room was also used in the evenings for school lessons. Prisoners who were unwell were accommodated in 'two wretched small huts, one with a bark roof' that were not conducive to healing. Detached cottages housed the superintendent and the catechist.[40]

La Trobe found the land to be 'good', and much of it was being cultivated. There were workshops on site for blacksmiths and carpenters. There was a good local supply of shells that were burnt for lime, and plenty of timber and clay. A 'good' road led to the Coal Mines, and to Cascades in the opposite direction. La Trobe stated that 495 convicts were stationed at Saltwater River when he visited. Many of the probationers there had formerly been at Port Arthur. La Trobe was agitated to find that quite a few of the third-class prisoners were mere boys: while 'a portion of the ward is railed off so that they cannot mix with the men', he nevertheless considered that 'their detention here under any circumstances is objectionable'. He saw some improvements at the station, but recommended more.[41]

Rowley's allotted time labouring as part of a probationary gang at Saltwater River was up on 6 April 1846. He was then assigned to a series of settlers. A number of these assignments were in the midlands, ranging from Tunbridge and nearby Oatlands to the larger centre further north at Campbell Town. He continued to accumulate offences while on assignment, including 'larceny under £5' in February 1848 and, in March the following year, 'being on the premises of Mr Vincent & making use of very abusive language when asked to leave'. Despite his chequered record, Rowley eventually received his ticket of leave on 16 April 1850, followed by a conditional pardon on 3 February 1852.[42]

Joseph Root's brother William was sent to Norfolk Bay for his initial period of probation, along with Nugent and Pickering. William Root accrued the highest number of offences of the three men. He was punished on nine separate occasions while under sentence for acts of misconduct. Three of these involved clothing – 'making away with a fellow prisoner's shirt', 'having a belt improperly in his possession' and 'altering and defacing slop clothing'. This latter offence could have involved the man making adjustments so that his regulation clothing fitted more comfortably, or altering its look with a view to being less readily recognised as a convict if he absconded. These three offences resulted in Root being given hard labour in chains for three months, seven days in solitary confinement, and hard labour in chains for another fortnight. His other acts of misconduct ranged from being 'absent from muster' to 'disobedience of orders, insolence and absence from his work'. On 24 November 1844 he was ordered to be flogged: he received 30 lashes for insolence.[43]

After his probationary period expired Root was assigned to a person called Rhodes in Murray Street, central Hobart, for just under a month from 10 March 1847. On 7 April he was reassigned to a colonist on Bruny Island, southeast of Hobart.[44] This island had formerly housed a government station for Tasmanian Aboriginal people in the 1820s and early 1830s, where they were issued with rations and taught rudimentary hygiene, Bible lessons and English. This had been a catastrophic failure: most of the Aboriginal people died within a year, likely as a result of dietary changes and introduced diseases, and the station was abandoned.[45] On 13 February 1849 Root received his ticket of leave. Rather than remain in the colony as required, his conduct record notes that on or around 13 November of the same year he absconded.[46]

When Dublin-trained medico George Nugent was released from hospital, he joined Root and Pickering at Norfolk Bay. Four offences were recorded against Nugent while he was under sentence: these involved 'making an improper statement in writing and addressing to Mr Crook', for which his probation was extended by one month; 'idleness', which earned him 10 days in solitary confinement; 'gross misconduct towards a female of respectability', which resulted in a sentence to hard labour in chains for nine months; and 'refusing to work'. Nugent had been privately assigned in 1845, but when he was sentenced to hard labour in November of that year he was sent to Port Arthur. He served another week in solitary confinement while he was there, for refusing to work. In 1847 and 1848 he was assigned as a convict servant to settlers in small towns in Tasmania's midlands, including Oatlands and Ross.[47]

Nugent also worked for a Mr F.C. Atkinson of Hobart, who hired him from the prisoners' barracks in April 1848. Atkinson was a homeopathic doctor who lived in Macquarie Street, one of Hobart's major thoroughfares, and he employed Nugent to work in a medical capacity. During this period Nugent was required to attend a coroner's inquest held in Hobart on 31 May 1848 to look into the death of Lawrence May. May's death was attributed to a fracture of his lower jaw and a resultant fever. Nugent had extracted two of May's teeth at the Nag's Head pub in Melville Street in central Hobart; and a third tooth, removed by the 'doctor's [Nugent's] boy', had apparently pained the patient considerably more than the earlier two extractions.[48] The jury's verdict implied culpability on Nugent's part, but this was not spelt out. The case attracted a lot of adverse publicity and was probably a strong contributing factor to the breakdown of the working relationship between Nugent and Atkinson. By 19 August Atkinson was taking out advertisements in the local newspaper dissociating himself from his former servant, Nugent, and cautioning people not to extend credit to Nugent in Atkinson's name without Atkinson's written authority.[49] Nugent, in the interim, received his ticket of leave on 13 June 1848. However, he fell foul of the authorities again on 16 December 1848 'in not proceeding to Green Ponds [a midlands town since renamed Kempton] in accordance with his pass'.[50]

On 31 January 1850 Nugent received his certificate of freedom. Once his sentence had expired in Van Diemen's Land he relocated within the

Australian colonies, reinventing himself in the process.[51] Posturing as a gentleman collector who had 'undertaken an exploratory tour ... some time ago in the neighbouring colony of New Zealand' and who had 'a materially scientific mind', he joined an expedition in the colony of Victoria that included William Blandowski and a Mr Jackson.[52] There seems to be no surviving evidence either to confirm or discount Nugent's story about having taken part in scientific exploration in New Zealand. Jackson, Nugent's companion in the Victorian expedition, was the landlord of the Keilor Hotel.

The leader of the expedition, Silesian-born Blandowski, was a noted naturalist – described by his biographer as an 'ambitious, eccentric, stubborn, impulsive, quarrelsome individualist' whose 'scientific integrity was sometimes questioned' – and a founding member of the Geological Society of Victoria.[53] In 1854 he became the first 'curator and collector of curiosities' of the Museum of Natural History in Victoria. Seeking specimens for the new museum's collections was the key purpose of his expedition with Jackson and Nugent. Their quest took them to Mount Macedon and surrounds, where Nugent later reported an extraordinary find 'on Mr Fawkner's run'. He was presumably referring to John Pascoe Fawkner, one of the colony's 'founding fathers' and publisher of its first newspaper. According to Nugent, the men had 'discovered some bones ... which resemble the bones of the "Moah Tonga," or large man-bird, which have been found in New Zealand'. Given the size of the bones, which likely belonged to one of the numerous species of megafauna that roamed across the Australian continent until the end of the last ice age, the men concluded that they must have found the remains of a creature 'more gigantic than an elephant'. The party located other fossils at the summit of Mount Macedon.[54]

Nugent evidently moved further north sometime after taking part in Blandowski's expedition. In August 1857 he was called on to give evidence at an inquest into the death of John Fogarty at the Hunter Valley. Fogarty, 'a notorious drunkard', had a knife wound to his arm and subsequently died from tetanus – or lockjaw, as it was called at the time. Nugent, who had resumed his prior occupation as a medical man, had treated the man's wound and, on considering it healed, suggested Fogarty return to work. Fogarty's health deteriorated, and Nugent's help was sought. However, he declined to assist as the person who summoned his aid did not have two guineas to pay him in advance. After the patient's death, Nugent's conduct earned him the censure of 11 of the 12 members of the jury.[55]

William Phelps Pickering was ordered to serve a notably shorter period of probation than his fellow *Portenia* convicts: he was sent to Norfolk Bay for 16 months. Shortly after his first Christmas in captivity in Van Diemen's Land, on 27 December 1843, Pickering's probationary period was truncated even further, to just 12 months. Annotations on his conduct record, inscribed in neat cursive script in the space provided for additional remarks, offer some explanation for his special treatment. The scribe wrote that 'the Governor of H.M. Gaol at Auckland recommended to the Principal Superintendent of Convicts this man'. The recommendation was based on Pickering's extraordinarily good behaviour – specifically his having provided the authorities with 'timely information' which saved the life of an assistant gaoler. New Zealand's Governor William Hobson was noted as having 'in the presence of himself [the governor of the gaol] commanded the High Sheriff to communicate to the prisoner that he had been pleased to commute his sentence to two years'. On 16 June 1844 Pickering was relocated to the Brown's River hiring depot. Pickering's New Zealand friends had not forgotten him in the interim: his relocation to Brown's River would have coincided roughly with the arrival from New Zealand of a petition written to plead his cause.[56]

The petition sent to Van Diemen's Land on Pickering's behalf, and related documents, are now held by Archives New Zealand in Wellington. The paperwork is badly water-stained and is, in parts, wholly illegible, but enough of the spidery nineteenth-century handwriting is readable to provide the gist of what was being communicated. The submission of Pickering's petition is attributed to Reverend John Frederick Churton, the man appointed by Hobson as the first vicar of St Paul's in Auckland. Churton reiterated how 'the late Captain Hobson had intimated ... that it was His Excellency's intention to commute the sentence of transportation from seven to two years'. Stains blot out most of Hobson's rationale, but the word 'death' has been preserved and ties in with earlier reports of Pickering having saved an assistant gaoler from death at Auckland. Tied up in the same water-stained bundle is earlier correspondence, written while Pickering was still at Auckland gaol, attesting to his good character and aiming to have him retained there while the matter of Hobson's apparent reduction of the man's sentence was addressed.[57]

As the 1844 petition passed through a number of hands in New Zealand and Van Diemen's Land, it accrued attached memoranda authored by various men, including James Coates, sheriff of Auckland, and James FitzGerald, a justice of the peace in Van Diemen's Land. Other correspondents in the penal colony included Comptroller General of Convicts William Forster and Colonial Secretary James Bicheno. Surviving evidence suggests that there were concerns in Van Diemen's Land that the royal charter did not give the lieutenant-governor any powers to remit convicts' sentences. Nor did any written evidence survive in Hobson's own hand attesting to his intentions with regard to Pickering. It did not end there. Lines written in FitzGerald's sloping hand drew a comparison between Pickering's case and that of another man, Francis Lethart, whose sentence had been reduced to one year's imprisonment rather than the three years to which the Supreme Court had originally sentenced him.[58] Quoting Virgil's lines for Queen Dido, '"Tros Tyriusve mihi nullo discrimene habetur" [Trojan or Tyrian, I treat them the same without discerning between them]', FitzGerald argued for 'the truly unfortunate prisoner Pickering' to be treated in the same way as Lethart.[59] There were references in the bundle of correspondence to Pickering having acted as a schoolmaster while at Auckland gaol, and to the pending outcome of his petition to Her Majesty for a pardon.[60]

No royal pardon was forthcoming, but on 20 June 1844 Pickering was released from the first stage of probation. His only offence while under sentence occurred later that same year: on 5 December 1844 he served 10 days in solitary confinement for 'misconduct in being on the Regatta Ground contrary to orders & presenting himself as a ticket of leave man'. After his release he was assigned to a Mr Lannigan in Hobart and then, from 20 February 1845, to Samuel Lessing. In January 1846 Pickering was granted a conditional pardon 'available within the limits of the Australian colonies and New Zealand'.[61] It was gazetted on 27 January 1846 and published in the *Colonial Times* two weeks later.[62] After his pardon Pickering travelled to Sydney where he soon married Jane Lightfoot Dodsworth.[63] Perhaps the young couple had met several years earlier when Pickering was in Sydney, or perhaps it was a whirlwind romance. Either way, by February the following year they had relocated to Auckland.

Charting Pickering's life course after he returned to the scene of his earlier crime shows clearly how the dreaded 'convict stain' failed to adhere to this white-collar criminal. He was demonstrably successful in pursuing both status and wealth – even more so than his shipmate Nugent. On 10 February 1847 Pickering was staying at the Prince Albert Inn from where he wrote to the colonial secretary for permission to travel to Wellington on a government vessel. He wrote that he had 'very large claims' against Peter Williams and David Scott, both formerly of Auckland. He knew that Scott, at least, had relocated to Wellington. Pickering intended to pursue judgments against both men, whom he described as being 'old land claimants'. He was very interested to know what lands may have since been granted to them both, with a view to staking his own claim to any such properties. Pickering enclosed a petition, also dated 10 February, in which he set out in more detail the money owed to him and the legal action he intended to pursue. A note written in the margin of his letter specified that Pickering's request could not be granted as passage on a man-of-war was available only to officers engaged in public business. A brief comment written in a different hand notes that Pickering was informed of this fact verbally two days later and, at the same time, he was told that information about deeds of grant to individuals was private and could not be divulged.[64]

Pickering made his own way to Wellington by August 1847, where he successfully obtained a judgment against Scott for around £600. However, following this 'most vexatious and expensive law suit' Pickering ended up with nothing after Scott put all of his property into the hands of trustees. Pickering included these details in another of his petitions, dated 27 June 1849. This time, he was keen to acquire a bush licence to sell 'fermented and spirituous liquors at Port Cooper [Lyttelton Harbour at Christchurch] in the middle island of New Zealand'. His application was successful. However, a note on the paperwork indicates that by 14 August he had had a change of heart: 'Mr Pickering', recorded the scribe, 'declines to take up the licence.'[65] Pickering decided to pursue less risky but nevertheless rewarding employment opportunities.

On 22 March 1849 Pickering wrote to Lieutenant-Governor Edward Eyre to inform him that he had met George Grey at King George's Sound and that Grey had promised Pickering 'when the new Canterbury settlement shall be formed, I will see what can be done for you there' – at least according to

Pickering, who requested interim employment until Grey's promise might be made good. Eyre replied that it was not within his power to employ Pickering. The former convict then found a position at the Royal Engineer's Office in Wellington, where he clerked from 1 August 1849 until he was retrenched (with a good reference) at the end of July 1850. Anticipating this, Pickering wrote to the colonial secretary a few weeks beforehand to remind him that he had experience working for the government. 'After Mr Seely [sic] was appointed Clerk to the Registrar of Deeds,' he wrote, 'I performed writing for the Clerk of the Legislative Council until the session closed.' He had also worked as a temporary clerk in the colonial secretary's office 'to copy the blue book', before he was employed at the Royal Engineer's Office. The colonial secretary replied that no additional government clerks were required at the time.[66] Blue books were detailed statistical records kept in all British colonies; they were compiled in New Zealand between 1840 and 1855. These records, some of which would have been written by Pickering, contain statistical and financial information of historical interest. Pickering had a hand in recording not only his own history in his surviving letters but also in recording the bigger histories within which his life can be framed.

Pickering entered the documentary record several more times, each time in relation to legal matters. One instance involved a court case, Salmon v. Pickering, heard before Chief Justice Martin at the Supreme Court in Auckland on 9 December 1851. It related to a financial fraud allegedly perpetrated by Pickering a decade earlier, around the time he had been found guilty of trying to pass himself off as an agent for the Sydney Banking Corporation and defrauding Israel Joseph. It seems that Pickering passed a bill of exchange to a man named William Webster. Webster had since gone to the Californian goldfields and had passed on the bill to Salmon, the plaintiff; it was then dishonoured by the Sydney Banking Corporation. Pickering was punished less severely this time round: he was ordered to pay Salmon £300 plus interest and court costs.[67]

Later in the 1850s and over the couple of decades until his death, Pickering bought land in central Wellington and as far afield as the Wairarapa, where he purchased a block in Greytown.[68] The most significant of his properties historically was the Karori Hotel on Tinakori Road (known as Karori Road at the time) in Wellington. The hotel provided a convenient place to take refreshments for people travelling between the town and the

Karori valley. Margery Renwick, whose ancestor George Dixon bought the pub from Pickering in 1861, has recorded how the Karori Hotel was the first to be built on Tinakori Road. Constructed between 1859 and 1860, it stood on part of Town Acre 516, owned almost entirely by Pickering who, by then, was living on the outskirts of Wellington at Loxley Hall, Kaiwharawhara. Like Barrett's Hotel, the Karori Hotel would have been a hub for community activities. Interestingly, it seems that one of the hotel's patrons was an elderly Edward Gibbon Wakefield – so it is possible that Wakefield and Pickering knew each other.[69]

Pickering was involved in yet another court case heard before two justices of the peace on 6 November 1863. This case attests to Pickering's feisty nature, and to the rural origins of Kaiwharawhara. A violent exchange had taken place after Pickering's neighbours' cow trespassed on his land. Pickering went next door to inform his neighbours – stock-keepers Dugald and Alexander Cameron – that one of their cows had strayed onto his property. The men accompanied Pickering to his place, and 'hard language ensued'. Pickering took an axe handle to Alex Cameron in an effort to persuade the men to leave. However, Cameron grabbed Pickering's weapon and used it to assault its owner. Given that Pickering had struck the first blow, the court was unimpressed when he pressed charges against the Camerons. The case was dismissed and costs of 23 shillings and tuppence were awarded against Pickering.[70]

In 1871 Pickering's wife Jane died at Molesworth Street in Wellington, aged 68;[71] Pickering was around 56 at the time. Two years later he remarried in Melbourne. The back story to Pickering's second marriage is rather intriguing for its connection with the New Zealand Wars and the flamboyant Prussian Gustavus Ferdinand von Tempsky. The well-travelled von Tempsky arrived in New Zealand from the Australian colonies, where he had worked on the Bendigo goldfields. The Prussian left Victoria to try his luck on the Coromandel goldfields in New Zealand. When the Waikato war broke out in 1863 von Tempsky became a leader of the Forest Rangers, 'an irregular colonial force which the authorities believed could match the bush fighting skills of the Maori'.[72] Pickering's nephew Alfred Pickering Palmer was a captain in the Patea Rifles, part of von Tempsky's Forest Rangers. Von Tempsky and Palmer were both killed in action in September 1868 during the Taranaki campaign at Te Ngutu o te Manu.[73]

Two years after Jane's death, Pickering visited his nephew's widow Grace Martha Palmer in Melbourne. It is rumoured that Grace fell pregnant to Pickering, who was much older than her. They were married on 29 August 1873,[74] and eventually returned to Loxton Hall in New Zealand, where they lived with Grace and Alfred's son (Pickering's great-nephew and now stepson) Alfred William Cobham Palmer, as well as their own three children, Loxley, Zealandia Hereford and Percy Pickering. On 26 August 1877, at the age of 62, Pickering died of pneumonia at Kaiwharawhara – by now a wealthy gentleman who provided generously in his will for his 'dearest friend Grace Martha' and the children.[75] The contrast with his fellow *Portenia* prisoners could hardly have been starker: having been segregated from New Zealand society, he had successfully reintegrated into it. The others had mostly absconded or died in relative obscurity.

CHAPTER 5

An otherwise untainted colony

B ritain's prisons were overcrowded by the mid-1840s. The British appeared to have an extensive, smoothly running convict system, yet its days were numbered. The colony of New South Wales was refusing to accept any more convicts, and there was mounting opposition to transportation in Van Diemen's Land. Aiming to circumvent colonial resistance to transportation, the British devised a scheme under which 'exiles' – men and boys who had completed part of their sentences in Britain – were shipped to the Australian colonies. Many of the adult prisoners had served time at London's Millbank or Pentonville prisons, and they became known in the Australian colonies as the Pentonville exiles. Some of the boys from Parkhurst Prison at the Isle of Wight were sent to the Australian colonies and to New Zealand.

New Zealanders were taken by surprise by the unexpected arrival of the first shipload of exiled boys. The outraged colonists subsequently prepared petitions and lobbied through London connections against the colony being used as a dumping ground for what many saw as England's refuse. They were already troubled by the flow of emancipated convicts into New Zealand from the adjacent Australian penal colonies. As Ron Palenski noted, the 'desire for New Zealand not only to be different from other British colonies, but also to be seen as being different' became 'an identity marker'.

He elaborated on this: 'one of the manifestations of this individuality was the desire shown by New Zealand not to be "tainted" by being a repository for unwanted British criminals'.[1]

Like the 'convict stain', a stigma attached to Parkhurst boys and followed the young men overseas. Used to surveillance and strict discipline at Parkhurst, they proved harder to control in their new urban environment once they had disembarked in Auckland. Moral panic ensued in New Zealand society, highlighting issues of class, race and respectability. Some colonial authorities were concerned about the boys mixing with and corrupting Māori. There were heightened concerns, too, around finding suitable masters to employ the youths and to train them to fit into colonial society rather than flouting its laws and mores. Over time, a number of Parkhurst boys found themselves before the law courts. Ironically, given their protestations about having these exiles in their midst, New Zealand colonists did not hesitate in eventually transporting three of these boys to Van Diemen's Land.

The first whiff of a scandal about to rock the fledgling colony of New Zealand was printed in the English-based *New Zealand Journal*. An agitated correspondent who signed their name as 'X' was dismayed by a statement printed in the *Times* on 14 July 1842 which revealed that 'the government has been induced to grant a free pardon to 60 boys who had been convicted of larceny, and to send them to New Zealand'. The source of the correspondent's agitation was that their own plan to emigrate had potentially been confounded, as they 'had hitherto imagined that New Zealand would be free of the odium which attaches to penal settlement'. The correspondent was particularly keen to be assured that neither Wellington nor New Plymouth was 'to become the receptacle of prison outpourings' and claimed to have become 'practically acquainted with the evils which result, not only to society in general but particularly to the aborigines, from the intercourse with the escaped of the colonial prisoners'. References in the letter imply that its author had likely spent time in New South Wales. The *New Zealand Journal* editor simply noted, 'we believe there is no intention of sending convicts to Wellington where they would not be encouraged in any way'.[2]

The *New Zealand Journal*'s colonial readership remained blissfully unaware of X's concerns as the *St George* docked at Auckland on 24 October 1842 with 57 boys from Parkhurst Prison on board – as the July edition had not yet reached New Zealand shores. These Parkhurst boys were juvenile delinquents. Operating between 1838 and 1863, Parkhurst Prison was progressive for its time, with its emphasis on housing youths in a discrete prison away from the adult prison population. Vocational training was provided for the young inmates, who could then be apprenticed out in the trades for which they were trained.[3]

Over time more than 4000 boys were marched through Parkhurst's gates, after travelling to the facility chained together in open third-class train carriages. Many of these boys were from the urban poor. As England industrialised in the eighteenth and nineteenth centuries, 'the professional and upper classes … could see physical differences between themselves and the working classes. They could see the effects of poverty, malnutrition, and disease.'[4] One practical outcome of such observable differences was the difficulty in accurately determining the biological age of malnourished youths. It is noticeable in juvenile delinquents' records that these often underprivileged youths' ages are not recorded with consistency. Take, for example, Edwin Rose from Cheltenham in Gloucestershire. Rose was estimated to be about 13 years old when, at the Lent Assizes in 1840, he was found guilty of stealing two loaves of bread from John Sier; he was sentenced to transportation for seven years and sent to Parkhurst Prison.[5] Yet just three years earlier, when Rose committed the first of five recorded offences (stealing two haddock from fishmonger Joseph Ward in Cheltenham), he was thought to be about eight years old. He stood 4ft 3in. tall at the time and, despite his relative youth, the brown-haired, round-faced boy with a dark complexion was recorded as being a labourer. Rose's other offences included stealing cheese, a loaf of bread and two other loaves of bread. He spent time in prison and was whipped for taking the single loaf and, later, was imprisoned for six calendar months and 'three times severely whipped' for taking two loaves.[6] All of his crimes related to pilfering food. It seems likely that the boy was simply hungry and that gnawing stomach pains drove him to reoffend. Nevertheless, as a recidivist he was sent to Parkhurst to be reformed and there trained as a farmer and shoemaker before he was exiled to New Zealand.

Of the English boys sent to Parkhurst Prison, records show that at least 1499 were transferred to Western Australia, Van Diemen's Land and New Zealand, where they were expected to start new lives. In addition to easing overcrowding in British prisons, the transportation of these boys was supposed to provide trained labourers for the colonies. The boys were all apprenticed to trades, and they all had experience on the land: each had done three hours of farm work a day during their confinement in Parkhurst Prison.

The Parkhurst boys were sorted into four different classes, ranging from free emigrants and apprentices to those who were considered reasonably orderly and, finally, boys with lengthy sentences of over 10 years. Those who were sent to New Zealand were classed as free emigrants or apprentices; the former received pardons when they arrived in the colony. This can be read as a sleight of hand on the part of the British government, designed to facilitate the arrival of the majority of these boys in New Zealand as free migrants rather than convicts.[7] From a colonial perspective the slips of paper recording the Parkhurst boys' pardons did not overwrite what was considered their innate criminality.

Given that their arrival in New Zealand was both unexpected and therefore unanticipated, it is not altogether surprising that extant records indicate a muted initial response. Nobody was quite sure what had just happened. Ensign Best, for example, recorded the boys' arrival in his journal the day after the St George docked with its 39 young tailors and 18 shoemakers on board. He referred to how 'their conduct having been good and their having been qualified to form useful members of society … they have been allowed to volunteer to come to this country'. He observed how some became free on arrival, while others were required to complete their apprenticeships before attaining liberty. 'Nothing', Best wrote, 'could have exceeded their clean and regular appearance on arrival.'[8] He did not seem overly concerned about the boys' criminal records or their potential to reoffend. Colonial officials were kept busy announcing the boys' arrival, seeking masters for the apprentices, creating indentures to be completed and issuing rules and regulations to provide for the governance of this new cohort of colonists. Auckland's harbourmaster David Rough, in his capacity as immigration agent, was given overall responsibility for the new arrivals, as the man sent out from England to assume that role had been redirected to Van Diemen's Land.[9]

Within two months of the boys' arrival colonists were venting their spleen in a growing moral panic. The *New Zealand Gazette and Wellington Spectator* stridently stated how the most powerful factor in New Zealand's popularity as a destination for intending British colonists was 'its total freedom from the baneful effects of "Convictism"'. It claimed that being free of convicts was a founding principle of the colony, and noted that while Governor Hobson voiced interest in using convict labour for roads and public works, the secretary of state for the colonies had adamantly refused to allow this, citing concerns over potential impacts on the 'aborigines' and 'on the administration of criminal law' in New Zealand. This the newspaper took to have been a 'pledge' given by Lord Normanby, which was now being broken by the Parkhurst boys being transported to the colony. The potential of this to deter a flow of 'respectable' and moneyed colonists was considerable.

'The recent introduction into this settlement of a number of boys from the establishment at Parkhurst,' the newspaper railed, could not be viewed 'without the most serious alarm'. They had, after all, 'been criminally convicted' and their very presence in the colony was likely to prove harmful to Māori and Pākehā alike. Indeed, according to the newspaper, the Parkhurst boys represented 'the systematic introduction of … evil' into an otherwise untainted colony.[10] In its next edition, the newspaper bemoaned the fact that New Zealand was already experiencing 'the disadvantage of being in the neighbourhood of penal settlements, in the influx of persons of questionable character'. The flow of Parkhurst boys into the colony was seen as augmenting this pre-existing problem. The colonists were upset about a potential escalation in policing expenses, a cost they fully expected would be visited on them rather than being met from England.[11]

In mid-January 1843 the *New Zealand Colonist and Port Nicholson Advertiser* reported that 'the whole of the emigrants from England, including the Parkhurst boys, had found employment from private individuals'.[12] In fact, while the 35 boys who set foot ashore at Auckland as free immigrants were all employed by private individuals, a few of the others were apprenticed out to Auckland tradesmen and some of the remainder were working for the colonial government. In his first half-yearly report on the boys who arrived on the *St George*, written at the end of March 1843, Rough stated that 'three boys remain disengaged'. By this stage Rough was a little disenchanted with the relocation scheme. He explained how 'one or two of the younger boys have shown inclinations to pilfer', and several of their older peers had 'betrayed such dispositions, as lead me to believe that they have not all been selected for immigration with the strictest regard for their reformation'. Perhaps he was understating the problems he was encountering with the Parkhurst boys, for in the same letter to the secretary of state for the colonies, Rough recommended that no further shipments of boys be sent out to the colony; he cited a lack of demand for apprentices.[13] Over the next few months Rough's concerns about some of the boys' behaviour must surely have been heightened after several incidents of antisocial behaviour. For example, in early April 1843 Chief Police Magistrate Felton Mathew reported to the chief colonial magistrate how two of the Parkhurst boys 'had been taken by the Police at the hour of Nine on Friday Evening, in a Public house of indifferent reputation and in which a number of men were at the time engaged drinking and fiddling'. The boys, Joseph Phips and Frederick Horne, had served apprenticeships as tailors but had been assigned to the survey and harbour master's departments respectively. Mathew enclosed depositions with his letter, including one from Rough in which the exasperated harbourmaster claimed to 'have done everything in my power to keep these boys from the town at night and totally forbidden them to enter public houses'. He asked that the police return to him any boys who were out on the town at night, other than those found in public houses; the latter he wanted locked up overnight and discharged the following morning. The correspondence indicates that Phips and Horne were 'severely reprimanded' on account of their behaviour; and that at least one government official saw the debacle as an overreaction on the part of those reporting on it.[14]

The same edition of the *New Zealand Colonist and Port Nicholson Advertiser* in which William Phelps Pickering's transportation to Van Diemen's Land was reported included a story about misbehaviour attributed (whether rightly or wrongly) to some Parkhurst boys. On 14 April 1843 Mrs Morton of Chancery Street went out early in the evening, leaving her dog behind. She returned three hours later to find her home ransacked and a box containing somewhere between £50 and £60, some jewellery and 'many valuable private documents' missing. The burglars broke into her residence through a back window. Despite no firm evidence as to the identity of the offenders the newspapers were quick to claim how, 'previous to the arrival of the "Parkhurst Seedlings," no such atrocious robbery had ever been committed in Auckland'. Such robberies were now 'but too common', the papers claimed. Aucklanders were reminded of the need to lock all their doors and windows when absent from home.[15]

A news item in the *Nelson Examiner and New Zealand Chronicle* claimed that Parkhurst boys were 'frequently brought before the magistrates for delinquencies and disorderly conduct' – although according to Rough's July 1843 report on his charges only one had been found guilty of an offence. Of the 57 boys, Rough said 42 were 'doing well', although the behaviour of the remaining 15 was 'unsteady and vicious'. It was proving difficult to find respectable masters for some of them.[16] Certainly 'many boys who had proven intractable and unresponsive were shipped from Parkhurst' to Point Puer in Van Diemen's Land, where they proved very difficult to reform in line with societal expectations.[17] It seems that some of the more difficult among the Parkhurst boys were also included among those exiled to New Zealand.

By mid-1843 New Zealanders were reading newspaper reports about their petitions against the reception of the Parkhurst boys being tabled in England. As Paul Buddee pointed out, the dating of these indicates that some colonists made up their minds within a month of the arrival of the *St George* that they did not want these boys in their midst. The first petition tabled in the House of Lords was from the New Zealand Society and was presented by the Earl of Lovelace. The petitioners were seeking to prevent 'the introduction of convicted prisoners into the colony of New Zealand'. This was followed by a petition presented by the Archbishop of Dublin, who likened 'a convict in durance, and an emancipated convict' to 'a wild beast chained, and a wild beast loose'. The Earl of Devon also lent his support to the New Zealanders' cause.[18]

Meanwhile, despite the colonial backlash, the *Mandarin* was setting sail for the Antipodes with 51 Parkhurst boys intended for Van Diemen's Land and another 31 for New Zealand.[19] This was, however, to be the last shipload of Parkhurst boys sent to the colony. At around the same time as the *Mandarin* set sail, the *Nelson Examiner and New Zealand Chronicle* reprinted some extracts from the *Hobart Town Advertiser*, brought to Nelson by a ship's captain. The reports indicate that at least some Vandemonians shared New Zealanders' views about these juvenile offenders. The boys were referred to as being 'almost exclusively thieves, nurtured in vice, and repeatedly convicted in the Police and Quarter Sessions Courts of London, until they finally appear at the Old Bailey'.[20] This, though, was an exaggeration. Some boys, such as Rose, had never appeared at the Old Bailey. Others, including George Bottomley, who arrived in New Zealand on the *St George*, were sentenced at the Old Bailey – although in Bottomley's case there is no surviving documentation to indicate a prior record. Bottomley was caught on 13 December 1839 by cheesemonger Jennison Barrett, after he took a piece of bacon from Barrett's shop window in Chichester Place at St Pancras, London. At the Old Bailey three days later, the 14-year-old claimed two other boys sent him to steal it. He was nevertheless found guilty of larceny and sentenced to transportation for seven years to the Isle of Wight. At Parkhurst Prison he, like Rose, was trained to be a shoemaker.[21]

While the *St George* boys were exclusively shoemakers and tailors, the mixture of trades of those on the *Mandarin* was a little more eclectic. Of the 22 boys sent out to New Zealand as free immigrants, there was one listed as both sawyer and carpenter, one carpenter and shoemaker, six carpenters, two coopers, three tailors, one shoemaker, two bricklayers, one plumber and glazier, two who were both coopers and shoemakers, one sawyer and shoemaker, one plasterer and bricklayer, and a farmer. The nine boys sent out as apprentices included a tailor and cooper, brickmaker and shoemaker, carpenter, two bricklayers and tailors, two tailors, a shoemaker and a farmer. Most of the youths were also considered suitably trained for farm work.[22] Almost all of these young charges behaved well during their long sea voyage from the Isle of Wight to the Antipodes. Their overseer from Hobart to Auckland described how 'whilst in my charge the boys were not guilty of any misconduct'. He added that this was 'with the exception of Edwin Rose who stole some bottles of gin' – and for that, there were extenuating circumstances. The letterwriter thought that another boy of 'exceedingly bad character' who had been offloaded at Hobart had induced Rose to help steal the gin. Sailors on board the vessel were also suspected of some involvement in the theft and had perhaps masterminded it. In Rose's favour, the overseer observed that the boy apparently 'bore a good character while in Parkhurst'. None of the other boys warranted a mention for any dubious behaviour, and a few had apparently shown themselves to be 'industrious';[23] these few were characterised as 'extremely good boys' and there were high hopes for their reformation. There was an obvious dichotomy between the colonists' moral panic and deep-seated suspicion of the Parkhurst boys and official reports of the almost exclusively 'good' behaviour of these youths en route to the colony.

On 14 November 1843, three days ahead of the *Mandarin's* arrival in Auckland, Felton Mathew wrote to the colonial secretary. The imminent arrival of more Parkhurst boys motivated him to complain about the 'very serious evils' that had befallen his community after the boys on the *St George* had disembarked. One interesting matter he highlighted was the propensity of some people, whom he viewed as being among 'the very worst characters' in Auckland, agreeing to be the master of some of the boys. Some of these 'masters' were emancipated convicts from the Australian penal colonies. They were no doubt hoping for a fresh start, but attitudes such as Mathew's typified the stigma associated with convicts. The chief police magistrate was convinced that Parkhurst boys who were associated with emancipated convicts 'who have long been hardened and experienced in crime' would find 'their former [criminal] tendencies ... awakened and fostered'.[24] Mathew's ideas were consistent with the thinking at the time that 'it was nurture rather than nature that was responsible for a person's criminal tendencies', and so the boys would be better nurtured by masters of high moral standing.[25] The fault in this logic, however, was that while the boys were considered capable of being reformed, former convicts who had already been reformed were still treated with suspicion. According to this schema, criminality was innate and reformation tenuous.

To underline what he saw as the Parkhurst boys' innate criminality, and as proof of his assertions, Mathews offered evidence of an upsurge in the number of robberies in Auckland after the arrival of the *St George* boys, some of whom, he claimed, had since fled to the Australian colonies or to Tahiti and other islands. He conceded that some boys who were assigned to rural masters of 'good character' had 'turned out extremely well'. In his view, happy outcomes such as this were because boys placed outside of Auckland could not readily associate with their former shipmates. He was also deeply concerned about interactions between some of the boys and local Māori; he blamed these delinquents for what he saw as an increase in criminal activities – particularly 'petty pilfering', as he put it – among some Māori. He advocated that no more Parkhurst boys be sent to New Zealand; that those boys already in residence be assigned to rural masters; and that those who behaved badly be sent to Van Diemen's Land.[26] Mathew's thinking echoed the prevailing British ideology relating to juvenile reformation. Juvenile delinquents were seen as being 'caught in a life of crime ... [with] corruptive friends and criminal connections'.[27] Severing these criminal connections by relocating the boys was considered crucial to their reformation.

As with the *St George* boys, Rough was instructed to take charge of those from the *Mandarin* when they arrived in Auckland. After a couple of years in this role he sounded exasperated when he told the governor that only about a third of the earlier arrivals seemed to be doing well; the remainder exhibited bad conduct and some had come before magistrates and been returned to him. The upkeep of many of these boys was being paid for from the public purse. The recently arrived *Mandarin* immigrants mostly declined offers of food, shelter and clothing from the government. They preferred 'to be at perfect liberty' and were steadfastly refusing to work for the government while they waited to be taken on by private employers. Rough was also having trouble locating masters willing to take on the small number of *Mandarin* apprentices.[28]

Colonial concerns about the boys evading scrutiny through being sheltered by Māori were eventually realised. Rough described to the governor how 'despite restraint [some boys] have escaped into the interior where the police cannot reach them and where they can live among the natives'. He asserted that Māori were willing to have these boys living among them.[29] On 21 March 1844 he wrote to the colonial secretary explaining how 'a boy named William Astell [sic] one of the apprentices from Parkhurst absconded about four months since and was retaken yesterday by a constable at the native settlement of Remuera'. William Astle, a 13-year-old tailor, had arrived on the *St George*. When Mathew questioned him, it was apparent that Astle was living a highly mobile life with his erstwhile benefactors – he had travelled with them to Whangaroa in Northland before relocating to Remuera. Astle described how his chores among Māori involved manual tasks such as carrying firewood and fetching water. He claimed to have been treated kindly by them. Mathew took issue with the boy being 'found of course almost in a state of nudity'. This offended his sensibilities and was seen as a sign that this white boy was starting to 'go native', having literally thrown off the material trappings of civilisation. He was also concerned that having Parkhurst boys among them was 'highly detrimental to the best interests of the Natives'. Mathew was not without compassion for Astle, however. He thought it likely that Astle had been wrongly accused of horse stealing – the offence for which he was transported to Parkhurst. He also observed how the youngster's physical development – like that of many other Parkhurst boys – appeared to have been retarded: Astle looked as if he was nine or 10 years old whereas, by the time he returned from living with Māori, he was actually 14.[30] In an interesting convergence between Astle's criminal record and his association with Māori, he appeared before the Supreme Court on Tuesday 2 September 1850 to answer another charge of horse stealing. Government interpreter Edward Meurant told the court that near the end of January 1850 he saw Astle leading a black mare 'along the road close to the Panmure Inn, having a few natives with him'. Several months later, in May, Corporal David Hazlitt of the Armed Police spotted Astle at Kawhia with the same black mare, now in a poor condition, and arrested the young fellow. Conflicting accounts were presented to the court about how Astle came by the horse. On the one hand he claimed to have bought the animal for £12 from a man named Pettit, who had since gone to California; on the other hand he was said to have admitted stealing the mare from outside the government domain. Probably because of this confusion – and the impossibility of checking Astle's story with the absent Pettit – the jury found him not guilty.[31]

Mathew, in the meantime, used the circumstances surrounding Astle's initial 'recovery' from Māori as evidence to bolster support for his plans for the *Mandarin* boys. He argued that Astle should be 'placed in the country under the care of a judicious master', well away from his former Parkhurst associates, to 'save him from ruin'.[32] Astle was far from being the only Parkhurst boy frequently at Remuera. In a letter to the colonial secretary written three days earlier than his missive about Astle's return, Mathew asked him to draw the governor's attention to some circumstances of deepening concern. He described how some of the unemployed boys 'have been for some time past in the habit of congregating in small parties, and wandering about the town & neighbourhood at all hours of the day & night … stealing linen and committing other petty depredations'. In many cases it had proven difficult to obtain sufficient evidence against the youths to secure convictions. Mathew had instead instructed his constables to apprehend the recalcitrant boys as vagrants on the basis that they were wandering around town at night with no visible means of support. Several such arrests had initially had a 'very salutary effect' on their erstwhile companions. However, the boys were now engaging in a new tactic that disturbed Mathew. He explained how 'these boys are in the habit of betaking themselves, in small parties, to "Remuera" & other Native settlements where they pass the day amongst the Natives & in the evening return to the town for the purpose of committing depredations'. Preventive action was necessary.[33]

The colonists put in place a two-pronged strategy. The chief protector of aborigines would warn Māori against harbouring any of these boys. As well as this verbal warning, Mathew ordered notices to be placed in the *Maori Gazette* reiterating the colonists' warning. Mathew was also asked to give 'most strict orders' to the constables to deal with the situation. The colonial secretary sought the attorney-general's opinion as to Mathew's capacity as police magistrate to deal summarily with the boys as vagrants. The attorney-general found that the English vagrancy law was applicable in New Zealand and considered that 'much of the vagrant act will avert the evil complained of [by Mathew]'. Paraphrasing section 4 of the 1824 Vagrancy Act 5 Geo., the attorney-general advised that the law:

> *enacts that any person wandering abroad and lodging in any barn or outhouse or in any deserted or unoccupied building or in the open air or under a tent, etc., etc., not having any visible subsistence and not having a good account of himself will be deemed a rogue and vagabond and may be summarily convicted before a magistrate and imprisoned for 3 months.*[34]

A reward was also offered to Māori who returned Parkhurst boys to the colonists. In a letter dated 28 June 1844 Mathew explained how two Parkhurst boys who absconded after being accused of burglary were 'apprehended and delivered up to the police by two natives'. To encourage such 'meritorious conduct' the police magistrate sought permission from the colonial secretary to reward the captors with two pounds of tobacco. His request was approved.[35]

Just a few trial records involving Parkhurst boys have survived. One is that of Henry Butler Dowie, reported in the *Southern Cross* in September 1844.[36] Dowie had appeared before the Old Bailey as a 15-year-old in 1838 and was found guilty of 'feloniously breaking and entering the dwelling-house of William Moody, on the 27th of May, at the Inner Temple': he had stolen spoons, sugar tongs and an eyeglass. He was sentenced to transportation for 10 years and was sent to the prison hulk HMS *York* for six months and then to Parkhurst Prison. While there he regularly pilfered food; the superintendent described the boy as 'quite devoid of moral principle'. Despite his chequered past, in 1842 Dowie was sent to New Zealand on the *St George* and arrived free in the colony.[37]

At the time of his arrest in Auckland Dowie was working for the surveyor J.P. Dumoulin. One Sunday he sought permission to attend chapel. Dumoulin also went out and, on his return, Dowie claimed the house had been ransacked in their absence. His story was disproven by the lack of any footprints in the garden beneath an open window that was allegedly used by the intruder. Dowie was charged with stealing money from Dumoulin. Evidence was presented to the court that Dowie had boasted 'the money was safely on the way to Sydney … and the name of a Parkhurst companion, who has actually sailed for that place in the "Terror" was mentioned' – although others said he had been joking. The jury was not amused: Dowie was found guilty and sentenced to transportation for seven years.[38]

Dowie was 21 by the time he arrived in Van Diemen's Land on 9 November 1844 on board the *John Pirie*. He was sent to Broadmarsh, a probation station on private property 12 miles from Brighton at the southern end of the midlands, to serve an initial period of probation of 15 months. Administrator La Trobe considered this station to be 'in a disgracefully neglected state' and said that the neighbourhood was 'not adapted for a Convict Station' because of the number of 'loose squatters' thereabouts. Dowie was later assigned to a handful of different masters and kept a clean sheet. He received his ticket of leave on 27 June 1848,[39] and was granted permission to marry Barbara Angus, a woman who had arrived free in the colony, on 15 October 1850.[40] Unlike many other working-class convicts transported to Van Diemen's Land from New Zealand, Dowie went on to experience commercial and political success. He established himself in the small town of Evandale, where he was a shop owner and a family man. In 1865 he was one of seven councillors elected from a pool of 15 to sit on the inaugural Evandale municipal council.[41] Dowie eventually died at home on 13 August 1889 at the age of 67. He was buried at the English burying ground at Launceston, north of Evandale.[42]

Two other Parkhurst boys were transported from New Zealand to Van Diemen's Land, albeit with markedly different outcomes from Dowie's. Like Dowie, Rose and Bottomley exhibited the type of behaviour Mathew complained about. Some of their exploits were detailed in the pages of the *New Zealander* in September and December 1845. The first of these reports described how seven boys appeared before the police court charged with 'having committed a burglary on the dwelling house of Mr. Alfred Jones, on Sunday afternoon, and stolen therefrom considerable sums of money, with various other articles'. The alleged offenders were named as Edward Rose, John Cotton, George Jay, Charles Brown, Frederick Miller, James McGuiness [sic] and George Bottomley. Rose, Bottomley and M'Guiness were all Parkhurst boys. After several witnesses were examined, including the aggrieved Jones, the magistrates discharged Cotton and Brown. The remaining five boys were remanded in custody overnight. Of these, Miller, Jay and M'Guiness were remanded for a few more days while more evidence was sought against them. There is no surviving evidence of these three being tried; this suggests that theirs may have been one of the cases that frustrated Mathew, where boys were released without charge. In the interim, evidence was produced to the court in relation to Rose and Bottomley. When Chief Constable James Smith arrested Rose and Bottomley, their rooms were searched and stolen property said to belong to Richard Webb was recovered. Webb later identified the property found in the boys' possession as his own. Rose and Bottomley were committed to stand trial.[43]

The two Parkhurst boys were brought before the Supreme Court in Auckland on 1 December 1845. A grand jury was sworn in to weigh up the evidence before them in relation to five cases, including several larcenies, breaking and entering a dwelling house, and stealing from a dwelling house. Rose and Bottomley were charged with 'feloniously receiving goods value twelve shillings, knowing the same to have been stolen, on or about the 23rd September last'. Within a week of the robbery, several stolen items were found in a box in a house the boys had rented. Webb told the court how he had been out for about half an hour in the evening. On his return he found that his house had been entered using a false key. A chest had been broken open and some items were missing; Webb itemised these as 'two blue shirts, one inside shirt, a pair of white moleskin trowsers, and one pair of boots'. While he could not swear positively as to the boots, he recognised one of the blue shirts as his property, as some white thread had been used to sew on the black buttons 'in a particular manner'. Specific stitching also marked the trousers as Webb's property. Shoemaker David Campbell testified that he had made a pair of boots for Webb; however, he could not swear to the recovered boots definitely being the same pair. The chief constable described recovering the property from the boys' house, after which their landlord, sawyer Joseph Hill, was called to attest to the boys having rented the house from him for three shillings a week.[44]

It was obvious to the judge and jury that Webb's property had been stolen and that at least some of the goods recovered from the house rented by Rose and Bottomley belonged to Webb. However, the boys' counsel argued that no account had been proffered as to how the goods came into their possession. A lengthy legal argument ensued in which English precedent was drawn on to further illuminate the case. Because the boys were charged with having received the goods rather than stealing them, they were found not guilty. Rose and Bottomley were detained in custody while a new bill was drawn up against them. They were indicted and arraigned for 'stealing goods to the value of twelve shillings, the property of Richard Webb', and the jury promptly found them guilty of that offence. In sentencing them the judge told them their offence was 'not attended by any of the ordinary circumstances of mitigation': they had not been tempted by the goods having been left lying around by their owner; instead they had taken property that was locked away under the owner's 'own roof'. The boys were considered to have used 'violent means' to avail themselves of Webb's possessions, having entered his home with a false key and broken into the chest in which his clothes were stored. The judge vowed to make an example of them: he told Rose and Bottomley that they would 'be each of you transported beyond the seas, to such place as his Excellency the Governor shall appoint for the term of Seven Years'.[45] Less than a week after their sentencing, on 8 December Rose and Bottomley were shipped to Van Diemen's Land on the *Cheerful*. The schooner, captained by a man named Patrick, carried a cargo that included gum, flax and timber, as well as two cabin passengers and three in steerage.[46] It was a slow voyage: the vessel took 28 days to reach Hobart, where it arrived on 8 January 1846.[47]

Timothy O'Meara travelled steerage on the same voyage as Rose and Bottomley. Originally from Tipperary, the 38-year-old architect and builder was another of the handful of white-collar criminals transported from New Zealand to Van Diemen's Land. Like William Phelps Pickering, he had committed fraud. O'Meara was sentenced in Wellington on 2 June 1845 to transportation for 10 years for 'forging a Govt. Debenture for £1'. A single man who was literate and a Roman Catholic, O'Meara explained how he arrived in New Zealand in March 1839 in the *African* from Launceston, Van Diemen's Land. He had originally travelled to Van Diemen's Land in the *Thomas* as a cabin passenger and a free man from the Cape of Good Hope to work in the island colony as a bobbin framer. O'Meara's 'stout made' body bore signs of conflict: his identifying marks included '2 bayonet marks [and] 2 cutlass marks on right arm'. While he was in the convict system he committed several offences ranging from 'making away with a knife' to wilfully damaging a government hut and, later, assaulting a fellow prisoner. Eventually on 10 May 1853 O'Meara received his conditional pardon.[48]

Yet another convict was transported from New Zealand to Van Diemen's Land for fraudulently trying to improve his financial situation. Joseph Massey, a joiner and carpenter originally from Alicante in Spain, was found guilty in September 1850 of having 'feloniously counterfeit 9 half-crowns, 13 shillings, and 20 sixpences, intending to resemble and pass for the Queen's silver current coin'. The coins and the equipment for manufacturing them were located at the prisoner's home at Freemans Bay in Auckland by the local constabulary.[49] It seems the authorities were tipped off when Massey's wife Anne was caught 'attempting to pass some of this base coin to an aboriginal native'. There was insufficient proof provided to the Magistrate's Court that Anne knew the coins to be counterfeit. She was discharged without conviction but her husband was later sentenced in the Supreme Court to transportation to Van Diemen's Land for 14 years.[50] Massey, who was 54 years old on his arrival in Van Diemen's Land, did not survive long under sentence; he died in hospital at Launceston on 17 July 1852.[51]

By the time Rose disembarked from the *Cheerful* in Van Diemen's Land he was 19 years old and 5ft 4in. tall. Bottomley was the same height but two years older. As young men they were too old to be sent to the boys' reformatory at Point Puer adjacent to Port Arthur; instead they were dealt with in the same way as any other adult male offender arriving in the penal colony. At 3am on the day the *Cheerful* arrived at Hobart, Rose saw a chance to escape and jumped overboard 'with his bundle'. He was recaptured and interviewed along with the other two prisoners later that same morning. Rose described how he had spent three and a half years at Parkhurst before being sent to New Zealand as an emigrant. He admitted stealing Webb's trousers and shirts, along with Bottomley. Bottomley, who said he was originally from Battlesbridge, an English village in Essex, had served two and a half years at Parkhurst before he was shipped to New Zealand. He admitted to being with Rose when the thefts from Webb took place. He flatly denied having served time in the Auckland gaol.[52]

Like O'Meara, Rose's body bore scars attesting to his life experiences: he was recorded on arriving in Van Diemen's Land as sporting a 'cut back of head, the hair off; cut between forefinger and thumb left hand; a pock mark on middle of his back'. And like O'Meara, he too was shorter than average and 'stout made'. He had a round, clean-shaven face and ruddy complexion with brown hair. His eyes were recorded as blue rather than the brown observed by the gaoler in Gloucestershire. Rose was punished for several offences while in Van Diemen's Land, including his first offence of trying to escape from the *Cheerful*. For that, he was given six months hard labour in chains. His probationary period was set at 12 months, which he served at Rocky Hills probation station.[53]

Located on the east coast of Van Diemen's Land not far from Maria Island, Rocky Hills was originally established to accommodate one of the many parties of convict road gangs that the government assigned to build infrastructure necessary for the colony's expansion. In 1847 when La Trobe inspected the site, 406 men were labouring there. When he inspected the buildings La Trobe found some reasonable huts existed, alongside others that were no longer being utilised. Prisoners who reached the first class were accommodated in huts of 30 men a piece. Second-class prisoners were allocated to small wooden huts in groups of 14. The 50 third-class men were housed in separate apartments that 'were kept extremely dirty'.

The probation station had an adequate brick-and-stone general store. A cookhouse and bakehouse were combined in one building, while the combined chapel and schoolhouse was just a shed. The hospital was one large room that was meant to have been divided in two, but that work had not been carried out. A very dissatisfied La Trobe reported on how the hospital fireplace had been destroyed through wood having been chopped on it. He found 'the tables dirty and the blankets black with filth, and no man's case written above his head'. La Trobe reported that there were 300 acres (121ha) of good land near Rocky Hills but it required proper fencing and draining so that more than the current 168 acres (68ha) under cultivation might also be farmed. His overall impression of the place was damning. 'The effects of bad management, inattention and inefficiency in the Officers of this establishment was evident in every detail,' he wrote. He found the prisoners 'noisy in the extreme'; they were 'badly clothed, their hair long, and about one half of them barefooted'. He put steps in train to have the superintendent and his team replaced, and he concluded that he saw 'little to recommend' Rocky Hills other than its inaccessibility.[54]

As well as serving time at Rocky Hills, Rose laboured at other probation stations, including Saltwater River early in 1847. From May 1847 he was assigned to private service, working for a number of masters located in central Hobart. This implies that he may have been putting his training as a shoemaker to use. While he was still under sentence Rose was found guilty of seven further offences. He was punished in December 1846 with 12 months' hard labour in chains for absconding. Other offences involved tobacco, being out after hours, being found drunk, and resisting a constable in the execution of his duties. There were more punishments of hard labour doled out to him. On 5 March 1850 Rose's application for a ticket of leave was refused. Near the end of the same year, on 12 November, he was advised to reapply for his ticket in six months. He successfully obtained this indulgence on 20 May 1851.[55]

Bottomley also carried identifying marks on his body, including 'marks of seton in nape of neck; scar on back of shoulder. 2 moles on breast; mark of a boil on left haunch ... wart on top of left forefinger'.[56] He was observed to be 'very stout made' with a large head, ruddy complexion, brown hair, blue eyes and a long clean-shaven face. Like Rose, he was initially sent to Rocky Hills. His first assignment to a private settler was on 23 February

1847 to the influential Quaker Edward Cotton at Great Swanport district
on the east coast of Van Diemen's Land.[57] His subsequent assignments were
mainly to other rural masters throughout the island, ranging from Oatlands
in the midlands to George Town in the far north of the colony. He also
worked for the Marine Board. While he was under sentence, Bottomley was
charged with five offences ranging from assaulting a fellow prisoner and
common assault to being out after hours and falsely representing himself
to be a pass holder. On one occasion he was found guilty of disturbing the
peace. For one assault, he was sent to Port Arthur in June 1849 where he
remained until April the following year. Bottomley received his certificate
of freedom on 17 December 1852, around 18 months after Rose obtained
his freedom.[58]

Rose and Bottomley later resurfaced in Victoria. Intriguingly, both men
adopted false names. Rose became 'William Williams'. Bottomley retained
his original name 'George' but tacked 'Williams' on to become 'George
Williams'; the men may have been trying to pass themselves off as brothers.
They were probably drawn to Victoria by the allure of the goldfields, like
so many other Vandemonians at the time. But it was not really a fresh
start. Bottomley, or George Williams as he was now known, ended up
in trouble with Victorian law enforcement. His name appears in several
Victoria police gazettes, the first of which lists him among 'prisoners to
whom tickets-of-leave have been issued during the week ending 6th July
1858'. He was named as 'Williams, George, alias Bottomly' and described as
having arrived in Van Diemen's Land on the *Cheerful*. As Williams, he was
tried in Melbourne on 2 December 1854 for larceny and receiving stolen
property and sentenced to five years' hard labour. The district in which he
was located was named as 'Wimmers, Pleasant Creek', a gold-mining town
since renamed Stawell.[59] The following year he was in the Geelong district
where he received a three-month sentence of imprisonment in May 1859
'for assaulting a constable in the execution of his duty'.[60]

It was under the name 'William Williams, *alias* Edwin Rose' that an
inquest into Rose's death was held in early September 1863. He died in
Bendigo Hospital as the result of a pistol shot fired at him by Constable
James Brien some weeks earlier on 25 July. The jury returned a verdict
of 'justifiable homicide' and was 'unanimously of the opinion that the
consideration of the Government and the warmest thanks of the public

are due to Constable James Brien for the determined action taken by him in successfully arresting the deceased and his companions'. According to Simon Henry, the landlord of the Queen's Head Hotel at Lockwood near Bendigo, Rose and four companions entered his premises on 25 July and over time became 'very rowdy'. He asked them to leave. Some time later Henry was told that the five men were robbing his piggery. The publican knew them to be armed and sent for the police. A group including Brien rode after the robbers; in the ensuing confrontation Brien received a small wound in the stomach, and Rose was fatally shot. Witnesses later declared that they had heard Williams (Rose) say 'they did not want to steal witness's pigs; they only wanted a feed'.[61] Life had come full circle for the boy who was punished and eventually transported for stealing food to assuage his hunger: he had grown into a man shot dead while stealing pigs for a feed.[62]

CHAPTER 6

The Queen's men

From the arrival of the first fleet in the Australian colonies in 1788 until more than half a decade after the end of the war in the Waikato, regiments of redcoats flexed Britain's imperial muscle across Australasia; they did not withdraw until 1870. Shortly after arriving in the Antipodes the role of these soldiers expanded considerably beyond guarding convicts. The redcoats became highly visible symbols of the imposition of the rule of law in the colonies. Colonists and indigenous peoples alike were considered to be British subjects. Indigenous peoples who resisted the imposition of British rule were 'pacified' by the military, sometimes with the support of opposing factions, and often with the assistance of shipboard or land-based vigilantes.

Despite being agents of British imperialism charged with the task of enforcing peace, some of the Queen's men disturbed the peace in various ways and were themselves subject to discipline and punishment. By 1847 colonial newspapers were reporting that 'the 65th regiment, stationed in New Zealand, is in a state of insubordination, and that upwards of one hundred and twenty men have been lodged in gaol'. According to the newspapers, Governor George Grey had asked that the 99th Regiment be sent to Wellington 'to keep the former regiment in check, until the offenders have been punished, and order restored'.[1] In the 1840s and early

1850s soldiers were disciplined before courts martial and in the colony's criminal courts. In a number of cases this resulted in the Queen's men being transported as convicts to Van Diemen's Land.

In 1840, as the proposed township of Russell was being 'marked out' at Kororāreka in the Bay of Islands, news broke of the murder of Patrick Rooney, a shepherd at Pukatuna. The alleged offender was Kihi, a Ngāpuhi man. He was handed over to the colonists on Good Friday and a hearing was held before Willoughby Shortland at the church in Kororāreka. Tempers flared. As the *New Zealand Gazette and Wellington Spectator* later reported, soldiers were sent for:

> who lost no time in coming to the spot, where they were joined by the inhabitants, and in a very few minutes proved to our sable brethren, that English law ruled the land. Great credit is due to the Police Magistrate and Colonial Surgeon on the occasion, for although no shots were fired, the natives appeared quite convinced that we were not to be trifled with.

After the arrival of the soldiers and the intervention of local missionaries, tensions were defused and peace was restored.[2] Kihi's was the first official trial for murder after the signing of the Treaty of Waitangi. It engendered some debate over whether, if found guilty, he ought to be hanged in accordance with colonial justice or shot – the preference expressed by some Māori. This became a moot point when Kihi died from natural causes before the conclusion of his trial.[3]

In the same article the journalist decried the way in which the fledgling colony had been 'forsaken' by emigrants from Sydney, who were not arriving in the anticipated numbers. 'We want men of capital,' the newspaper reiterated, 'men willing to work as mechanics and agricultural labourers.'[4] While New Zealand colonists continued to dream of a new society with a hierarchy of urban and rural labouring classes and men with sufficient capital to employ them, redcoats were required to be on the ground to ensure the security of England's latest colonial venture.

The first serious skirmish between Māori and Pākehā involved warriors and civilians rather than soldiers. At Wairau on 17 June 1843 a violent episode occurred that James Belich has attributed to misunderstandings arising from ambiguous wording about sovereignty in the Treaty of

Waitangi; tensions over British interference in Māori affairs; and Māori desires to continue trading with the newcomers – compounded locally by 'careless land purchasing' on the part of the New Zealand Company. When 50 armed colonists from the New Zealand Company settlement of Nelson set out with Captain Arthur Wakefield and police magistrate Henry Thompson to enforce their claim over land in the Wairau Valley, conflict ensued. The colonists thought they owned the land fair and square. However, their stance was contested by Ngāti Toa paramount chief Te Rauparaha and his nephew Te Rangihaeata. The colonists tried to arrest Te Rauparaha with the intention of settling the dispute in accordance with the colony's English-derived colonial laws. This was ironic, given that they had pre-empted the land commissioner's pending investigation into ownership of the valley by attempting to have it surveyed. On that fateful day in June, a trigger-happy colonist fired a shot that killed Te Rangihaeata's wife Te Rongo. In the resulting affray three more Māori died, along with 22 colonists. The deaths of the colonists, including Wakefield, attracted considerable controversy. Some were killed by Te Rangihaeata in retaliation for the death of his wife, after they had surrendered to Ngāti Toa. After the incident, colonists – particularly in Nelson, Wellington and the Hutt Valley – were fearful of further violence.[5]

Conflict on a larger scale was avoided until 1845, when the Northern War erupted. The war was fought between March 1845 and January 1846 around the Bay of Islands in Northland. The first of the New Zealand Wars was far from being merely a case of Māori fighting against the European colonists; instead, motivated by complex factors, different factions of Ngāpuhi opposed each other. One faction collaborated with the crown and the other faction was warring against it. Those who fought alongside the redcoats were led by Tāmati Wāka Nene, Mohi Tāwhai, Patuone and Makoare Te Taonui. The opposing faction was led by Hone Heke and Kawiti. After the sacking of the colonial settlement at Kororāreka on 11 March 1845, Governor Robert FitzRoy summoned reinforcements from the Australian colonies. A detachment of the 96th Regiment was sent to New Zealand, as was the 18-gun sloop *Hazard*. The 140 soldiers, sailors and marines augmented a 200-strong force made up of armed locals and volunteers from merchant ships moored nearby. Yet more military men – 215 soldiers from the 58th Regiment – arrived from the Australian colonies on 22 April 1845 when Auckland appeared to be under threat. The troops were commanded first by Lieutenant-Colonel William Hulme and later by Colonel Henry Despard. These military leaders reported directly to the Sydney-based Commander of Forces General Sir Maurice O'Connell. Despite the colonists' high hopes of victory aided by imperial soldiers and 'friendly' Māori, ultimately 10 months of war concluded with what Belich described as 'defeat for the British and limited victory for Heke and Kawiti'. In the meantime, Governor FitzRoy was dismissed and was replaced on 14 November 1845 by Captain George Grey, who had just completed his term as governor of South Australia.[6]

Between 2 June 1847 and 2 November 1850, 51 imperial soldiers were transported from New Zealand to Van Diemen's Land. Some were currently serving soldiers; others had been discharged. The average age of the soldiers was about 25 – six years younger than that of the civilian male convicts at just over 31 years.

The oldest convict transported from New Zealand was former soldier William Spyke, who claimed to be 68 years old on his arrival in Hobart; he had deserted from the 96th Regiment eight years earlier after 15 years of service. However, Spyke's connections with the British Army dated back to childhood – he grew up in Portugal with the 7th Dragoons. At Nelson on 1 October 1847 he was sentenced to seven years' transportation for larceny. Adding to a growing record of criminality, Spyke stole a shirt from Mr Watkins; this earned him a passage to Van Diemen's Land. Spyke had other earlier brushes with the law, including allegedly stabbing a farm labourer with a clasp knife at Whanganui, and stealing wheat from Isaac Colley in the Hutt Valley.[7] No record seems to have survived of the outcome of the Whanganui matter. At the Hutt, there was 'strong suspicion' against Spyke, but insufficient evidence to satisfy the jury of his guilt.[8] Robert Burnett has also described Spyke as breaking into the home of surveyor Charles Heaphy and stealing from him. Shortly after the burglary Spyke, who seems to have be an itinerant, was found carrying the stolen property wrapped up in his bedding. As Burnett has mentioned, by the time of the burglary Heaphy was enjoying a 'slight reputation' as an artist. There is no mention of any of his artworks being found in Spyke's possession, which indicates that the works probably went untouched.[9] In Van Diemen's Land Spyke changed his

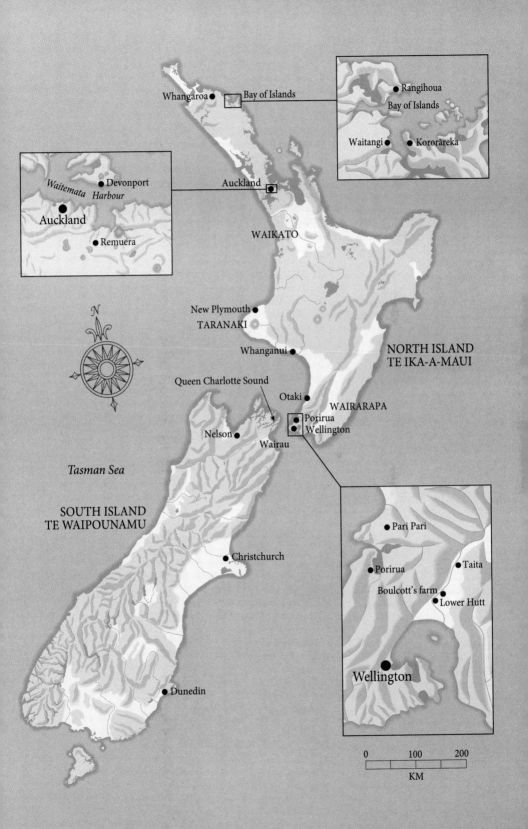

Whangaroa
Bay of Islands

Rangihoua
Bay of Islands
Waitangi ● ● Kororāreka

Auckland

Waitemata
Harbour ● Devonport

Auckland
● Remuera

WAIKATO

New Plymouth ●
TARANAKI

Whanganui ●

NORTH ISLAND
TE IKA-A-MAUI

Queen Charlotte Sound

Otaki ●
WAIRARAPA
Porirua
Wellington

Nelson ●
Wairau

Tasman Sea

SOUTH ISLAND
TE WAIPOUNAMU

Christchurch ●

Dunedin ●

Pari Pari ●

Porirua ● ● Taita
Boulcott's farm
● Lower Hutt

Wellington

0   100   200
KM

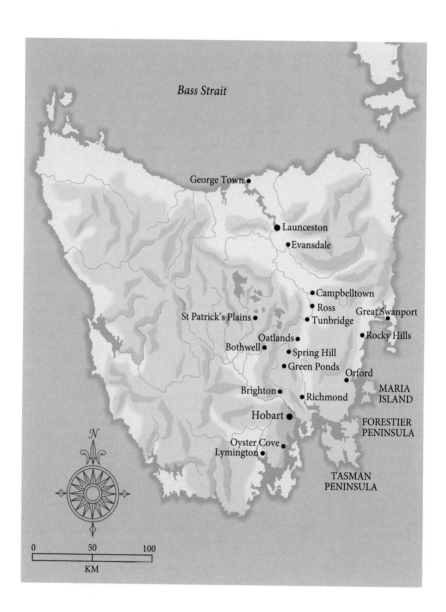

Bass Strait

George Town

Launceston
Evansdale

Campbelltown
Ross
St Patrick's Plains   Tunbridge   Great Swanport
                    Oatlands   Rocky Hills
       Bothwell   Spring Hill
                    Green Ponds   Orford
              Brighton   MARIA
                          Richmond   ISLAND

       Hobart   FORESTIER
                                                PENINSULA
       Oyster Cove
Lymington

                                        TASMAN
                                        PENINSULA

N

0   50   100

KM

ii

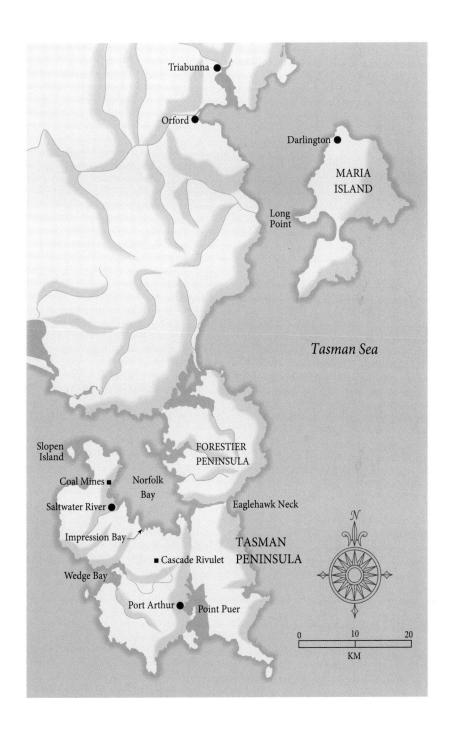

Triabunna ●

Orford ●

Darlington ●

MARIA
ISLAND

Long
Point

Tasman Sea

Slopen
Island

Coal Mines ■ Norfolk
Bay

Saltwater River ●

FORESTIER
PENINSULA

Eaglehawk Neck

Impression Bay

■ Cascade Rivulet

TASMAN
PENINSULA

Wedge Bay

Port Arthur ● Point Puer

N

0   10   20
KM

ABOVE: *William Phelps Pickering with his first wife, Jane Lightfoot Dodsworth.*
Private collection

RIGHT: *William Phelps Pickering with his second wife, Grace Martha Palmer, and children.*
Private collection

After his return from Van Diemen's Land, William Phelps Pickering amassed a property portfolio that included Karori Hotel in Wellington.
Edward Smallwood Richards, Alexander Turnbull Library, 1/2-027926-F

Loxley Villa at Kaiwharawhara, home of William Phelps Pickering and his family, stood as testament to his material success after the former convict's return from Van Diemen's Land. Private collection

Barrett's Hotel on the Wellington waterfront was used as a temporary courthouse. Samuel Charles Brees, Alexander Turnbull Library, A-109-027

Convicts labouring in Hobart.

George William Evans (painter), Richard Reeves (engraver), Hobart Town, Van Diemen's Land *(1828), National Library of Australia, nla.gov.au/nla.obj-135297750*

Convicts Patrick Mullins, Henry Rogers, John Coghlan and Joseph Root from the Portenia *each served part of their sentence at Impression Bay probation station on the Tasman Peninsula.* Unknown artist, W.L. Crowther Library, *SD_ILS:125211*

ABOVE: *View of Auckland from Margaret Reardon's sister's home at Smale's Point.*
Patrick Joseph Hogan, Alexander Turnbull Library, C-010-015

RIGHT: *Pari Pari, north of Wellington, where the Māori warriors were captured before being transported to Van Diemen's Land in 1846.*
Samuel Charles Brees, Alexander Turnbull Library, B-031-020

COOKS-STRAITS
PARI - PARI

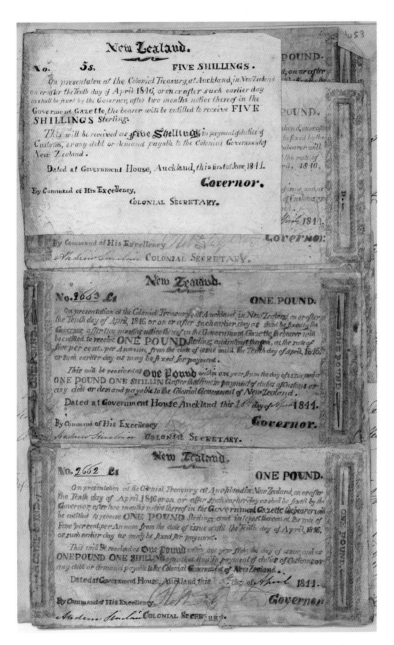

Government debentures forged by architect and builder Timothy O'Meara from Tipperary, one of the few white-collar criminals transported from New Zealand to Van Diemen's Land. He was sentenced in Wellington on 2 June 1845 to transportation for 10 years. Timothy O'Meara, Archives New Zealand, ACGO 8333 48/ 1846/452

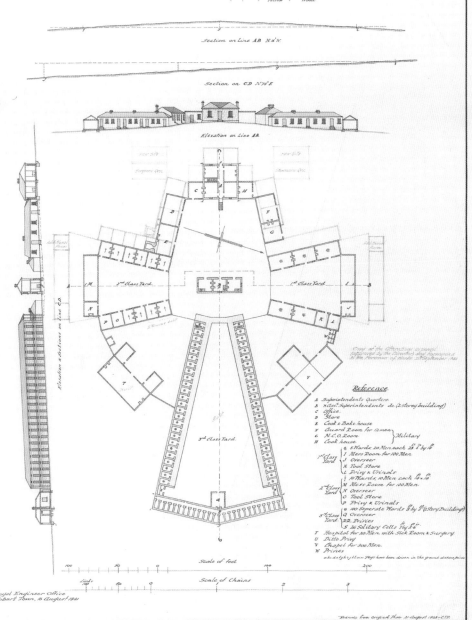

ABOVE: *Almost half of the convicts transported from New Zealand to Van Diemen's Land were, or had been, British soldiers.* Samuel Charles Brees, Alexander Turnbull Library, A-109-034

ABOVE: *Maria Island, where the Māori convicts were sent in 1846.* Curzona Frances Louise Allport, Allport Library and Museum of Fine Arts, SD_ILS:84499

LEFT: *It was highly unusual for deceased convicts' graves to be marked with a headstone, yet one was erected over the grave of Hōhepa Te Umuroa at Maria Island, where it still stands.* Photograph: Jack Thwaites, Tasmanian Archive and Heritage Office, NS3195

Te Kūmete's portrait was one of five portraits of the Māori prisoners at the Hobart penitentiary painted by watercolourist John Skinner Prout. John Skinner Prout, British Museum, Oc2006, Drg.30, AN76380001

Maketū was the first person to be judicially executed in the fledgling colony of New Zealand, pre-dating the execution of Joseph Burns. Joseph Jenner Merrett, Alexander Turnbull Library, E-216-f-141

*The only female convict transported from New Zealand, Margaret Reardon
served part of her sentence at the female factory in Hobart.* John Skinner Prout,
Allport Library and Museum of Fine Arts, SD_ILS:100631

*Margaret Reardon's conduct record. Convicts' details were recorded in
conduct registers in Van Diemen's Land.* Tasmanian Archive and Heritage Office,
CON40-1-8, 292

name but not his habits: as William Burns he was found guilty on 27 May 1854 of stealing a petticoat and was imprisoned for two months with hard labour. Spyke was 'discharged to freedom' in November 1855.[10]

The transported soldiers came from four British Regiments: the 58th (Rutlandshire) Regiment of Foot (the 'black cuffs'), 65th (2nd Yorkshire North Riding) Regiment of Foot, 96th (Manchester) Regiment of Foot, and 99th (Lanarkshire) Regiment of Foot. All four regiments arrived in the region having served as guards on male convict transports, and the 58th had also taken over garrison duties in New South Wales from 1843. The majority of the soldier convicts were tried at Auckland, where 17 faced a general court martial and another 16 appeared before the Supreme Court. Others were tried at Wellington, where seven were court-martialled and 10 were tried in civil court cases. Spyke was the only soldier tried at Nelson, although two civilians were also tried there: John Green was sentenced on 1 October 1844 to 10 years' transportation for killing a bullock and stealing the carcass; and a year later, on 1 October 1845, Richard Conway got 15 years' transportation for assaulting Constable William Harding with a firebrand at a public house with intent to maim him. Conway, a stonemason who had grown up at Greenock, nominated Rome as his 'native place' and, when interviewed at Hobart, claimed to have been 'with Captain Wakefield and the survey party'.[11] He may have been one of dozens of colonial men hastily armed and sworn in as special constables to accompany Wakefield to the Wairau Valley as tensions heightened over ownership of the fertile land there.

The crimes committed by the soldier convicts fell into five main categories, with some overlap: desertion; larceny, burglary, stealing and highway robbery; striking superior officers or shooting at fellow foot soldiers; insubordination; and robbery or forgery while in a position of trust and responsibility. Those tried by the civil authorities were soldiers who, having deserted, committed further offences that generally involved property – although two were tried for manslaughter. In instances where general courts martial had been convened in New Zealand, the proceedings and outcomes were communicated to, and approved by, the commander of the forces in Sydney.[12] Once his approval was granted these proceedings and outcomes were made public by being published as general orders. Unfortunately these general orders seem no longer to be extant. Colonial newspapers were not permitted to report in any depth about courts martial proceedings and outcomes until they had been formally approved. Varying levels of detail about such proceedings have survived in newspaper columns.[13] In instances where court-martialled soldiers were sentenced to transportation under the provisions of the Mutiny Act, they were handed over to the civil authorities who arranged for them to be shipped to Van Diemen's Land under guard. The associated costs were met by the British government.[14]

By far the largest cohort of soldier convicts transported from New Zealand – 26 men – were from the 58th Regiment. Of these, 11 were convicted of robbery, larceny or burglary, one for drunkenness and firing at a sergeant, another for firing at a soldier in the barracks, two for striking a superior officer, one for subordinate conduct, two for manslaughter and eight for desertion. Three of these eight were also found guilty of stealing property. A further 14 soldier convicts were from the 65th – 10 of whom were convicted of robbery, larceny or burglary (one of whom also struck a superior officer); one struck a superior officer; and one deserted from the regiment and stole property. Two of the soldiers from the 65th betrayed the trust placed in them while in a position of responsibility: John O'Donnell forged a cheque on the regimental bank while serving as colour sergeant, and William Brown stole money from the Treasury while on sentry duty. They were given sentences of seven years' and 15 years' transportation, respectively.[15] Two soldier convicts, one of whom was a deserter, were transported from the 96th Regiment for stealing property, and another nine were from the 99th Regiment. Seven of those nine were deserters, one struck an officer and one was found guilty of rape.

The first of the Queen's men transported from New Zealand to Van Diemen's Land were William Lane, George Morris and John Bailey – all Protestants – and an Irish Catholic, Richard Shea. These men were four of the nine soldier convicts from the 99th Regiment. When they were interrogated on their arrival in Van Diemen's Land, Lane, Morris and Bailey claimed they had been 'taken by the Natives'. Bailey explained that this happened at Hokianga, north of Auckland, and that the men had been held captive for around four months.[16] A brief record of their general court martial reveals a story at odds with this tale about being kidnapped by Māori.

In June 1846 Lane, Morris, Bailey and Shea were shipped from Wellington to Auckland on a government brig 'to headquarters to be tried by a Court Martial'.[17] In October, it was eventually recounted in several New Zealand newspapers how 'privates Lane, Morris, and Bailey, of the 99th regiment ... deserted from Her Majesty's forces to join the ranks of the rebel chief Kawiti'. From this tantalising but all too brief account it seems that the three soldiers were following in the footsteps of early Pākehā toa – 'a group of shadowy, semi-legendary figures, the fighting Pakeha Maori' who participated alongside Māori as combatants in the inter-iwi musket wars.[18] While these earlier men lived beyond the reach of the long arm of colonial law, redcoat deserters in colonial New Zealand were subject to military justice.

As Phillip Hilton explained, former soldiers were overrepresented in the convict system in Van Diemen's Land. Of the 60,000 male convicts transported from across the British Empire to the penal colony, 3275 were former soldiers and marines. The majority of the soldier convicts, 2000, were transported after a court martial. At least 1200 more men 'confessed upon arrival to having previously taken the King's shilling'. Within the British Army desertion was 'an insidious problem' – in 1796 it accounted for a staggering 84 per cent of soldier offences. Although this figure fell substantially, by the mid-nineteenth century desertion remained the most common cause of soldiers being transported to Van Diemen's Land. Technically, desertion attracted the death penalty, but many of the younger rank and file were given another chance by being sentenced to transportation or some other punishment. Hundreds of these men were branded with the letter 'D' on their left hip to shame them: they were marked bodily as a deserter forever after, and they were identifiable as a deserter if they ever again tried to sign up for military service. It was generally the more poorly paid soldiers or those who had been severely disciplined who ran away. Many of the transported soldiers had already accrued records of punishments for offences committed while in the British Army.[19]

After the court martial of Lane, Morris and Bailey, the *New Zealand Spectator and Cook's Strait Guardian* reported that the 'sentence [to transportation] of the court which sat some months ago' had been approved by O'Connell.[20] At the time, O'Connell was not only the highest-ranking military officer in the Australasian colonies, he was temporarily also the highest-ranking civil authority. From July to August 1846 he administered the government of New South Wales after the departure of Sir George Gipps and before the arrival of the new governor, Sir Charles FitzRoy.[21] Appointments such as O'Connell's were not unusual in Britain's antipodean colonies where naval and, later, military men of standing regularly held high office as part of the apparatus of the civil administration. In societies riven by frontier conflict, such men were viewed as strategists who were well trained and well placed to execute required duties in times of war.

Not everyone approved of such appointments, though. Some people thought military men had been 'chosen for posts which they were utterly unqualified to fill, from their previous habits of life, and from the *sic volo sic jubeo* [thus I will, thus I command] tone which they have been accustomed to employ in the everyday transactions of common life'. The person who wrote this '[did] not deny that there have been several instances where naval and military men have shown themselves well qualified for civil office', but considered that 'they are exceptions in proof of the rule'. The writer thought it wise to guard against the possibility of despotic rule by not combining the offices of governor and commander of the forces in one person.[22]

In the same newspaper article in which the sentence to transportation of the three soldiers was confirmed, the fate of their fellow private Richard Shea was also made public. He, too, was sentenced to transportation for life. He had 'struck Lieutenant Johnson at Porirua', an act he later described as having been carried out using his firelock when on parade.[23] In a similar case, the *New Zealander* reported in June 1850 that, prompted by an incident on Karori Road in Wellington in which Private John Smith of the 65th Regiment struck Judge Henry Samuel Chapman, 'it appears that Smith desired to be transported, and committed the offence with the expectation that he might thus secure that object'. The soldier was, at the time of the offence, performing hard labour along with a two-year term of imprisonment for 'an outrageous assault on a married woman'. Rather than being transported to Van Diemen's Land, however, Smith was flogged: he received 50 lashes 'at the gaol before the assembled prisoners'. The newspaper railed against the punishment: it claimed that flogging failed to reform bad characters. Instead, such 'punitive discipline [resulted in] the vast majority being hardened and rendered reckless, rather than reclaimed by it'. The *New Zealander* did not provide any particular evidence as to why it was supposed that Smith hoped to be transported; it is unclear whether he gave evidence to this effect or if this was simply speculation.[24]

A clue as to whose opinion was being reported can, however, be found in an article from the *New Zealander* published more than three years earlier, on 6 February 1847. It was likely Chapman himself who supposed that two soldiers from the 65th Regiment – Michael Fitzgerald and Patrick Brady – stole a silver watch from a man's home in Epsom in Auckland in order to be transported to Van Diemen's Land. Judge Chapman, who grew up in London and later worked in Amsterdam and Quebec, had been admitted to the Middle Temple at London on 12 June 1840. Earlier that year he began publishing the *New Zealand Journal* in London – the publication where the article railing against the transportation of Parkhurst boys to New Zealand had appeared. In 1843 Chapman was appointed as a judge of the Supreme Court of New Zealand for the southern district, which included the New Zealand Company towns of New Plymouth, Wellington and Nelson.[25] However, it was at Auckland that Chapman sentenced Fitzgerald and Brady to 12 months in Auckland gaol with hard labour. In doing so, the judge observed how 'it appeared very clear, their chief object in stealing the watch, was to commit a crime of sufficient enormity to cause them to be transported'. Their motivation, he claimed, was to 'thus get clear of their Regiment'.[26]

If it was Brady's desire to be transported, his wish was eventually granted. He was among the six soldiers transported from New Zealand to Van Diemen's Land for striking a superior officer. An Irishman, originally from Dublin, he arrived in Hobart on 5 April 1849 on the *Perseverance* to serve a life sentence for striking an adjutant. After keeping a near-clean sheet, Brady received a conditional pardon on 28 April 1858.[27] Intriguingly, Phillip Hilton's extensive research into British soldiers within the Vandemonian convict system revealed that more than 80 per cent of soldiers transported for mutinous behaviour were sentenced for 'individual acts of mutiny and insubordination', rather than having taken part in a group uprising. He found that offences involving mutiny and insubordination, including striking an officer, were noticeably more common beyond British borders. Some of the offending soldiers were likely lashing out from frustration, or were perhaps suffering from some psychological illness; others stated unequivocally that they preferred the prospect of transportation over continuing to serve in the British Army.[28]

After arriving in Hobart on the *Castor*, Lane, Morris, Bailey and Shea stated their offences and detailed the length of their military service. They were interrogated about their prior offences and punishments. Such admissions were extracted from all the soldier convicts transported from New Zealand, and inscribed on their indents in Van Diemen's Land. Bailey had completed seven years of military service with the 99th Regiment with no prior convictions. His comrades Lane and Morris, who served four and five years respectively as part of the same regiment, both admitted to having previously been disciplined. Lane had received 150 lashes for drunkenness, and Morris was made to serve six months' hard labour for desertion.[29] Shea admitted to having been court-martialled for drunkenness, for which he had served three months' hard labour.[30]

Shea was being flexible with the truth. Drunkenness was part of one of three charges he had faced, alongside fellow privates Michael Tobin and John Power, at a garrison court martial held in the mess room of the 99th Regiment in Barrack Square, Sydney, in late December 1844 or early January 1845. The first charge related to the three soldiers 'forcibly entering the Crispin Arms public-house, between seven and eight o'clock, on Christmas evening'. The second charge pertained to their having destroyed property on the premises, valued at £8 and upwards; and the third charge was for 'rioting in the streets'. The case against the prisoners and the defence they mounted went unreported in the *Sydney Morning Herald* in early January 1845, 'as it is not usual to report the proceedings of Courts Martial until the sentence has been formally announced'.[31] As in New Zealand, the commander of forces would review the case before the details were promulgated to the military through general orders and relayed to the civilian population through colonial newspapers.

When Shea arrived in Hobart with Lane, Morris and Bailey, the four were ordered to serve an initial period of probation for 30 months at Norfolk Island. The colonial administration favoured Norfolk Island penal station as a site of incarceration for soldiers and former soldiers from across the British Empire. As Timothy Causer has pointed out, 'there were significant numbers of soldiers – and former soldiers – detained at Norfolk Island'.

There was an obvious correlation between the sites the soldiers were court-martialled at and regional disturbances. For example, numerous British redcoats were transported from Upper and Lower Canada in 1839 and 1840; many ended up at Norfolk Island.[32] New Zealand bucked this trend, however: of the 46 soldiers transported from New Zealand during the 1840s and early 1850s, no redcoats other than the four already mentioned ended up serving their probation at Norfolk Island.

Norfolk Island is located about 900 miles east of Sydney. It was claimed by Britain in 1774, but it was not settled until 1788. Because of logistical problems caused by its distance from Britain's Australian colonies, the first settlement on the island was abandoned in 1814. The island was recolonised by the British in 1825 and operated as a penal station for the next 30 years.[33] It gained notoriety as a site to which 'prisoners convicted of heinous offences' were sent.[34] Colonial traveller Godfrey Charles Mundy referred to Norfolk Island as 'a college for rogues, of which New South Wales and Van Diemen's Land are merely preparatory schools'. To his way of thinking, convicts had to 'have matriculated, graduated, and become professors [of crime], in order to be entered on the books' there.[35] In short, the men sent to the Norfolk Island penal station were thought to be beyond redemption. The regime under which the men laboured also gained a reputation as being extremely sadistic, rendering the island a living hell.

Causer's revisionist history of the second penal settlement at Norfolk Island has resulted in a nuanced historical understanding of this complex site. Many of the hoary old myths and rumours that abounded about the place have been shown to have been just that. Despite various colonial governors seeking to use the island as a dumping ground for doubly and trebly convicted prisoners, only around half of the men sent there had been convicted of more than one offence. Causer described the 'ruling structure' at the penal station as 'fairly well-delineated', yet at the same time he highlighted multiple ways in which the authority wielded by the ruling elite was regularly challenged by civilian officers, some of whom were convicts filling minor administrative roles. The convicts themselves employed strategies to avoid work or to improve their own conditions, and they enjoyed leisure activities in their spare time just as convicted men and women did elsewhere within the Australian penal colonies.[36] Norfolk Island was, however, first and foremost a site of punishment. During the time that Shea, Lane, Morris and Bailey were forced to labour there, the use of leg irons was routine. Floggings were commonplace too, and while most men were flogged on only one occasion, the average number of lashes received per beating was a lot higher than was usually the case in either New South Wales or Van Diemen's Land.[37]

None of the first four redcoats transported from New Zealand was flogged while at Norfolk Island, where they arrived on 24 June 1847 – although all were punished. Two of the Englishmen were charged with multiple offences. Lane was sentenced to stints of imprisonment with hard labour in chains on five separate occasions, ranging from 14 days for being found with tobacco in his possession and a month for 'improperly receiving meat from a fellow prisoner' to four months for idleness. Another offence that resulted in 14 days' imprisonment with hard labour in chains involved 'improperly allowing Mr Moore to be in his master's garden'.[38] Morris was imprisoned for four calendar months with hard labour in chains for 'being drunk and arming himself with a fowling piece to prevent his lawful apprehension on the morning of the 26th of Jan'. Interestingly, he too was charged with a food-related offence: he was sentenced to three months' imprisonment with hard labour for trying to smuggle sugar out of the gaol cookhouse.[39] Both Morris and Lane were likely participating in a convict-operated black market. Prisoners were keen to supplement their diet with whatever additional produce and other rations they could acquire, or to relieve their boredom with banned substances such as alcohol and tobacco.

Their companion Bailey's conduct record was relatively clean. Early in his sentence he narrowly avoided being punished for having lost his pannikin when the lost item turned up; and he served 10 days in solitary confinement in June 1849 for an unspecified act of misconduct.[40]

Lane, Morris and Bailey all arrived back at Hobart on 31 January 1850 on the *Lady Franklin*. Shea, who had been imprisoned just once for 14 days with hard labour in chains for having tobacco in his possession, had arrived back in Hobart several months earlier, on 12 November 1849.[41] After his return, Shea, fresh-faced with brown hair and blue eyes, was assigned to several different masters in Hobart before being sent to labour in rural locations. The Irishman eventually completed his sentence in the colony's capital, where he worked for masters in the centre of town at Harrington

Street and then Elizabeth Street. He accrued three further offences, including being found drunk, before he received his ticket of leave on 19 September 1854; this was followed by a recommendation for a conditional pardon on 16 October 1855, which was granted on 21 November 1856.[42]

In stark contrast Lane, who accrued the most offences of any of the four while at Norfolk Island, was ordered on his return to Van Diemen's Land 'not to be allowed to reside in the Hobart or Launceston districts until further orders'. Given that he was a brickmaker by trade and therefore could have proved very useful to townsfolk, relegating him to rural areas marked the concern the convict administration felt about his lack of progress towards reformation. Urban living would have posed too much of a temptation to the unruly convict, who was likely considered to be lacking in self-discipline. Despite his poor reputation, the Englishman with brown to red hair, hazel eyes and a sallow complexion accrued just five more offences while under sentence. Drunkenness was on his conduct record.[43] His offences spanned the period over which he was single and then after he became a married man. Lane received permission on 7 February 1853 to marry female convict Rosina Morgan, who arrived in the colony on the *Cadet*.[44] A laundress with dark-brown hair and black eyes, Rosina disembarked in Van Diemen's Land on 12 April 1849 at the tender age of 16 to serve a seven-year sentence to transportation for stealing a coat. She came from Newton Bushel in Devon, England.[45] Lane received his ticket of leave the year after their marriage, on 8 August 1854. This was followed by a recommendation for a conditional pardon on 3 July 1855, which was granted in May 1856.[46]

The Englishman John Bailey, a grey-eyed farm labourer with light-brown hair and sandy whiskers, had notably fewer masters than his erstwhile companions in Van Diemen's Land. This could reflect his temperament and work ethic – or it might be an indication of the value of a labourer to those trying to earn a living off the land on an island where farm servants could be hard to come by. Bailey accrued just two further offences, one of which involved 'harboring a female on his master's premises', for which he received a reprimand. He, too, received his ticket of leave on 8 August 1854 and was recommended for a conditional pardon on 28 August 1855. This was granted on 22 July 1856.[47]

The clean-shaven George Morris, with blue eyes and flaxen hair, was originally from Halifax in Nova Scotia. Like Bailey and Shea, his conduct

record listed his occupation as 'laborer'. He, like Lane, was not allowed to
live in Hobart or Launceston 'until further orders' and was initially sent
to Tunbridge in the midlands. He laboured for masters in New Norfolk
to the west of Hobart and eventually in Hobart itself. Towards the end
of his sentence Morris was assigned to the noted botanical collector
Ronald Campbell Gunn. He accrued eight offences before he absconded
on 21 September 1854 – including being drunk, 'resisting a constable in
the execution of his duty', being out after hours and being absent without
leave. After he was recaptured Morris was sentenced to 18 months' hard
labour with 12 months' probation to be served at Port Arthur, in addition
to his existing sentence. This punishment delayed his ticket of leave to 27
January 1857. On 19 January 1858 he was recommended for a conditional
pardon, which was granted on 31 August.[48] By then, Morris had married.
He received permission in September 1857 to tie the knot with Mary Ann
Jackson, a hazel-eyed and brown-haired cook who arrived in Van Diemen's
Land on the *Duchess of Northumberland* on 21 April 1853 to serve a
sentence of transportation for seven years for receiving stolen property.[49]
Her conditional pardon was approved on 28 April 1848, several months
ahead of Morris receiving the same indulgence.[50]

When it came to desertion, each of Britain's colonial sites exhibited its
own peculiarities. As the *New Zealander* explained, 'this country [New
Zealand] affords more than ordinary facilities for desertion; a fact which
is notoriously exemplified in the case of soldiers, who desert so frequently,
notwithstanding the strict guard under which military regulations place
them'. Reporting in the context of exiles – men who had served most of
their sentence in Britain – possibly being shipped to the colony, the *New
Zealander* opined that the New Zealand bush was well suited to providing
refuge for escapees, and 'no practicable amount of surveillance' was
adequate to guard against these men availing themselves of opportunities to
take off. Colonists saw male escapees as potentially posing a risk to Māori,
particularly to women, who would 'rapidly become more and more corrupt'
because of the 'gross [sexual] immoralities [that] would almost certainly
prevail'. The Parkhurst boys were depicted as agents of depravity. While
some of the boys were known to have 'turned out well', many had allegedly
'relapsed into crime, and corrupted others, until their name passed almost
into a proverb for lawlessness and vice'.[51]

But although the allure of the bush and the possibility of joining the ranks of Māori warriors may have attracted the likes of Lane, Morris and Bailey, other redcoats serving in the British Army during the New Zealand Wars seem to have deserted for quite the opposite reason. Four of the six soldier convicts who arrived in Van Diemen's Land on the *Julia* on 2 June 1847 were court-martialled in Auckland in August 1846, where they were sentenced to transportation for 'deserting in the vicinity of hostile natives': it seems that fear motivated the men to desert their posts, fellow soldiers, regiment and military responsibilities. One of these soldier convicts, Michael Tobin from County Cork, explained on his arrival in Van Diemen's Land how he had been sentenced to transportation for life for deserting from the 99th Regiment with two other soldiers, John Robinson and Bernard McNally. Tobin had also struck his superior officer, Captain Armstrong. He admitted to being punished previously during his five years of military service 'for being drunk and breaking into a public house'[52] – the same incident in which Richard Shea was involved a few days after Christmas 1844 in Sydney.

Robinson, who was originally from Whitehaven in England, also served for five years with the 99th. Like Tobin, he accrued a record of being punished for drunkenness. His sentence was to transportation for 14 years.[53] McNally volunteered that their desertion was from Paruru, near Auckland. The groom and dairyman, originally from Dublin, served in the 99th for five years and eight months, during which time he was charged four times with offences related to drunkenness. McNally was flogged on one of those occasions – he received 100 lashes for insubordination while drunk. Interestingly, he added that when they had deserted in New Zealand, 'friendly natives' had returned the three soldiers to their regiment. McNally, like Robinson, received a sentence of transportation for 14 years.[54]

Another foot soldier transported on the *Julia* under the name James Brearly claimed on his arrival in Van Diemen's Land that his first name was really Isaac. He, too, served five years with the 99th and was twice punished for desertion before he was sentenced to transportation for 14 years for 'desertion in the vicinity of hostile natives'. Court-martialled in Auckland on the same day as Robinson and McNally, Brearly also claimed to have been 'brought back by friendly natives'.[55]

The 'friendly natives' were those Māori who were considered loyal to the crown during the New Zealand Wars. By the 1860s Māori who maintained a neutral or loyal and 'friendly' stance towards the crown were often referred to as kūpapa Māori. This term has since changed in meaning. As Ron Crosby observed, by the end of the twentieth century kūpapa was considered to have just one meaning – and that was 'traitor'.[56]

Cultivating collaborative relationships with select local indigenous people was a strategy used by Europe's imperial powers across their colonies in different parts of the world. To cite just a couple of examples, at the Cape colony (which is now part of South Africa) the Dutch elevated men from among the local indigenous Khoi population who proved willing to negotiate, and endowed them with staffs of office as symbols of their status in the newly emerging colonial order. Over time, these newly anointed 'captains' usually passed down the staff and the responsibilities attached to the office it represented to their sons.[57] Across the Australian colonies the British used a range of methods to secure Aboriginal collaboration in endeavours ranging from tracking escaped convicts and guiding exploratory expeditions through to serving in 'native' police forces and providing labour across the cattle and pearling industries and as domestic servants.[58] As in New Zealand, 'friendly' natives were sometimes rewarded for their services, albeit usually not as generously as colonists, while 'hostile' natives often felt the full force of the relevant European empires' punitive power.

As with almost all the soldier convicts who arrived as small groups in Van Diemen's Land, Tobin, Robinson, McNally and Brearly were initially sent to the same probation station. In their case this was Lymington at Port Cygnet, south of Hobart. When Administrator of Van Diemen's Land Charles La Trobe visited this probation station it was relatively new. He described the buildings as 'superior ... being of stone, brick and wood'. The huts at the site were capable of accommodating 400 men, although only 230 were living there. A mess room used by the first- and second-class convicts also served as a chapel and school room. Some solitary cells were built, and there were plans for a further six. The site was well served with 'capacious' storerooms and surrounded by 'abundant good land', some of which was under cultivation. Parts of the surrounds were lightly forested, and some more heavily so; La Trobe imagined that these 160 acres could be 'cleared with comparative facility'. He observed 'excellent clay for bricks and rough stone for foundations', as well as good water. This was a site at which self-sufficiency might truly be achieved. When it came to accommodation for the third-class prisoners, however, La Trobe found their separate apartments 'not substantial'. Annoyingly to the administrator, the convicts could readily converse with those in adjoining apartments. One of the main gripes La Trobe had about the site, though, was that it was virtually impossible to prevent the convicts communicating with local settlers.[59]

McNally laboured at Lymington between 13 June 1847 and 5 May 1848, after which he was relocated to Parson's Pass on the east coast of Van Diemen's Land, north of Hobart. He completed the latter part of his probation period at nearby Triabunna and on Maria Island, off the east coast of Van Diemen's Land, where he laboured at Darlington at the north of the island as well as at Long Point, near the isthmus that joins north and south Maria. Essentially, convict labour was redirected to where it was most required at any given moment. After becoming a passholder on 8 September 1849 McNally served the remainder of his sentence under a range of masters across the north, middle and south of the island at places including the West Tamar, Fingal, Richmond, New Town and Hobart, among others. While he was under sentence he was punished for 10 more offences, including being drunk, lying and larceny.[60]

In an episode with immediate ramifications for the hazel-eyed man with black hair and whiskers, just two days after being sentenced to hard labour for three months for 'misconduct in being found in bed with a woman', McNally was on 8 January 1858 granted permission to marry.[61] His wife-to-be was his erstwhile illicit consort, an Irish woman from Dublin named Ann Currie who, at the age of 21, arrived in Van Diemen's Land on the *Duchess of Northumberland* to serve seven years. She was hazel-eyed, had dark-brown hair and stood just 4ft 9in. tall. Tried in Edinburgh for 'theft with another' and transported to Van Diemen's Land, Currie also accumulated numerous additional offences, including being found drunk and absconding. Her record notes an undisclosed act of 'misconduct' – related to McNally – on 6 January 1858, for which she was sentenced to three months' hard labour.[62]

McNally's conditional pardon, recommended in August the previous year, was granted to him on 31 August 1858.[63] The Irishman died a pauper just 15 years later on 25 October 1873, aged 61 – at the time he was at the Brickfield Pauper Establishment in North Hobart. His death was attributed to bronchitis.[64]

Tobin's record is as peppered with transfers and offences as McNally's, and the two men were transferred to the same probation stations. Interestingly, Tobin was also charged with misconduct involving a woman. He was found in September 1852 'in the bedroom of Mr Johnstone's female servant' at Hobart. The former soldier absconded on several occasions but eventually received a conditional pardon on 26 July 1859.[65] Like McNally, Tobin married in Van Diemen's Land. His wife was Elizabeth Bracken, who arrived free in the colony. The couple married on 24 May 1858 at Launceston. By then Tobin, aged 30, held a ticket of leave and had retrained as a tailor; his bride, aged 21, is recorded in the marriage register simply as 'spinster'.[66]

There are no records relating to permissions to marry for Robinson or Brearly. Robinson's record reads much the same as his two companions. He was sent to the same probation stations as they were, committed numerous offences while already under sentence, and was regularly transferred between masters. After having served part of his sentence in chains, Robinson received a conditional pardon on 28 September 1858.[67]

Unlike the other three soldiers who deserted in the vicinity of so-called hostile natives, Brearly's conduct record is almost a clean sheet. The sallow-complexioned young man with brown hair and hazel eyes could not entirely escape the shame of his past, though, as – like so many other soldier convicts before him – he was branded with 'D' on the left hip, permanently marking him as a deserter. Brearly, like the other three, was transferred to Parson's Pass but he was not sent to labour at Triabunna or Maria Island. He worked for far fewer masters than McNally, Tobin or Robinson as a probation passholder. His record indicates that he spent most of the remainder of his sentence in the constabulary. His sole offence occurred in June 1852 – drunkenness, for which he served 14 days in solitary confinement. On 11 April 1854 he was recommended for a conditional pardon. He received this indulgence on 30 January 1855.[68]

Patrick Shea and Henry Hodges were the two other soldiers who arrived in Hobart along with McNally, Robinson, Tobin and Brearly on the *Julia* in midwinter of 1847. Shea, a 23-year-old Irishman from the 58th Regiment, was court-martialled in Wellington on 12 January 1847 for drunkenness and firing on another soldier in the barracks. He was sentenced to transportation for life. Like his fellow soldier convicts, Shea was initially sent to Lymington to serve his probation before being transferred to Parson's Pass. In the first year of his sentence Shea absconded but was recaptured; his brief taste of freedom cost him 14 days in solitary confinement.[69] The authorities were unable to hold Shea for long. He fled into the bush again, this time with John Sullivan, James McGough and Andrew Duffey. The four escaped convicts formed a gang of bushrangers led by Duffey. Such renegades were usually escaped convicts, but occasionally former colonial officials joined their ranks. Bushrangers were often heavily armed and survived by robbing other people. The young former soldier's gang ended up in a shootout with the police on the east coast of Van Diemen's Land, in which one of their number was killed.[70] Shea, Sullivan and McGough were captured, then tried at Oatlands in the midlands before the chief justice and a jury. All three were found guilty of shooting at a Constable Kelly with intent to murder him.[71] At the end of 'the longest sittings ever held' in Oatlands at the time, the three bushrangers were sentenced to be hanged. McGough 'turned round laughing, put on his hat, and with two of the others made a desperate rush on the constable, with a view to escape'. They were detained, however, and returned to the gaol.[72] Shea was hanged at Oatlands on 9 May 1848.[73]

Unlike the other soldiers transported on the *Julia*, Hodges' trial was a civil one. His case was heard before Judge Chapman at the Supreme Court in Wellington on 1 September 1846: he was charged with raping a widow, Ann Cording. The woman told the court that she had lost her way on returning home to Thorndon Flat after visiting Mr Blathwayt and had ended up in a swamp. A soldier on guard at the nearby gaol answered her cries for help. He accused her of being drunk; she claimed she was ill. After helping her partway towards her destination, the soldier raped her. She later swore that Hodges was the rapist – she said she recognised his voice. Other witnesses were called who testified to the woman's state following the assault and to the soldier's muddiness that night. Hodges was found guilty and sentenced to transportation for life.[74] On his arrival in Van Diemen's Land he said that he had served seven years with the 99th Regiment before his conviction. He, too, was sent initially to Lymington, then to Parson's Pass; he completed his probation at the two stations at Maria Island, Long Point and at Darlington. After becoming a probation passholder on 4 May 1850 Hodges was assigned to masters in Hobart and further south at

Peppermint Bay. He was punished only once for misconduct while under sentence before receiving his ticket of leave on 8 August 1854, followed by a conditional pardon on 22 July 1856.[75]

The only other convict transported from New Zealand for rape was a civilian, William Wright, a 40-year-old labourer originally from London who was married with two children.[76] Found guilty in the Supreme Court at Wellington of raping 16-year-old Fanny Jenkins, Wright persistently asserted his innocence; he claimed to have been with his wife at the time of the alleged assault. He was sentenced to transportation for life.[77] Wright's determination to prove his innocence was so strong that he absconded from Van Diemen's Land and returned to New Zealand to try to clear his name and salvage his reputation. Correspondence amounting to 78 pages sits in Wright's file at Archives New Zealand in Wellington. It includes a petition to Governor George Grey written on Wright's behalf and signed by dozens of petitioners, in which they wrote of having 'seen with pain his [Wright's] prolonged punishment in heavy irons', prompting them to intercede on his behalf. The petitioners described Wright as a 'good neighbour and a kind father' and sought the governor's mercy.[78] Their pleading was to no avail. Wright was tried on 1 September 1852 at the Supreme Court in Wellington for being illegally at large and received another sentence to transportation for life. He was returned to Van Diemen's Land on the *Exchange* and then the *Circassian*, along with the final four convicts transported from New Zealand to Van Diemen's Land.[79] Wright was sent to Port Arthur to serve one year's probation in heavy irons, labouring as part of the quarry gang. On 9 December 1853 an order was given that he be released from heavy irons; these were to be replaced with light irons and Wright was to remain in the quarry gang. Wright eventually became a probation passholder on 1 June 1856. He received his ticket of leave on 8 June 1858 and a conditional pardon on 24 January 1860.[80]

The last two soldier convicts transported from New Zealand to Van Diemen's Land – James Woods and Michael Morrissey – were both discharged soldiers who had served with the 65th Regiment. The two men were 'indicted for robbing J Church, on the 1st of last November [1852], of £10 in bank notes and twenty shillings in silver, and also of taking from him a silver watch, and putting him in bodily fear'. The matter was heard before Justice Stephens at the Supreme Court in Wellington, where it was revealed that both defendants had prior records. Morrissey had already served two years' imprisonment with hard labour for a similar offence, while Woods had previously received three months' imprisonment for 'keeping a disorderly house'. Both defendants were found guilty and sentenced to transportation for 15 years.[81] Woods, a 41-year-old married man originally from County Tyrone in Ireland, was sent to Port Arthur on his arrival in Van Diemen's Land. He accrued four more offences while under sentence before receiving his conditional pardon on 2 February 1858.[82] Morrissey, the younger of the two, was aged 26 when he arrived in Van Diemen's Land, a single man originally from County Cork in Ireland. He was sent to Cascades, down the Tasman Peninsula, to serve his probation. Morrissey was found guilty of just one offence while under sentence when, on 28 May 1855, he was punished for 'misconduct in refusing to enter eligible service at a fair rate of wages', for which he received six months' hard labour. His ticket of leave was granted on 30 November 1856 and he received his conditional pardon just over three years later, on 24 January 1860.[83]

CHAPTER 7

In open rebellion

The British argued that Australian Aboriginal people were British subjects. As such, they were nominally protected under colonial laws – but also obliged to comply with those laws. The New Zealand colonial judiciary mounted substantially the same legal argument about Māori, who were considered to have become British subjects after Lieutenant-Governor Hobson's 1840 proclamation of British sovereignty over New Zealand.[1] As John Pratt has explained, 'the onset of formal colonisation in New Zealand and the importation of British punishment practices meant the two systems [Māori and Pākehā] with their irreconcilable differences could not live together'.[2] The British intended for Māori to be assimilated into colonial society over time. From the 1840s, regardless of whether and to what extent Māori understood colonial laws, any contravention on their part meant they could be brought before the courts and punished – although alternative mechanisms were also used to resolve disputes.

New Zealand law courts emulated their Australian colonial counterparts in providing interpreters and legal counsel for Māori defendants, to provide the semblance of a fair trial. The colonists' insistence on treating Māori as British subjects meant that attacks on settlers' persons and property were criminalised, regardless of the underlying motivation. Instead of being made prisoners of war, during episodes of frontier skirmishing or open

131

warfare Māori were taken into custody and put on trial in the criminal courts. When conflict in the Wellington region was at its height Governor George Grey declared martial law over the area. This led to captured 'rebel' Māori – controversially at the time and since – being subjected to courts martial, as a result of which one warrior was hanged, another died while in custody in Wellington, and five warriors were sentenced to transportation for life to Van Diemen's Land. This was the first time that Māori had been transported to Van Diemen's Land – but it was not the first time indigenous New Zealanders had been sentenced to transportation.

The first court of quarter sessions, convened in Wellington in October 1841, heard several cases involving intercultural conflict. The defendants in two of the cases were named as 'natives E'Wara and E'Tonghi [Pukewa]'. In opening the session, Chairman Edmund Halswell felt a need to 'mention these cases in particular'. He reiterated to the court:

> I am desirous of letting the public know that the natives are in truth
> and in fact British subjects, and are to be treated in every respect like
> any of ourselves; they have the same right to protection of the Law, and
> they must be held equally amendable for any breach of it: but in order
> that they may be shielded from the consequences of their ignorance, or
> presumed ignorance of our laws and customs, counsel will be assigned
> them by the court, and a sworn interpreter will faithfully translate all
> that is important for them to know.[3]

He reiterated such sentiments on several occasions, stressing the equality of all before the law as well as the responsibilities of each British subject, whether Pākehā or Māori, to uphold the law.

The intercultural matter brought before the court of quarter sessions was heard on Tuesday 5 October 1841. Colonist John Collyer stood accused of stealing a gun from E Tuma, 'an aboriginal inhabitant of New Zealand'. In this instance, British law protected the Māori man's property rights. Collyer was found guilty and sentenced to three months' hard labour.[4] Later that same day Pukewa was charged with stealing from Alfred Hornbrook's shop a blanket that he allegedly coveted and could not afford. Pukewa was provided with counsel, Dr Evans, and John Knox was sworn in as interpreter. In Pukewa's case, before the jury was sworn in, Evans entered a plea that 'by the Treaty of Waitangi, all the rights of chieftainship were reserved to the New Zealanders [Māori]; and that among those rights, was that of administering justice among the inhabitants of their own tribe'. Crown Prosecutor Hanson objected; he claimed that the court 'could not take cognizance of the Treaty of Waitangi unless it was produced'. After some discussion the case was adjourned until the following day.[5]

On Wednesday Evans withdrew his plea as to jurisdiction but requested that Pukewa's case be determined by a jury that was '"*de medietate lingua*" [sic], – composed half of natives, half of Europeans'. 'The prisoner,' Evans reminded the court, 'was not a native born English subject.' The crown prosecutor objected: he countered that the defendant was 'clearly a British subject'. 'So soon as New Zealand became a British Colony,' Hanson told the court, 'all the natives became *ipse facto* British subjects.' After Evans lost this argument, a jury comprised entirely of Pākehā was empanelled. The trial lasted five hours. Pukewa was found guilty, but the jury strongly recommended mercy on the grounds that 'he was the first native who had been tried under English law'. He was sentenced to seven days' hard labour.[6]

Just a few months later, at the court of quarter sessions in Wellington on Wednesday 4 January 1842, Pukewa appeared before Halswell and three justices of the peace – this time charged with stealing from James Pribble two blankets valued at 15 shillings. Pukewa allegedly took the blankets off a clothes horse outside the door of the Pribble family's home. Mrs Pribble sent her 14-year-old daughter to Pipitea pā in search of the stolen property. The daughter confronted Pukewa, who was 'putting the blankets on'. He ran away, and later tried to sell the blankets to another settler. In his defence the prisoner claimed to have bought the blankets from a Mr Blake. Constable Thomas Floyd told the court that the prisoner claimed to have a receipt for the purchase but 'he only saw some maori words on it'. It seems no attempt was made to retain the alleged receipt or to have it translated for the court. Pukewa was found guilty and sentenced 'to be transported to Van Diemen's Land, or any other place which his Excellency the Governor might think fit, for the period of seven years'.[7] Pukewa became the first Māori person in the colony sentenced to transportation to Van Diemen's Land; however, the lack of any indent or conduct record in the Tasmanian archive suggests that his sentence was never carried out.

Halswell opened the first session of the county court for the Southern District of New Ulster several months later, on Wednesday 20 April

1842. After reading the usual proclamation against vice and immorality, he explained the constitution and jurisdiction of the new court to those assembled. Halswell then took the opportunity to reiterate how he 'deemed it of essential importance that the Native population should be made to understand that, whilst their persons and property would be carefully protected against aggression by Europeans, yet that they were amendable to British law, and would undoubtedly be punished for violating it'. 'The determination of the Court,' he stated, 'was to enforce the law against Natives as well as Europeans, as least as far as that was practicable without endangering life and property.'[8] While this approach may on the surface have seemed fair-minded and even-handed, it failed to take into consideration cultural and linguistic differences or tikanga Māori (lore, etiquette and protocols used to determine appropriate behaviour and to correct transgressions).

Throughout the 1840s Māori continued to appear before the colonial law courts, sometimes as plaintiffs and sometimes as defendants. Court cases involving intercultural conflict in Wellington in the mid-1840s were held against a backdrop of rising tensions over the right to cultivate the particularly fertile land at the Hutt Valley. As early as May 1843 newspapers were reporting 'an attack by a body of Maories upon some half-dozen industrious Scotch settlers, who have made a joint purchase of a country section up the Hutt'. It was understood by colonists at the time that 'The Natives, in that case, are part of Rangihiata's [sic] tribe, who say like the rest, with few exceptions that, they have not sold the land in question, and will not suffer any white people to settle upon it until they get the *utu*.' Some Māori were also known to have complained that a few of the colonists had broken their side of the bargain by taking lands that were already being cultivated by Māori, rather than clearing virgin forest themselves.[9]

This was the crux of the matter. Māori who the settlers considered were local to Port Nicholson were 'satisfied' with the New Zealand Company's land purchases at the nearby Hutt Valley. The British colonists thought it 'nothing but fair to suppose that the residents [local Māori] had greater claims and rights to the district, than strange aborigines who had never, until they took forcible possession, seen the valley of the Hutt, and who had been living some hundreds of miles away from that place'. Reflecting in 1845 on the initial British occupation of the valley, the colonists asserted that 'the European first made an inroad on the primeval forest; they did not drive the natives either from their pahs or their cultivations, for the Hutt valley was one unbroken wild'.[10] The colonists, though, failed to appreciate 'the increasing pressure that had developed through the 1830s as a result of major influxes into the Otaki area of Ngāti Raukawa from Waikato and of Te Ātiawa and its related Taranaki iwi such as Ngāti Ruanui'. These newcomers travelled into the region at the invitation of Ngāti Toa relatives already living there. The resultant increase in population led to competition for the land and its resources and to crop raiding and, ultimately, to several battles between Māori. Ron Crosby has explained how this constellation of issues led to Te Ātiawa feeling under threat from Ngāti Toa rangatira Te Rauparaha. As a consequence, they sought to divest land at Whanganui a Tara and Heretaunga (the Hutt Valley) to the New Zealand Company. In return, they hoped to arm themselves with more muskets and use the Pākehā as a buffer between Ngāti Toa and themselves.[11]

By 1845 tensions were boiling over. The colonists understood the New Zealand Company to have purchased land at the Hutt Valley from Te Ātiawa in good faith. However, while Te Ātiawa were utilising land in the lower reaches of the valley, Ngāti Rangatahi who originated from around the Upper Whanganui River and Ngāti Tama from north Taranaki were occupying the valley's upper reaches. None of the proceeds from the land sales entered into between Te Ātiawa and the New Zealand Company were shared with Ngāti Tama and Ngāti Rangatahi, who understandably felt aggrieved by this. The colonists did not seem to appreciate the complexities of Māori land ownership or the grievances over the land purchases in the Hutt. Rather than negotiating a peaceful settlement, Governor Robert FitzRoy and Major Richmond, superintendent of the Wellington region, decided to utilise imperial soldiers and citizen militiamen to drive off those Māori who were still occupying the 'purchased' land.[12]

Meanwhile, colonists who were worried by rising tensions at the Hutt attended a public meeting at the Aglionby Arms on Thursday 19 September 1844 to discuss 'the seizure of their lands by the natives'. The crowd was so large that many were forced to stand outside. At the time, around 650 to 700 British settlers lived at the Hutt, most of them agriculturalists. These concerned colonists demanded action and decided to petition the governor. The land question, they reasoned, had hovered over their heads for three years already. The delay in settling the matter had seen 'the demands and aggressions of the natives ... daily increasing'. Colonists were being driven off the land, their houses destroyed and their crops uprooted. To add insult to injury, in some cases the very same Māori whom they had paid to clear the land were those now driving the colonists away. Displaced settlers were also annoyed that the law provided no compensation for people who lost everything. The colonists made a point of reiterating that none of the aggressions against them had been at the hands of those occupying the land on their arrival at the colony. Instead, they attributed blame to 'remnants of vagabond tribes, from all parts of the North and South Island' who built fortifications in the Hutt and made a handsome profit from selling potatoes and pigs to the settlers in nearby Wellington. All told, the colonists considered 'that in common with the other settlements founded by the New Zealand Company, [we] are suffering under hardships unparalleled by those of any other of her Majesty's subjects – and unexampled in the history of modern times'. The 118 petitioners were all 'inhabitants of the Hutt' who called on the governor to redress their grievances or, if he was unable to do so, to forward their petition to London to the secretary of state for the colonies.[13]

During this period of heightened tensions, on 25 March 1845 the New Zealand government passed a Militia Ordinance. Under its provisions it became 'lawful for his Excellency the Governor to call together, arm, and array as a militia' colonists who would be trained by officers appointed to command them. 'Every man ... between the ages of eighteen years and sixty years, being a British subject, and not an aboriginal native, who shall reside within the colony' became liable to serve in the militia. Those with afflictions such as lunacy, blindness, deafness or lameness could be excused from service. An adjutant with experience in the British Army would oversee each body of militia and 'would be recompensed eight shillings per diem'. Under the same ordinance it became lawful for the governor to constitute courts martial and to grant his commission or warrants to officers commanding the militia to convene those courts, too. Any militiaman who deserted could be punished for mutiny and desertion in accordance with the articles of war. The results of any regimental court martial were to be submitted to the commandant of the regiment for his approval. The commandant was empowered to execute, mitigate or remit sentences as he saw fit.[14] The Hutt Valley colonists who petitioned FitzRoy now had a legal framework within which they could take up arms against Māori.

Against this backdrop of impending war, and in the aftermath of the Wairau incident and the northern wars, skirmishing was taking place at the Hutt in the mid-1840s. Because Māori were seen as British subjects they were brought before the colonial judiciary to answer for their 'crimes'. Some were even threatened with transportation. The trial of Te Kūmete, who was later transported to Van Diemen's Land, and fellow defendant Wiremu reveals a typical process of acts of frontier war being criminalised.

Both men appeared before Justice Chapman and a grand jury sitting under a special commission at the Supreme Court in Wellington on Friday 27 March 1846. Their trial filled 55 pages of Chapman's notebook in his scrawling hand, with crossings out and marginalia documenting his thought processes as the case unfolded.[15] Te Kūmete and Wiremu faced charges of carrying out robberies with violence and of 'cutting and maiming a pig'.[16] They were arrested in the Hutt Valley in the company of Sub-Protector of Aborigines Henry Kemp. Kemp had earlier told Māori at Kaipara in the north of New Zealand, when he was seeking jurisdiction over their affairs, that 'the able interference of the Magistrates among the Natives who had committed robberies had been patronized and approved of by the chiefs or masters of the respective culprits, and was a great preventive of future depredations'.[17] Making Māori subject to colonial law had the blessing of their rangatira and would, Kemp thought, function as a deterrent. Kemp was pressed into service as an interpreter at the trial of Te Kūmete and Wiremu.

The first charge alleged the defendants were part of a larger party of Māori who robbed the house of the settler Hughes at Taita on Sunday 1 March 1846. Te Kūmete and Wiremu were described as 'among the most active of them and also as having been with an armed party of natives similarly engaged in the neighbourhood about the same time'.[18] Hughes' neighbours Arbuthnot Burnett and Mary Burnett said that they saw Te Kūmete carrying a sword; another witness, Charles Collis, said Te Kūmete had come to his house on the same day 'with a drawn sword'.[19] Despite extended discussion about Te Kūmete's moko (facial tattoo), and about the existence of another man who closely resembled him, all six prosecution witnesses swore positively to Te Kūmete's identity. Only Hughes positively identified Wiremu. This did not bode well for Te Kūmete. After hearing evidence, including alibis for Wiremu provided by local Māori, the jury retired for one and three quarter hours. Wiremu was acquitted. Te Kūmete, however, was found guilty of robbery – a crime Chapman described as 'one equally recognised as an offence amongst the natives'. He sentenced Te Kūmete to 10 years' transportation.[20] Within two months Te Kūmete regained his liberty, as evidence presented to Chapman after the trial 'induced his Honour the Judge to believe he [Te Kūmete] was not the guilty party'.[21] However, Te Kūmete's release enabled him to join in the May 1846 attack on Boulcott's farm.

The attack on the heavily fortified Boulcott's farm by about 200 warriors under the command of Te Rauparaha's nephew Te Rangihaeata and his ally Hēmi Tōpine Te Māmaku on 16 May 1846 became a key event in the conflict at the Hutt.[22] At the time of the unexpected dawn raid, 50 soldiers from the 58th Regiment were camped at the farm, which was one of a series of military posts throughout the valley. Six soldiers died in the attack and four other men were wounded. Some Māori were wounded or killed in the confrontation but were carried away from the site by their compatriots, so the exact numbers of casualties could not be determined. When the warriors had retreated out of range of the colonists' muskets they performed a haka.[23]

Initially the colonists did not know who had orchestrated the raid; they were later alarmed to hear that it had been led by Te Māmaku. Over the following months the colonists continued to seek the aggressors. As winter approached, a combined force of Hutt militia and their Te Ātiawa allies intercepted a large contingent of Whanganui Māori warriors at Pāuatahanui, north of Wellington, where one of the Whanganui rangatira, Te Whareaitu (also known as Martin Luther) was captured and handed over to the regular soldiers. His brother Te Rangiātea was too ill to escape his pursuers and was also captured. Both were related to Te Rangihaeata and, more distantly, to Te Māmaku. However, Te Rangihaeata and his substantial tauā (war party) remained elusive.

In August 1846 the colonists heard that some of the Māori 'rebels' were leaving their position in the Horokiwi Valley to the north of Wellington. British ally Wiremu Kīngi was asked to intercept the wanted men.

Inclement weather made for difficult living conditions, and this drove some of the sought-after Māori down to the coast near Pari Pari in search of food. Pari Pari was the residence of Te Puke: his village, according to Edward Jerningham Wakefield who visited it in 1840, was 'situated on a terrace of the hill, about fifty feet above the beach'. Wakefield, who was the son of Edward Gibbon Wakefield, recorded how he saw 'two or three canoes ... hauled up under some karaka trees' near the beach, while 'the old men of the pa were sitting beneath their shade, enjoying their pipes'.[24]

In mid-August 1847 some of Kīngi's men, led by Āperahama Ngātohu and Nepetarima Ngāuru, captured eight of the hungry Whanganui warriors near Pari Pari: they located Hōhepa Te Umuroa, Te Kūmete, Te Waretiti, Matiu Tikiahi, Te Rāhui, Tope, Mataiumu and Te Korohunga after smoke from their fire gave away their position. According to a report filed by Major Edward Last, commander of the 99th Regiment, 'a good deal of firing was heard in the direction of the Pari Pari'. Te Rangihaeata's forces put up some resistance. The eight men, who later became known as the Pari Pari prisoners, were handed over to the armed police at Waikanae, transferred into British military custody then incarcerated on the HMS *Calliope* with Te Rauparaha, who had already been taken prisoner. Governor Grey later paid the Māori captors £30 for 'having surrendered Te Kūmete and seven other rebels, with their arms, over to Government'.[25]

While Te Kūmete and his fellow prisoners waited on the *Calliope*, Grey dealt with Rangiātea and his brother Te Whareaitu. Grey instructed Last to convene a court martial of officers from his British regiment at Porirua, north of Wellington, to try the prisoners. Neither man was provided with legal representation. One of the militiamen acted as interpreter. Rangiātea pleaded guilty to 'being found in possession of a spear' but denied a second charge of 'having taken part in an attack and massacre of Her Majesty's troops at the Hutt'. The ailing prisoner was found guilty of both charges and was sentenced to imprisonment for life on the grounds of insanity. He was admitted to hospital in Wellington, where he died just two months later. Te Whareaitu faced similar charges, 'that he had resisted and wounded a friendly Maori of the Ngatiawa [Te Ātiawa] tribe' and 'of aiding in rebellion by taking part in a skirmish in the Hutt Valley three months before'. The military officers found Te Whareaitu guilty of open rebellion, and he was sentenced to death. Te Whareaitu said he 'was not afraid to die, and only regretted that he was not shot or tomahawked instead of having been taken prisoner'. The sentence attracted opprobrium from the press and some of the settlers, however. The military had difficulty finding somebody to fill the role of hangman. Eventually 'a purse of gold' was offered to a soldier who agreed to be the executioner. When the soldier-hangman drowned little more than a year later in shallow waters his comrades attributed the death to his role as executioner; they claimed that his share 'in the killing ... had clung to him like a curse'.[26]

The Pari Pari prisoners were also subjected to a court martial, ostensibly because Grey had imposed martial law.[27] Martial law had been declared around Bathurst, New South Wales by Governor Thomas Brisbane over a four-month period of intercultural conflict from August 1824, and across parts of Van Diemen's Land by Lieutenant-Governor George Arthur in 1828 during the height of the Vandemonian War. In all of these cases these declarations both recognised and reflected the reality of frontier conflict, contrasting with the criminalisation in the colonial law courts of warriors who ought to have been treated as prisoners of war but whose military endeavours were masked by civil legal proceedings. Grey's declaration of martial law was questioned by a correspondent who wrote to the *Wellington Independent* using the nom de plume 'An Englishman'. The writer carefully stated that he was not censuring the governor, but he reminded readers that 'it is under the best rulers that the liberties of the people are most liable to be infringed'. He enquired whether circumstances in the Wellington region warranted the imposition of martial law – this was a measure usually resorted to in extreme circumstances only, and its imposition suspended people's rights to be tried before the civil courts. The writer was concerned that living under martial law 'tacitly allowed that Englishmen forgo their privileges on moving to a British colony'. With regard to the Māori prisoners taken after the Hutt war, the writer noted, 'they have now been in custody for over two months. They are not notorious criminals. They were taken in a foraging expedition. To try them now by court martial, and then hang them, now that there is no necessity for such a proceeding, would be a gross act of wanton barbarity.' He asked whether there was 'the slightest reason to suppose, either that witnesses would be intimidated, or that a jury would be unwilling to convict them if they were tried legally?'[28]

Grey was not swayed by such critiques. Two days after Te Whareaitu's execution, he had the Pari Pari prisoners 'who had been taken with arms in their hands, in open rebellion' brought ashore from the *Calliope* to face a court martial. The *Wellington Independent* speculated that 'there is every probability that Te Kūmete and two or three other notorious characters will be hanged for their offences'. Major Last seemed less keen on the process than Grey, however, and sent the eight Pari Pari prisoners to Wellington to be tried before the civil courts. Richmond, though, refused to try the men, saying the declaration of martial law had stripped him of the authority to do so. Grey sent the prisoners back up the coast to be tried in a newly convened court martial in Porirua on 12 October 1846, presided over by Last and comprising four of his officers.[29]

Last's commanding officer Lieutenant-Colonel Hulme gave the youngest prisoner, Te Korohunga, his freedom as he was still a boy.[30] This set a precedent that was followed at a court martial in April 1847, after an altercation between colonists and Māori that came to be known as the Gilfillan killings. On 16 April 1847 Nga Rangi, described as a 'minor chief', was receiving his wages from Lieutenant Holmes, a young naval officer from the *Calliope* for whom he worked, when Holmes accidentally discharged his pistol and severely wounded Nga Rangi. Attempts to placate local Māori in the aftermath of the incident failed. Utu was demanded to restore balance. On Sunday 18 April the outlying settler John Gilfillan arrived at Whanganui. He was severely wounded and was worried that his wife and children might have been killed by a party of six Māori. The following day his wife and three of their six children were found dead at their home; one young daughter was severely wounded but still alive; and two infants were unharmed. The six warriors who had carried out the attack were pursued. One escaped into the bush but the remaining five were captured and court-martialled. Early on Monday 26 April four of the men were hanged: they were named in a letter to the *Wellington Independent* as Te Ua Wiri, Te Ware Kuki, Te Awa Uri and E'Taka. The fifth, described as a 'boy named Pu-pu-tai, who appeared to have taken no part in the murders' was nevertheless 'sentenced to transportation for life'.[31] The boy, who was thought to be aged around 12, ended up having his sentence suspended on condition that he serve on the government's brig *Victoria*. He was eventually pardoned and released from the vessel in April 1850.[32]

The seven remaining Pari Pari prisoners at Porirua faced three charges: '[having] been taken in arms, and in open Rebellion against the Queen's Sovereign Authority and Government of New Zealand'; 'aiding, siding and assisting the Rebel Chief Te Rangihaeata'; and being 'unlawfully … in possession of a firelock, the property of Her Majesty the Queen, marked 58th Regiment H. No. 62 … The said firelock having been so unlawfully detained since 16th May 1846 at which time it was in the possession of Private Thomas Bolt 58th Regt. who was shot in the attack by the rebels on 16th May 1846'. As before, the prisoners were not provided with legal representation but were given an interpreter, which ensured they could be said to have understood the proceedings.[33]

Four Māori witnesses attested to the guilt of the defendants, who had in any case already pleaded guilty to all three charges. Three witnesses gave evidence under oath through the interpreter Ensign Servantes. The fourth, Te Witu, was not a Christian but gave evidence after being 'cautioned to speak the truth'. Te Witu's evidence, as interpreted by Servantes, was that he had taken the musket bearing the mark of the 58th Regiment from Te Kūmete. Te Kūmete then asked Te Witu whether he was 'positive that you took the musket marked 58th Regt. 62 from me?' Te Witu stated he was. After this, evidence was taken from several of the military, one of whom had been at Boulcott's farm and confirmed that the weapon belonged to the deceased soldier, Bolt, and had not been seen again until it was found in the possession of the Pari Pari prisoners.[34] In their defence, the Pari Pari prisoners agreed that they were followers of Te Rangihaeata. However, they denied killing anyone. They were nevertheless found guilty of all three charges and were sentenced 'to be transported as felons for the term of their natural lives'.

The prisoners were shipped to Auckland on board the naval steamer *Driver* to await their passage to Van Diemen's Land. Grey gave orders for Matiu Tikiahi and Tope to be detained in Auckland as potential witnesses against Te Rauparaha, should charges be brought against him. Despite this, when the *Castor* set sail for Van Diemen's Land at the end of October 1846, Matiu Tikiahi was one of the five Māori prisoners on board; Mataiumu and Tope remained behind.[35]

CHAPTER 8

Perfectly European

I n the early and middle decades of the nineteenth century more than 90 Australian Aboriginal men were incorporated into the convict system in the Australian penal colonies. Their presence within the convict system excited little interest or comment from British colonists at the time. Many of these warriors died in custody. In 1835, shortly after the Vandemonians had successfully exiled the remnants of the island's once numerous Aboriginal population to an offshore island, Lieutenant-Governor George Arthur and his executive council expressed their extreme reluctance to accept a group of Aboriginal convicts from New South Wales. The presence of these warriors would be unwelcome in a colony where the killing times remained fresh in everyone's memory. Colonists would be alarmed by their presence, the authorities thought, and the few remaining Tasmanian Aboriginal people might be incited by the newcomers to a state of discontentment with their lot.[1]

The Vandemonian colonists, despite the way they had waged war against and ultimately banished the remnant Aboriginal population from the island they inhabited, were incensed at what they saw as the poor treatment meted out to Māori by New Zealand's colonists. The Vandemonians viewed Māori as superior to Tasmanian Aboriginal people. Their strength of feeling was such that when the *Castor* arrived in Hobart from Auckland on 16

November 1846 with Hōhepa Te Umuroa, Te Kūmete, Te Waretiti, Matiu Tikiahi, Te Rāhui and several Pākehā convicts on board, Hobartians flocked to the waterfront to witness the unfamiliar spectacle of Māori warriors dressed in traditional attire and to advocate strongly for the men to be treated with leniency.

The newly arrived convicts were taken to the government paddock to be interviewed. The Māori prisoners were allocated police numbers 765 through 769 and their details entered meticulously into the conduct register. Te Umuroa and Te Kūmete could read and write in Māori, it was noted. Most of the men were described as 'laborer' and all five were 'single'. After they had been processed, the men were lodged in the nearby Hobart penitentiary to await their transfer to a work gang at Port Arthur.[2]

In a letter sent with the prisoners, Governor George Grey reasoned that had the Māori been prosecuted under their own law for their 'several murders and many robberies' they would have received a death sentence. Transportation was, he claimed, a merciful alternative. Grey thought:

> *a great advantage would result to this Country [New Zealand], if these men were from time to time really kept to hard labour, and if they could be allowed to correspond with their friends … In this manner many of the turbulent chiefs would ascertain that the government really intended to punish severely all those who connected themselves with murderers and robbers, and would find from the letters of their friends in Van Diemen's Land, what the nature of that punishment of transportation really is.*[3]

He intended their punishment to be exemplary and to be used as a tool to pacify Māori who continued to resist the processes of colonisation.

Ironically, it had almost the opposite effect. The transportation of Māori cemented a growing opinion among some settlers that the colonists themselves were contributors to conflict. For example, 'Justice' wrote to the editor of the *New Zealander* to explain how 'the report that a man was hanged, and that others were transported, merely because in their own country, lords of their own soil, they ventured to fight with the Pakehas, is rapidly spreading through the island, and natives who formerly looked upon us with respect are now beginning to call us murderers'. The letter writer urged the governor to circulate information to confirm that the trials were fair and based on evidence rather than on rumours of the men's activities that were not examined properly in court.[4]

When news of the judicial execution of Te Whareaitu was relayed to Van Diemen's Land, the *Colonial Times* claimed, 'it is impossible to characterise in terms sufficiently expressive of abhorrence the detestable crime of Governor Grey (Captain, as he is, to the disgrace of the army, called), in the murder of the gallant New Zealand chief Wareaitu'.[5] The Vandemonians were not yet ready to reflect critically on their own record when it came to the treatment of indigenous people – including having hanged several of their number – or the resultant catastrophic mortality of Aboriginal peoples in their own colony: they were far more comfortable chastising their neighbours across the Tasman. Remarkably, *The Britannia and Trades' Advocate* condemned the British colonisation of New Zealand as 'unjust … [and] an act by which the British name and character were tarnished'. Vandemonians viewed Māori as superior 'natives' fighting to defend their country. The *Colonial Times* declared that Grey ought to have gone 'at the head of the troops' to 'fight the New Zealand patriots like a man'. The more conservative *Hobart Town Courier* claimed that it would not 'censure … the decree which subjected a native chief [Te Whareaitu] to the heaviest penalty of the law' yet stated emphatically, 'if we have nothing to say of the dead, we have much to plead for the living'.[6]

The newly arrived Māori were admired as warriors but were also seen as naïve 'children of nature', in much the same vein as colonists viewed indigenous peoples across the British Empire. One of the main concerns voiced in Van Diemen's Land was that these intelligent yet 'simple-minded' men would be corrupted at Port Arthur. *Hobart Town Courier* staff visited the prisoners at the Hobart penitentiary and spoke with them through an interpreter. The newspaper railed against the men being sent to 'mingle with masses of moral guilt and doubly convicted crime' – as would be the case if they were sent to the penal station. It was suggested that compared with the fate awaiting them at Port Arthur 'the doom of their Chief was mercy'.[7]

The *Hobart Town Courier* asked the five men whether they thought it wrong that a New Zealand chief (Te Whareaitu) had been hanged. One of the men answered that he 'didn't know'. Te Umuroa, Te Kūmete, Te Waretiti, Tikiahi and Te Rāhui were reportedly 'unwilling to express freely any opinion on the hostilities in which they were engaged, or on the justice of their sentence'. They claimed 'that they were only "fighting those who came against their country"' and denied committing murder. When quizzed about their condition the men confirmed they had been given plenty of food and clothing, were not expected to labour and were getting sufficient rest. But they were not happy with the poor quality of their drinking water. According to the *Hobart Town Courier* the men described it as 'wimouri kakena', which the interpreter translated as 'very bad water'. The men were, after all, used to being able to 'quench their thirst from the crystal springs and rivulets' of New Zealand.[8]

Artist William Duke, who had spent some time in New Zealand, visited the men and painted a portrait in oils of Te Umuroa that now hangs in the National Gallery of Australia in Canberra. Using artistic licence, Duke completed Te Umuroa's moko in his portrait of the warrior although, in reality, Te Umuroa's facial tattoo was only partially complete at the time of his transportation. In Duke's depiction of Te Umuroa, the warrior grasps his tokotoko firmly in his right hand and wears a sombre expression. Noted colonial watercolourist John Skinner Prout also visited the prisoners. He created poetic likenesses of the five Māori convicts, relying on simple tones of black, sepia and white that created a light, ephemeral impression. The individual portraits show each man cloaked in his traditional attire. A pounamu earring hangs from Te Kūmete's right ear. He also has a moko, as do two of his companions, Te Waretiti and Te Umuroa. Te Kūmete's moko fits the description provided at his civil trial before Justice Chapman in Wellington in March 1846. Prosecution witness Thomas Jackson Hughes from the Hutt Valley claimed that when he had first met Te Kūmete some 18 months to two years earlier, he 'was tattooed on the chin' but had since had 'an outer line from the cheekbones around the face' added sometime within the previous month.[9] In each of the Prout portraits the subject wears a serious expression, ranging from Tikiahi's rather pensive look to the forthright gaze of the slightly older Te Kūmete. When the portraits were completed, each signed his portrait in his own handwriting using a lead pencil. These engaging, luminous watercolour paintings form part of a larger collection of 36 of Prout's works now held at the British Museum in London.

Duke was not the prisoners' only visitor who had formerly resided in New Zealand. When conflict first arose between colonists and Māori over contested land in the Hutt Valley, Thomas 'Quaker' Mason and his family temporarily relocated from Taita in the Hutt Valley to Hobart. Not only was Mason concerned about the likelihood of war breaking out, he disapproved of the way colonial authorities were treating local Māori, some of whom were his friends. He was also worried about Jane, his wife, whose health was suffering. After they arrived in Van Diemen's Land in 1845, Mason began working as a bookkeeper and later opened a small school for Quaker children. He became part of the inner circle of well-known Quaker missionary and humanitarian George Washington Walker who, with the minister James Backhouse, left England in 1831 to undertake a nine-year mission to the Cape colony and the Australian colonies. Walker settled in Hobart in 1840 where, with Backhouse, he founded the Society of Friends in Van Diemen's Land.[10]

When Mason visited the Māori convicts at the penitentiary shortly after their arrival he 'was immediately recognised as an old friend and received with great joy'. He noticed how his friends' appearances had changed. Three had become tattooed since Mason last saw them.[11] He read this as 'a sign that they have thrown off the restraint of Christianity', and he informed Comptroller General of Convicts Dr John Hampton of this when Hampton asked his advice on how best to treat the men. Mason told Hampton that tattooing was 'strictly forbidden by the missionaries'.[12] His views are consistent with a Pākehā 'shift from awed fascination to shrill disgust' when viewing tattooed faces.[13] Despite Mason's concerns about the warriors' possible shift away from Christianity, all five men carried copies of the Bible printed in te reo Māori, which they were seen to read. They had possibly come into contact with the Catholic Church through Father Comte, who established a mission at Otaki in 1844 and who worked extensively with around 200 Māori associated with Te Rauparaha.[14] Mason advised Hampton to separate the Māori convicts from the rest of the convict population. He also advocated for them to be provided with Christian instruction. He suggested the lightest possible approach in physically restraining the men. He also advised refraining from commenting on the fairness or otherwise of their court martial; if a pardon came from London, it would then be seen as a boon rather than an automatic right.

While the Māori prisoners were at the Hobart penitentiary, the administrator of Van Diemen's Land Charles La Trobe made sure they were kept 'secure ... from association with the common herd of Prisoners'. He was concerned about the legality of the court martial under which the men were sentenced, and decided to treat the five Māori convicts differently from other convicts arriving in Van Diemen's Land.[15]

Usually when prisoners were sentenced to transportation for life they were sent to penal stations such as Port Arthur or Norfolk Island. However, La Trobe came under increasing pressure from the Vandemonian public to treat the Māori newcomers with leniency. He found it expedient to rule out sending the men to either location. He wrote to the Home Office in London on 30 November 1846 to draw Earl Grey's attention to the case; he informed Grey that although procedure demanded it, 'I cannot resolve to send them either to Norfolk Island or [Port Arthur at] Tasman's Peninsula to be classed and associated with the transported felons congregated in those settlements'. La Trobe enclosed as background information copies of both Governor George Grey's letter and Mason's advice on how to treat the prisoners. He then had to wait many months to receive advice from London. In the meantime, the *Hobart Courier and Government Gazette* reported it was 'good to learn ... that the most repulsive provision' of the men's sentence (sending them to Port Arthur) had been overturned; they were instead destined for the probation station at Darlington on Maria Island, just off the coast northeast of Hobart.[16]

The preferential treatment received by the Māori convicts extended beyond sending them to a probation station rather than a penal station. They were also fast-tracked through the probation system. As instructed by the Colonial Office, the men were 'allowed all the freedom enjoyed by the holders of Tickets of Leave' – an indulgence not usually granted before 12 years into a life sentence. This meant the men could immediately be given the free pardon La Trobe was seeking on their behalf from London if and when it was approved. In the meantime their status as ticket-of-leave holders entitled them to greater privileges than other convicts at a similar stage of incarceration.[17]

The probation station at Darlington on Maria Island was quite new when La Trobe decided to send Te Umuroa, Te Kūmete, Te Waretiti, Tikiahi and Te Rāhui there. Opened just five years earlier, it was one of two on the island; the other was the smaller station, about half its size, located to the south at Long Point. Darlington probation station was considered sufficiently large to house at least 730 men. It had its own hospital, chapel, laundry, cookhouse, bakehouse, windmill and mess hall, and provided exercise yards by day and sleeping wards for the men at night. There were also separate cells 'on the Pentonville plan' that could be 'made perfectly dark by leather placed around the sides of the doors' for the purpose of punishing any convicts who committed misdemeanours while already under sentence. The convicts wore clothes issued by the government that included caps 'marked in the front with the Police number and at the back with the Station number', by which they could be readily identified. Flat land around the probation station on the otherwise hilly island was cultivated with wheat, hops, potatoes, flax, turnips and other vegetables taking up around 360 acres (145ha). In addition to tending these crops, convict labourers worked to make baskets and rope mats and also burnt lime in kilns to be exported from the island for use in the building industry.[18]

The five Māori convicts, in the interests of their wellbeing, were to be worked and housed separately from the other convicts at Darlington –unlike Australian Aboriginal and other indigenous convicts, the overwhelming majority of whom were housed and punished alongside everyone else. As a precursor to relocating the men, the authorities sought a suitable overseer. Mason was an obvious contender but had family and work commitments that necessitated his remaining in Hobart, so the authorities were forced to look elsewhere. They managed to find another colonist with prior experience in New Zealand. Indeed, one of the local Tasmanian newspapers described John Jennings Imrie as having been 'many years a resident amongst the tribe and well acquainted with their language, and [able] to afford them every facility and advantage of religious and moral instruction'.[19]

In fact, Imrie had previously lived at Nelson, the New Zealand Company settlement, rather than at Whanganui where the Māori convicts came from. He ran a store in Bridge Street, 'J.J. Imrie & Co', between 1841 and 1843, where he sold a wide range of merchandise including 'black and green teas of fresh quality … fine Irish butter and English cheese … vinegar in bottle and cask … frying pans, girdles, etc., starch and blue, soap, cigars … Highland whiskey and old rum in bottles, garden seeds in assorted packages … A choice assortment of native mats'. In Nelson, Imrie was simply known as 'Mr Imrie'. The title of 'Dr' he adopted later in life seems not to have been earned – he failed to complete the medical degree he enrolled in as a young man at Edinburgh University.[20]

A story of how Imrie and his family had fled Nelson penniless and in peril of their lives was another of his exaggerations – in fact, in July 1842 he had advertised 'a splendid new oak boat, English built' for sale. The auctioneers Fell & Harley sold on his behalf 'town section 270' at Nelson 'situated in Cambria Street north of the Wood, together with the dwelling house erected thereon, now in the occupation of Mr Imrie, containing 3 rooms and a passage, brick chimney, oven, fowl and pigeon houses, etc. etc.' When the Imrie family sailed for Van Diemen's Land on the brigantine *Sisters* on 30 September 1843, their relocation was planned well in advance and was fully funded.[21]

By the time Imrie was employed as overseer to the Māori convicts, the Scotsman's English wife Etty had delivered three of their eventual family of eight children. The elder two, Henry and Eliza, were born in England in 1836 and 1839 respectively, while their younger sister Jessie was delivered in New Zealand just 28 days before the family's departure from Nelson. Etty was pregnant when the family sailed for Maria Island on the government schooner *Mary* with the five Māori convicts. La Trobe and Hampton accompanied them – presumably to see the small party settled in at Darlington and to check that the probation station was running smoothly.[22] The mountainous and heavily forested Maria Island is clearly visible from the Tasmanian coastline. By the time the Māori convicts arrived there on Sunday 20 December 1846 it was home to 291 convicts. During the summer months, Maria Island convicts rose at 5:30am and laboured until 6pm. The Māori convicts, who were initially housed about half a mile from the Darlington probation station, were not required to adhere to such a strict regimen. In the middle of the week after their arrival, Imrie's diary entry for Wednesday 23 December reads: 'At 6am visited the Maoris hut all fast asleep'. Later in the morning, they spent time reading and writing and received several visitors. That afternoon, they hunted unsuccessfully for crayfish.[23]

On Christmas Day when Imrie went to visit his charges at 7am he 'found them all reading'. Young Henry Imrie had already been visiting the Māori men for two hours before his father's arrival at their hut. In the afternoon, they all 'took a walk in the bush'. The day ended, as per their usual routine, with evening prayers in the men's hut. On Boxing Day a general muster was scheduled for all of the convicts. The Māori convicts cleaned their hut before being inspected and included in the overall count. Within days of their arrival, they were building new huts. This initially involved selecting and cutting timber and putting up the framework, and later they gathered wattle. Undertaking this task on the damp and cloudy Tuesday 19 January resulted in all five men becoming 'very fatigued'. The next day Te Waretiti was 'indisposed from the fatigues of the preceding day' and remained unwell throughout February and March. In the meantime, the walls for the new huts were built using the wattle-and-daub construction method typical of colonial housing. Latticed frameworks for the walls were constructed from strips of wood. The men made a mixture from clay and other locally available materials, and plasterers used this to finish the walls. The convicts thatched the roofs. They moved into their new hut on Sunday 7 February 1847, and they then helped the Imries shift into their new home. Later in the week, the men were building an outhouse when Matiu Tikiahi cut his thumb quite severely.[24]

The weather throughout February was very warm. At one point a bushfire erupted in the foliage beyond the Imries' hut so the men cleared some of the land around the huts to give them better protection. When they were not kept busy building, the Māori convicts were cleaning, doing laundry or carrying water. Occasionally Imrie provided them with a half day's instruction in reading and writing. Their weekends were quite relaxed and often included fishing expeditions or possum hunts. Sunday mornings were spent in prayer with Imrie. As summer progressed into autumn, the men created and fenced a vegetable garden. With Te Waretiti still ailing, from Monday 15 March Imrie had the men knock off at 12:30pm each working day. They spent their afternoons in a leisurely manner. Sometimes the men would go fishing or catching crayfish. Other times they would read or take a walk in the bush or along the beach with the Imries. The gentler routine did not help Te Waretiti, so at the end of March Imrie 'applied a blister' to his neck.[25] Fortunately, by Easter Sunday he was 'much better'.

One wet Monday in mid-April Te Umuroa complained of pain in his side. Imrie arranged a footbath for the patient and a dose of salts. While his companions cut and carried wood and sowed peas in the newly dug vegetable garden, Te Umuroa was confined to bed. By Saturday 24 April his health seemed to be improving and he joined the others on their afternoon stroll after their Sunday prayers. However, on Monday he was suffering from 'severe Rheumatic pains'. The following day, Tuesday 27 April, Etty Imrie gave birth to a son, John – named after his father. The Māori convicts were given a day off to mark the occasion.[26]

On Saturday 1 May Dr Brownell visited and checked on the health of mother and baby and also looked in on Te Umuroa, whose health continued to worsen. Throughout May, as the men were employed in planting out cabbages, lettuces, gooseberry cuttings and potatoes, Te Umuroa's health seemed to be improving a little. However, after having rallied he went into a steep decline. Brownell visited on Friday 25 June and found his lungs 'in a very bad state'. The doctor ordered a blister, but the treatment was unsuccessful – Te Umuroa remained gravely ill with tuberculosis. On Sunday 18 July he asked to see Etty Imrie and the two read prayers together. Imrie was worried about Te Umuroa and stayed by his side until midnight. When Imrie returned to the men's hut at 4am he found 'Hohepa very nearly gone'. An hour later, the patient 'breathed his last without a struggle'. The following morning a small funeral was held at the cemetery at Darlington where Imrie 'read the service in his [Hohepa's] native language'. Unusually for a deceased convict, an ornate headstone was erected over the grave, engraved in te reo Māori.

After their companion's death, the others continued their work in the vegetable garden, and cut and carted firewood. Their lives as convict labourers were punctuated with prayer and fishing expeditions as well as walks along the startlingly white sandy beaches and through the scrubby Australian bush. Some of their Sunday afternoon walks now took them up the steep, grassy hills to the small cemetery northeast of the probation station to visit their friend's grave. Several of the men suffered minor ailments in the months following Te Umuroa's death. For example, in September 1847, Te Waretiti experienced swelling in his neck that required lancing and a poultice; and in November, Te Rāhui and Te Kūmete both suffered from influenza.

In the meantime, officials based in London, New Zealand and Van Diemen's Land exchanged correspondence that was to determine the fate of the surviving Māori convicts. In May 1847 the Home Office wrote to Grey about the Māori prisoners; they suggested that 'it must have been some

Proclamation by you of martial law under which they were tried'. The official thought it a 'question of grave doubt' that under such circumstances the men 'could lawfully be treated as Convicts in V.D. Land'. Courts convened during times of martial law were not 'legal tribunals'. The problems arising over the probable illegality of the original sentences could be addressed in Britain only by an Act of Parliament – a difficult and inappropriate course of action. Similar sentiments were conveyed to La Trobe in response to his initial inquiry to London.[27]

Early the next year, in February 1848, welcome news arrived from England that the Māori convicts were officially pardoned: the men were free to return to New Zealand once the appropriate arrangements could be put in place for them to do so. In the meantime, Imrie accompanied them on one last visit to Te Umuroa's grave. Mason arrived at Maria Island to visit the freed men and, during March, spent several days with them. The day after Mason left, the *Lady Denison* collected the Imries and their former charges. Te Kūmete, Te Waretiti, Matiu Tikiahi and Te Rāhui left Hobart for New Zealand on the *Lady Denison* on 10 March 1848. In Hobart, the *Colonial Times* reported how 'under Dr Imrie's attentive care the prisoners were as comfortable as they could be rendered consistently with their situation, the loss of liberty and their expatriation being their principal sources of sorrow and regret'. Their incarceration was represented to Hobart's reading public as beneficial: in captivity the men had apparently 'become perfectly European in their habits and general demeanour' through following Imrie's example.[28]

Despite Grey's determination to make an example of Te Umuroa, Te Kūmete, Te Waretiti, Tikiahi and Te Rāhui, the return of the surviving four to Auckland in April 1848 hardly rated a mention. The *Wellington Independent* reported that 'four out of the five natives of New Zealand, who were transported to Van Diemen's Land for bearing arms against the Queen's troops during the late disturbances at the southward, are returned liberated, by order of Earl Grey, the fifth having previously died'. No graphic descriptions of the horrors of the convict system were printed and there is no evidence that any of the men wrote to their relatives in New Zealand while in captivity. It does, however, seem probable that those who returned in 1848 told their friends and relations about the conditions under which they had laboured and the broader implications of having convicts within

British colonies – adding their voices to the many who had visited Sydney.

On 5 May 1849, Te Ātiawa, Ngāti Raukawa, Te Paneiri and Ngāti Toa signed a letter to Queen Victoria petitioning her to ensure that British convicts or those with tickets of leave would not be sent to New Zealand. They assured Her Majesty that there were plenty of 'whites … [and] ourselves the natives' to perform the necessary labour in the colony. The signatories wrote 'we have heard a bad account of that class of persons [convicts] from … some of our own people who have been at Port Jackson and Hobart Town'. They were concerned to ensure that New Zealand did not become like the Australian penal colonies and had already experienced the presence of former convicts at Kapiti Island who had urged Māori not to adopt Christianity. More than 300 people described as the 'leading men of the tribes' signed the petition.[29]

Another prisoner, Te Āhuru, was returned from the penal colony after a short stay in 1851, just weeks into his seven-year sentence to transportation for stealing. He was one of the last convicts transported from New Zealand to Van Diemen's Land. Apparently he could 'not speak a word of English'.[30] Earl Grey had sent a despatch from London to Governor Fitzgerald at the Swan River Colony, instructing him to keep Aboriginal prisoners sentenced to hard labour separate from the general convict population. Lieutenant-Governor Denison in Van Diemen's Land felt bound by Grey's despatch but was concerned about the cost and impracticalities of separately accommodating Māori prisoners. He therefore expedited Te Āhuru's return to New Zealand. After this, Grey made arrangements for Māori prisoners that no longer involved transportation to the Australian penal colonies.[31]

For more than a century and a half Te Umuroa's headstone has intrigued visitors to the small colonial cemetery near Darlington. Throughout the different eras of occupation on Maria Island thousands of visitors have paused to read the words, which are still visible: 'Dei Roarei Tokotoia Metau Tinana Ehoa [Here lie the remains of] Hohepa Te Umuroa, Native of Wanganui, N.Z., who died July 19, 1847'.

In the early 1970s, Tim Hume from Launceston in Tasmania's north became intrigued with the life story of Te Umuroa after seeing the headstone at Darlington. He corresponded extensively with John (Jack) Tattersall at the Hawke's Bay Museum and Art Gallery in Napier. The men shared knowledge that enabled both to build a more complete picture of the events surrounding the Māori convicts. Much of this material was later included in a pamphlet published by the museum.[32]

The following decade, in 1985, 10-year-old Sarah Heald was sufficiently moved by the experience of seeing the headstone to tell her father, expatriate New Zealander Chris Heald, about it. At the time, Heald worked for Australian Federal Minister for Justice Senator Michael Tate and was well positioned to enquire into the circumstances surrounding Te Umuroa's internment and to advocate for his repatriation. He worked closely with Chris Batt, a Tasmanian parliamentary candidate, to campaign for the remains to be repatriated to New Zealand.[33]

Once it was established that Te Umuroa was Ngāti Hau of Te Āti Haunui a Pāpārangi from Hiruharama (Jerusalem) on the Whanganui River, local kaumātua became involved in seeking the return of their whanaunga. Arrangements were made for six kaumātua – Matiu and Lei Māreikura, Hoana Akapita, Te Otinga Te Peehi (George Waretini), Joseph Wānihi and Nohi Wānihi – to travel to Maria Island in July 1988. The New Zealand delegation also included John Tahuparae, a cameraman with Māori language news bulletin *Te Karere* with Whanganui connections, and David Cresswell from the Department of Maori Affairs. After an overnight stop in Christchurch the contingent flew to Hobart.[34]

On Saturday 30 July 1988 the New Zealand delegation arrived at Hobart International Airport. Tasmanian Aboriginal elders Dawn and Athol Smith welcomed them 'to country' and presented the New Zealanders with an Aboriginal flag. Batt (by then an elected member of the House of Assembly) presented the visitors, on his own and Chris Heald's behalf, with a print of Prout's evocative watercolour portrait of their ancestor. Hobart-based Adam Ranui, representing Māori living in Tasmania, also welcomed the Whanganui Māori and wished them success in their quest.[35]

The New Zealanders were honoured guests at a hāngi on their first evening in Tasmania. On Sunday morning the visitors attended Mass. They then visited Port Arthur, the penal station to which Te Umuroa and his companions were to have been sent. From there they travelled up the east coast until they arrived at the small town of Orford. Maria Island lies clearly visible across the channel of water that sets it apart from the Tasmanian mainland. At daybreak the following day, Monday 1 August, the visiting

Māori prayed at the nearby beach. This began a pattern of morning and evening prayers that framed each of the next five days, emulating the prayerful lives their ancestors led as convicts on Maria Island.[36]

When the kaumātua approached the cemetery at Darlington where their whanaunga had lain waiting for them for so long, the rest of the contingent hung back out of respect as the Whanganui Māori greeted Te Umuroa. This opening ritual was later described evocatively on the front page of one of Melbourne's major daily newspapers: 'while wild Cape Barren geese honked nearby, two Maori women sat by the stone, bowed their garlanded heads and wept'. Prayers were also said for others who rested in the cemetery, and thanks were given for their care of Te Umuroa during his time among them. Photographs of the kaumātua by Te Umuroa's headstone were printed on the front page of the *Age*.[37]

After the ceremony 'the first sod was turned by a Māori hand' then archaeologists Richard Morrison and Brian Prince, assisted by Darryl West (a Tasmanian Aboriginal man with expertise in recovering ancestral remains), began the official excavation. On the third day West indicated wordlessly that he had located the head of the coffin. While the designated experts took a deliberately long lunch the 'Wanganui River archaeologists' removed the earth down to the level of the coffin. By midday on Thursday 4 August a long, narrow coffin with faint lettering beginning with 'H' was exposed. The kaumātua had found their whanaunga.[38]

On Friday 5 August 1988 Te Umuroa returned to Hobart for the first time in more than 140 years. He rested temporarily within the sacred confines of St Joseph's Church, an elegant convict-built sandstone structure with pews hewn from New Zealand kauri. St Joseph's opened in 1841, making it Hobart's oldest Catholic church; it was consecrated only five years before Te Umuroa and his companions first arrived in Van Diemen's Land. The following day Te Umuroa's relatives accompanied him back to New Zealand where he rested briefly at St Mary's Cathedral in Christchurch before returning to Whanganui.

A tangi for Te Umuroa was held throughout the night of Sunday 7 August. The Reverend Father Wiremu Te Āwhitu officiated at Te Umuroa's burial the following day. As Te Āwhitu led the congregation in prayer for Te Umuroa, three different sets of male pallbearers took it in turns to carry the coffin to the prepared grave at the Roma cemetery at Jerusalem. Images of the event were reproduced in the *Wanganui Chronicle*. As Matiu Māreikura revealed to the journalist who attended the ceremony, 'we felt he was calling us to come and take him home ... His long 141-year wait has finally come to an end.'[39]

Despite his reinterment, Te Umuroa's return to New Zealand was not quite complete. A Melbourne-based Māori woman, Delphina Crapp, learned about the warrior's repatriation. She realised that a tokotoko she had purchased at an auction was probably the property of Te Umuroa, and this was later confirmed when an expert identified the designs on the tokotoko as being specific to the Whanganui area. After several unsuccessful attempts to return the tokotoko by post, Crapp flew to New Zealand and returned it to Te Umuroa's people in person. The warrior's journey home was finally completed.[40]

CHAPTER 9

A woman's place

T hroughout the 1840s New Zealand's colonial population grew. Those who lived in towns and cities felt particularly secure by sheer force of numbers. Memories of intercultural conflict in the mid-1840s were starting to fade, but the names of murdered colonial families still brought rapid recall, and the mere mention of the names of certain Māori still filled the settlers with dread. So it was easy for Aucklanders to believe that Māori were culpable when, in the middle of the night in spring 1847, most of a colonist's family were slain in their beds. Local newspapers sensationalised the murders in columns sprinkled with rumour and innuendo, and speculation about Māori violence and utu hung over Auckland for months. The crime, meanwhile, remained unsolved. But over time it became apparent that all was not as it first seemed. A tale gradually unfolded of impoverishment, jealousies, class distinctions, covetousness, domestic violence, death and perjury. Such was the prelude to the transportation of the only female exiled from New Zealand to Van Diemen's Land.

News of the murders of Lieutenant Robert Snow, his wife Hannah and their youngest daughter Mary in the early hours of Saturday 23 October 1847 shocked Auckland, a settlement that 'had been so long proud of its own comparative security'. Snow was the inaugural officer in charge of the colony's first naval base at Flagstaff (later renamed Devonport) on

Auckland's sparsely populated north shore, a role he filled for six years. Reporting on the tragedy a few days after its discovery, the *New Zealander* thought the event more 'frightful ... than any of those which have stained the other settlements'. By way of comparison, the incident at Wairau was 'at least, unpremeditated', while the 'murders' of the Gillespie family in the Hutt and the Gilfillans at Whanganui 'took place at a period of high excitement, and in a time of war' for which, the newspaper argued, 'we ourselves are confessedly to blame'. Tellingly, a reference was then made to 'Makatu' (Maketū), whose murder of Thomas Bull and Elizabeth Roberton was attributed to a 'mere appetite of blood in the savage who committed it'. 'Even that,' stated the newspaper, 'was unaccompanied by such circumstances of additional atrocity, as, in this case, we have too much reason to fear.'[1]

After its breathless preface, the *New Zealander* recorded its hesitation in providing any details of the Snow murders on two grounds: an ironical unwillingness 'to pamper that craving for excitement ... which finds its most congenial food in records of crime and misery', and a reluctance to jeopardise an eventual jury trial. On balance, however, the editor decided to go ahead anyway. He reported how sometime between midnight and 1am on Saturday morning a light in the Snows' home caught the attention of Quartermaster Benjamin Baker on the ship *Dido*. This seemed odd to Baker. Shortly afterwards, flames broke out. He reported this to the officer of the watch, Lieutenant Gough, who informed the captain. Captain Maxwell immediately ordered the cutter lowered – this took around 20 minutes. By the time the cutter's crew reached shore the Snows' home, built from highly flammable raupō, had collapsed. At that point in the newspaper's narrative, its earlier reference to intercultural conflict became clear as it reported how 'two canoes were observed to steal out from underneath the shore, seen, though hardly noticed by the crew of the cutter, who had no suspicion at the time of foul play'. As soon as it became known that foul play was involved, though, suspicion fell on Māori as the likely perpetrators.[2] While the cutter's crew worked to extinguish the flames, Gough hurried to the nearby house of a man named Oliver, who was 'in charge of the cattle on the run', to check whether the Snow family had sought shelter there. Failing to locate them, he then checked with the signalman Duder, who had not seen the Snows either. This led Gough to the horrible conclusion that the Snow family was likely buried beneath the smouldering remains of their home.

At this point the *New Zealander*, despite its avowed wish not to whet the appetites of readers craving excitement, went on to describe how Gough ascertained the probable location of the Snows' bed then 'ordered the ashes to be shovelled away from thence, with great care'. 'After a little while', reported the newspaper, 'the foot of the man appeared.' His dead wife and daughter lay nearby. The damage to their partially burned corpses made it obvious that something other than falling rafters had caused their fatal injuries.[3]

A group of armed men from the *Dido* found 22 Māori sleeping nearby and took them into custody. After a local clergyman pledged that all 22 would reappear on the day of the inquest the group was set free, much to the disgust of the newspaper, which proclaimed: 'there can be no doubt but that natives were perpetrators of the foul deed'. To be fair to the *New Zealander*, the perception that Māori were behind the arson and murders was not only that of Pākehā: the newspaper reported how 'our native police pronounced the wounds to be Maorie handiwork at once'. They thought the way the flesh had been cut from all three corpses, and the parts of the body that had been hacked off, was consistent with Māori practice. The newspaper could not resist further sensationalising the story: 'what was done with that flesh, we leave our readers to suppose'.

Snow was known to have had recent altercations with local Māori: he chased away one man who was intent on lighting his fire near a powder magazine, and another who wanted to take a loaf of bread from Snow's house. Whether the murders were a political act or one of private revenge, the *New Zealander* opined, remained to be seen. Its report concluded with the news that several days after their deaths, on Tuesday 26 October, men from the *Dido* carried the coffins of Snow, his wife and child as part of their funeral cortege. The procession included 'a long train of Naval officers and … inhabitants of Auckland, anxious to pay a last tribute of respect to a family so long known and esteemed amongst them'.[4] The Snows' daughter Eliza Ann had been away from the family home at the time and so had survived the tragedy. Captain Maxwell later took her into his care and was seeing to her education and future needs.[5]

The inquest into the Snows' deaths was held on Monday 25 October, the day before their funeral. The proceedings took place before Coroner J. Johnson at the Caledonian Hotel – like Barrett's Hotel in Wellington, a large public house that doubled as a venue where colonial officials carried out their public duties. Witnesses attested to motive on the part of local Māori. Signalman Duder from the nearby signal station said that some 18 months to two years previously Snow had fallen out with Māori who owned the schooner *Lucidan* and who came to cut raupō. Snow took some of the cut raupō and, when it was traced to his property, refused to return it to those who had gathered it. In response, the Māori who confronted Snow about his theft of their property had reportedly threatened to burn down the man's house. Quartermaster Baker also testified to seeing two canoes pulling away from the shore at about the time Snow's house was set alight. A picture was emerging of Māori revenge that had been years in the offing.[6]

Other witnesses were called, some of whom added to the evolving narrative of Māori culpability. The clerk from the *Dido*, William Warburton, told the inquest that Snow spoke to him about telling some Māori not to light a fire near the powder magazine. Snow told Warburton the Māori had since treated him with 'great respect'. Warburton and another witness, coxswain George Brombeck, said they saw at least one canoe making away after the conflagration at Snow's house. A man named James Harp said he had encountered Snow at a local store a few days earlier, where Snow told Harp about evicting a Māori man from his house at gunpoint as the intruder tried to steal a loaf of bread from Snow's table; some distance from the house the intruder allegedly threatened Snow that 'he would make the *pakura taihoa* (he would be revenged by and bye!)'. Other witnesses were called to give evidence about the mutilated bodies of the deceased. Near the end of the proceedings a Māori man referred to as 'Thomas, a native chief' was called. He told the inquest that he was in the bay on the night of the fire and was woken by the flames. Thomas and some others had arrived earlier that night in two canoes and some of their party had gone ashore to sleep. Others, including Thomas himself, slept on board the canoes. He saw no other canoes that night. Nor had he heard any voices until the cutter from the *Dido* put in to shore. The final witness, gunner John Rogers from the *Dido*, said he saw canoes heading away from the scene and told the inquest how he 'did not think that the natives who belonged to them, could see the canoes that were going away; they seemed to start from a bay farther eastward'. Without retiring the jury returned a verdict of 'Wilful Murder against some person or persons unknown'.[7]

Over the following months a massive hunt ensued to find the person or people responsible for the Snow murders. As Christmas 1847 approached suspicion still fell on Māori. Rumours abounded. One story told of some Māori travelling by canoe between the Hauraki Gulf and the Waikato and putting in to shore en route, at which point one of the men 'dressed himself in a grey linen blouse, a white shirt, and a pair of new trousers of drab woollen stuff, and put on a straw hat, with a narrow turned-up brim, and a black ribbon tied round it'. The hat, reported the newspaper, was too small for the wearer – and it was said to be strikingly similar to a hat belonging to the late Lieutenant Snow. The inference was clear to readers. The same newspaper reported how some among the highest echelons of Māoridom were providing support in identifying and apprehending the offenders. Waikato rangatira Te Wherowhero and 'other influential chiefs in the neighbourhood' promised to identify those responsible. 'The natives around us,' reported the newspaper, 'have determined … to find out the true guilty parties, and deliver them up to justice.' That being the case, it was thought that 'the perpetrators of the foul deed will be speedily arrested'.[8]

Rumours of Māori culpability circulated well into 1848, and several suspects were named in the *New Zealand Spectator and Cook's Strait Guardian*. The principal offender was said to be Ngamuka from the 'Ngatiruru' tribe of the Waikato, and two 'Ngatitematerā' men were rumoured to have been his accomplices. The newspaper named the chief of the latter tribe as 'Taraia'. The *New Zealander* revealed that both Ngamuka and Taraia, in the company of a number of other Māori, had visited Government House, where the governor interviewed them. As Ngamuka remained free, the *New Zealander* concluded that he 'has sufficiently exculpated himself in the eyes of His Excellency' but regretted that the matter had not been brought before the magistrates' court so that the general public could be privy to the proceedings.[9] The resident magistrates' courts were constituted just a year earlier under an 1846 ordinance passed after George Grey superseded Robert FitzRoy as governor. Under the ordinance, magistrates were empowered to hear matters involving Pākehā or Māori. In the case of Māori, the courts replaced the earlier system under which rangatira and protectors of aborigines had jurisdiction over crimes involving Māori.[10]

In what initially appeared to be an incident completely unrelated to the Snow murders, on Tuesday 28 December 1847 a Joseph Burns (or Byrnes) was seen drunk at Tutty's bar in Auckland as early as 11am, after which he attacked two women who were well known to him. In his drunken state Burns went to the home of William and Sophia Aldwell near Smale's Point at Commercial Bay – his third visit that week. Burns had been living with Sophia's sister Margaret as his common-law wife for almost five years. Their relationship had soured, though, and when Burns travelled to the Australian colonies for a month, Margaret Reardon (or Byrnes, as she was sometimes known) had moved with her two young sons from Burns' shack at Shoal Bay to her sister's place. It was the sisters Sophia and Margaret that the drunken Burns went to see after leaving Tutty's bar. Reardon later recalled how Burns told her melodramatically that he 'had come to bid me goodbye forever'. Her sister Sophia claimed that she had been cutting bread for one of Reardon and Burns' children at the time when Burns had knelt before her and asked her to 'strike him with the knife'. When Sophia refused, he pulled out a white-handled razor and used it to cut Margaret's neck several times, inflicting injuries that left her bedridden for a fortnight. He tried to attack Sophia with a black-handled razor and also tried to cut his own throat before he was taken into custody.[11]

Burns' trial took place before Chief Justice William Martin at the Supreme Court in Auckland on 1 March 1848. At the trial Colonial Surgeon John Johnson (wrongly named in the press as James Johnson) described him as a seaman who had been in Auckland since 1840 and had previously sailed on HMS *Victory*; he had apparently suffered a fall on board that had left him with a fractured skull. Johnson told the court that, since he had recorded in his notebook in 1840 that Burns had 'contused wounds of the head', he did not recall seeing him again until he attended Burns in hospital six weeks before the trial to treat his neck wound.

The court also heard evidence from medical officers who had treated Reardon; from boatman William Pierce, who had tackled and restrained Burns on the day of the attacks on the two sisters; and from the policemen who had arrested Burns. A claim that Burns' previous injury led to a state of 'temporary derangement' during which he had committed the assaults was discredited by the attorney-general, and the chief justice dismissed any notion that being drunk could diminish his culpability. 'The law of

England,' he told the court, 'had never adopted the principle of permitting drunkenness to be an excuse for crime.'[12]

The jury retired for 12 minutes before returning a guilty verdict against Burns for 'intent to do grievous bodily harm'. Burns was sentenced the following day to be 'transported beyond the seas, to such place as His Excellency the Governor shall appoint, for the term of your natural life'. Martin told Burns that the guilty verdict ought to be seen as 'an impressive warning to others' that 'intemperance shall not excuse crime'. Burns was remanded in custody while arrangements were made to transport him to Van Diemen's Land.[13]

A little over a week later a curious article appeared in the *New Zealander*. It reported that Margaret Reardon 'is detained in custody' as it seemed she might be able assist the police to 'throw further light upon the melancholy fact of the late murder of Lieutenant and Mrs Snow and child'.[14]

A week after Burns' trial, on Wednesday 8 March 1848, the *New Zealander* reported on a matter before the resident magistrate's court. Together with four justices of the peace, two of them high-ranking military men from the 58th Regiment, the resident magistrate spent several days investigating a startling confession made by the prisoner Burns at the gaol on the evening of Thursday 2 March. After an earlier visit from Margaret Reardon, Burns had told the authorities that it was he who, in the company of his former shipmates Thomas Duder and a man known as Oliver, had murdered the Snows. The *New Zealander*, when it reported Burns' confession, regretted its role in incriminating Māori in the murders and stated that it would be 'among the first to offer reparation for the stain that we ourselves have innocently contributed to fix upon them'.[15] Burns' story was backed up by Reardon, who said that on the night of the slayings she had hidden in some bushes and had overheard a discussion between Burns and Duder. She said Duder talked about some money that Snow allegedly had hidden in his home – with a view to stealing it and hiding it under the flagstaff. Duder had allegedly tried to convince Burns to accompany him but, Reardon said, Burns expressed his reluctance and instead went to bed.[16]

After telling her story to the authorities, Reardon was called on to repeat it in court in front of the accused, Duder, on Saturday 4 March. Just as she was doing so, dramatic news was received at the magistrate's court that Burns had cut his throat and was 'bleeding to death'. Johnson rushed from the court to the gaol. He eventually returned to say that Burns was no longer in any immediate danger of dying. However Burns, while he was seemingly at death's door, had retracted his confession. This left Reardon's evidence as the only 'facts' against Oliver and Duder. The newspaper described her as a 'woman of notoriously bad character' whose 'evidence … had been received by the public universally … with a degree of caution amounting to suspicion'. Reardon then confessed that she had made up her story. Oliver, against whom the evidence was scant, had already been released, and now Duder was also set free.[17]

Speculation abounded that the former couple's motivation in lying about Oliver and Duder stemmed from Duder having provided information that led to Burns' dismissal from his job for stealing and butchering his employer's stock.[18] Burns had then fallen on hard times. He was evicted from his farm cottage and built a rough shack on the North Shore in which he lived with Reardon and their young two sons. Like numerous working-class couples throughout the colony, the family were forced to make shift[19] – they just scraped by on what Burns could earn through labouring for local rangatira Eruera Maihi Patuone and by eating vegetables that Reardon grew.[20] The man named Oliver whom Reardon tried to implicate in the Snow murders had replaced Burns in his former job as a stock-keeper, thus fuelling the notion that the aggrieved former employee was seeking his revenge by having these men implicated in the Snow murders.[21] This, though, was not the whole story and, as the New Zealander reported, 'it is an old and true saying "Murder will out"'.[22]

By the first of the following month, April, Burns himself was brought before the Supreme Court to face charges of having murdered the Snow family. While he was in custody awaiting transportation for his previous offence, Margaret Reardon went to the police station to collect his tool chest. Captain Atkyns had entered into a conversation with Reardon at the station, during which she initially complained about Burns' treatment of her and then hinted that they could both reveal more about the Snow murders. Atkyns subsequently interviewed Burns in prison, and Burns confessed a second time to his part in the murders. The transcript of Burns' trial is no longer extant, so historians have to rely on newspaper accounts of the proceedings and archival records of the depositions taken before his Supreme Court hearing to ascertain the gist of the evidence presented.[23] In court, Reardon claimed she heard Burns say that he intended to rob and kill Snow. She said she saw him leave home at 6pm armed with a tomahawk and a bayonet. The tomahawk was found in Burns' tool chest, and a forensic examination revealed rust and blood stains that implied it was likely to have been used to kill Snow and his family. Reardon added that when Burns had returned at 1am he claimed that he murdered the family and showed her one pound 'in silver' taken from the Snows' property. She also told the court about Burns' earlier assault on her and claimed that he was desperate and had tried to force her into marriage, then turned violent when she spurned him. It is interesting to note that if she had married Burns, Reardon would not have been able to give evidence against him in relation to the Snow murders. Reardon claimed that she first raised this legal complication with him as they were returning home from town in a boat – at which time they had seen the Snows with some shopping and allegedly also with a large amount of cash. In other words, she said she had aired this concern at the moment at which the plan to rob and ultimately to murder the Snows was being hatched. As Terry Carson has pointed out:

> the court was supposed to believe that Margaret Reardon's first thought on being told that a murder was about to take place was to consider her legal options and lack of legal privilege due to not being legally married to Burns. It seems an unlikely first thought for a woman of her background.[24]

What seems more likely, as Carson has suggested, is that Reardon had been schooled thoroughly by the colonial authorities as to what she ought to say in evidence, and that Burns' assault on Reardon could have been motivated by their dispute over some land he wanted to sell and Burns' plans to use the proceeds to leave the colony, taking one of their sons with him.[25]

Other witnesses were called to give evidence against Burns. Colonial Surgeon Johnson stated that the Snows' wounds were likely to have been inflicted by a tomahawk and bayonet, and another witness testified that he saw Burns spending a lot of money. It took the jury 45 minutes to find Burns guilty. On hearing their verdict Burns cried out in court, 'My God, I'm as innocent as the child unborn!' He was condemned to be hanged at midday the following Saturday at the site of the murders – a punishment generally reserved for the most heinous of crimes.[26]

In his final days Burns was ministered to by men of the cloth, who encouraged him to confess. The prisoner steadfastly refused to do so and blamed Reardon for having incriminated him. He insisted that she, too, was guilty. Burns threw allegations at Reardon when she visited him in his cell – allegations that she vehemently denied. The day before the execution the former couple's children were brought to the cell to say goodbye to their condemned father. The *New Zealander* described their separation at the end of the visit as 'most harrowing' and told its readership how the youngsters had to be literally 'torn from his embrace'. By evening Burns was more contrite: he thanked the sheriff for his care throughout his incarceration, and implied that he was on the verge of confessing. Several prayerful hours followed and, ultimately, one of the ministers, Churton, heard Burns' full confession. It was written down and signed by the prisoner half an hour before midnight on the eve of his execution.[27]

In his confession Burns claimed that when he and Reardon returned home from town on Friday 22 October 1847, she had told him that Mr and Mrs Snow had been in town too and had 'got a lot of things'. He claimed that Reardon had then suggested they ought to avail themselves of some of the Snows' property and observed that their flimsy house would be easy to break into and enter. In Burns' account of what happened next he claimed that Reardon was his accomplice. The pair had dressed in blue clothing – presumably to conceal themselves well in the dark – before taking their punt around near to where the Snows lived. They walked up the path to the family home, both armed with a tomahawk. His, Burns claimed, was large and was not the weapon produced in evidence against him in court. The smaller weapon allegedly used by Reardon was the same tomahawk Burns claimed to have later seen at her sister's house, along with a knife used in the murders (the utensil Sophia Aldwell was using to cut bread for her young nephew). Burns stated that when Lieutenant Snow answered their knock at the door, he had struck Snow; but he said that it was Reardon who fatally cut the man's throat. He then said that he killed Mrs Snow while Reardon murdered the child, Mary. According to his account, Reardon then robbed the dead couple of their linen, the large knife that was later seen at the Aldwells' home, and £2 in silver – which was all the money they could find. He then set fire to the house, and Reardon burned most of the deceased family's stolen clothing several days later. Burns claimed that Reardon kept and wore '2 chemises with Mrs Snows initials on them in red silk', and a few other 'trifling things'.[28]

Despite Burns' persistence in incriminating Reardon, the police do not seem to have seriously investigated her as a suspect in the murders or as an accessory after the fact. Ultimately it came down to his word against hers as to her level of involvement in planning, committing and covering up the crime. It is not possible to say with absolute certainty whether and to what extent she was involved, although it is interesting to note that she likely instigated the cover-up story whereby suspicion was briefly and erroneously cast on Duder and Oliver. Her motivations for committing perjury could relate to her having had some level of culpability although not necessarily to the extent implied by Burns.

Early on the morning after his confession Burns read from the Bible. His irons were then removed and he was taken into the yard to be loaded onto a cart. Escorted by police, a strong detachment of soldiers from the 58th Regiment, several public officials including the sheriff and accompanied by Churton, Burns was taken to Official Bay. Many boats were in the bay, including numerous Māori waka whose crews were ferrying paying passengers to the scene of the impending execution.[29] According to the *Daily Southern Cross* the government intended the execution to be 'as imposing a spectacle as possible'; it was rumoured that 'official notice of the execution has been sent to the natives for ten miles around Auckland, in order to secure a large attendance'. Towards this end, the execution was scheduled for 'the unusual hour of midday'. Not everybody approved of this – the *Daily Southern Cross* railed against the brutality of such 'disgusting and inhuman exhibitions' as public hangings which, it considered, might have a 'powerful effect' on good men but would have almost none on the 'inferior' classes in society for whom such salutary lessons were intended.[30]

Burns was taken across to the North Shore in the *Ann* then marched to the temporary scaffold. He sat on his own coffin while Churton wept and prayed over him. Burns apologised to his former shipmate Duder for trying to incriminate him in the Snows' murders, but he continued to blame Reardon for inventing the falsity. In accordance with the usual procedure, the prisoner's handcuffs were removed and his arms pinioned at his sides before he mounted the steps of the scaffold. Burns' final words were spoken on his behalf by Churton, who told the gathered crowd of onlookers that

Burns attributed his downfall to 'his fondness for bad women, and his love of drinking'. His public confession was meant to convey contrition but was also intended as a cautionary tale. After he had prayed for forgiveness of his sins, the bolt was drawn, the platform fell and Burns became the first Pākehā to be judicially executed in New Zealand.[31]

In keeping with the practice at the time, Burns' remains were buried in the yard of the Auckland gaol. However, to make way for a market to be held in what had become the old gaol yard the bodies of Burns and several other men also hanged for murder were exhumed in 1866. The *New Zealand Herald* reported how 'the bones were placed in fresh coffins and conveyed to Symonds-street' for reburial 'in a remote and unused spot' within the cemetery there.[32] Symonds Street cemetery was also the final resting place of the late Lieutenant Snow, his wife Hannah and their daughter Mary.[33]

Given that Reardon's false testimony in March 1848 against Duder and Oliver could have resulted in the execution of two innocent men, she was held in custody to be called to account for lying to the court. This necessitated alternative arrangements for the care of her young sons. Resident Magistrate Thomas Beckham wrote to the colonial secretary on 10 March 1848 to explain that Reardon was being held in custody to provide evidence against Burns. He sought permission from the governor for the alienated couple's two children to receive government rations as they were 'wholly dependent on her [Reardon] for support'. Beckham's request was approved. An annotation on the reverse of his letter indicates that rations were 'supplied accordingly' to the boys.[34]

After six months in custody Reardon appeared before Chief Justice William Martin at the Supreme Court in Auckland on 1 September 1848, charged with 'wilful and corrupt perjury' but notably not with murder. She pleaded not guilty. Damning evidence of Reardon perjuring herself was presented by the prosecution, including a copy of her deposition to the magistrate's court in which her false accusations about Duder were dutifully recorded by the clerk James Elliott. Elliott testified to the veracity of the document and confirmed to the Supreme Court that the mark on it was Reardon's. Several witnesses testified that Reardon had given her evidence in an unhurried manner. She had been cautioned at the time to tell the truth. The governor of the gaol, George McElwain, told the court that he recalled Reardon's evidence at Burns' trial: on that occasion she admitted to the Supreme Court that 'she knew her former evidence [against Duder] to be a lie'. The youngest witness was George Watson, a boy of 11. He testified that he was living at Duder's house at the flagstaff at the time of the Snow murders. He confirmed that Duder had not left his house all night, and Duder himself said the same in court. Eventually Reardon was asked if she had anything to say in her own defence. In response, the registrar Mr Outhwaite read a statement from the 'wretched woman' in which she said the story she told about Duder and Oliver was born out of fear after Burns had threatened to implicate her in the Snow murders, or to murder her. Reardon claimed Burns 'always boasted that he would soon shake the fetters off him; and would never be transported'. She had felt 'compelled under fear' to lie. Despite these extenuating circumstances, the jury took only five or six minutes to find her guilty.[35] The next morning Martin told Reardon she had been convicted of 'perjury in its worst form'. He said there could be 'no excuse for so foul a crime' as charging an innocent man with murder, even though Reardon had later retracted her story. He informed her that 'the sentence of the Court is that you, Margaret Reardon, be transported beyond the seas to such place as His Excellency the Governor may appoint, for a term of seven years'.[36] With that judgment, Reardon became the only woman to be transported from New Zealand to Van Diemen's Land.

Not everyone was entirely happy with the verdict. The *Anglo-Maori Warder* bemoaned the fact that Reardon was put on trial – not out of any concern for the wellbeing of her or her children, but because suspicions remained that 'more actors than one' were at the scene on the night of the Snow murders. With Reardon about to be transported, 'her evidence, which might possibly again be required, is now entirely lost'.[37] The public was left with a sense that perhaps not all of the facts had been uncovered. Justice was seen to have been only partially served.

Over the many decades that have passed since the Snow murders numerous stories have circulated about Burns and Reardon, and different interpretations have evolved regarding her positioning both in colonial society generally and in relation to the events that took place in Auckland in 1847 and 1848. Megan Simpson, for example, has observed how colonial society was quick to condemn Reardon as a woman of bad character – a positioning that 'deemed her to be at odds with the good moral character of most female settlers'. Reardon was represented to the public as part of 'the criminal underclass who frequently came before all levels of the judiciary'. While this certainly seems to have been the case, Simpson has also argued that Reardon was condemned by society 'for her supposed depravity, regardless of the strong evidence of abuse, cruelty and hardship she endured'.[38] More recently Terry Carson, a retired barrister who spent several years poring over surviving documentation relating to the Snow murders, has thrown doubt on the notion that Reardon was a long-term victim of domestic abuse. Aside from Burns' attack on her when he visited her sister's house there is no other record of a violent relationship between the two; on the contrary, Reardon was comfortable talking with her former partner on her own outside the house just a few days before the attack, and was confident she had information that could send him packing. Carson concluded that to state Reardon's 'actions were totally due to fear of Burns is an oversimplification … not borne out by the available evidence'. Surviving evidence, according to Carson, demonstrates that Reardon was 'probably lucky that perjury was all that she was charged with' as her actions implied that she may well have been at least an accessory to murder.[39]

The intercolonial trading vessel *Sisters* was contracted to transport Reardon to Van Diemen's Land after her conviction for perjury. As well as carrying paying passengers and occasionally prisoners, the *Sisters* regularly brought trade goods across the Tasman. One of the Auckland traders, Thomas Lewis of Fort Street, advertised a range of goods that the schooner had delivered to Auckland in October 1848 before it made the return trip to Hobart with Reardon on board. The goods included 'seventy-four bags [of] fine flour and '124 bags [of] Biscuit'. Other goods ranging from vinegar and Roman cement to glue and drapery also arrived on the *Sisters* although it is unclear whether these were imports from Van Diemen's Land or brought up from Wellington.[40]

En route to Auckland the *Sisters* suffered a mishap off the east coast of the North Island. Despite strong winds near East Cape, Captain Clark decided to go ashore for fresh provisions. He took the ship's boat manned by two passengers – fishermen by trade – along with several of the *Sisters'* apprentices. When they made land Māori traders encouraged Clark back out to sea to put in further down the beach where pigs could be loaded. A local pilot was provided to guide them. Shortly afterwards a tremendous breaker rolled in, swamping the ship's boat and washing its captain and crew into the water. One of the fishermen rescued an apprentice before making for shore. The Māori pilot clung to the boat but it started to drift further out to sea, so he too swam to shore. Clark stripped off, and he and the other fisherman tried to save the apprentices from drowning. Eventually the exhausted captain struck out for the beach; four Māori women swam to his aid and helped him to safety. Meanwhile Robert Tholburn, the second fisherman, drowned, as did two apprentices – William Blackman and James Clarke. The *Wellington Independent* heaped praise on local Māori, who provided food, clothing, warmth and comfort to the survivors and brought them safely back to the *Sisters* the following day.[41] The unfortunate incident served as a reminder of the precariousness of life and the dangers involved in sea voyaging.

Life on land, too, could also be hazardous – as Clark experienced when he arrived at Auckland. While he and another man, Maxwell, were watching cattle being offloaded from the *Elizabeth and Henry* at Freemans Bay, an 'enraged ox' broke loose and charged Maxwell. The beast was deterred by a whip, whereupon it changed course and went directly for Clark. The 'gallant tar' fled, looking back over his left shoulder to keep an eye on his bovine assailant. As the ox closed in on him Clark leapt to one side. The momentum of the furious animal carried it forwards over a cliff, beneath which it lay 'apparently dead' for several hours. The colonial newspapers printed and reprinted this story as a cautionary tale. It confirmed the wisdom of the recent relocation of stock ships from Official Bay to a site further from the town centre. If the relocation had not occurred, reported the media, 'we might, in all probability, have been called upon to record the fatal results at a Coroner's inquest'.[42]

Perhaps it was a relief for Clark to leave Auckland. By the morning of Tuesday 3 October 1848 the *Sisters* had safely returned south to Wellington. On board were 'for Van Diemen's Land, one woman and seven men, under sentence of transportation'. The men included three soldiers from the 58th Regiment – Thomas Warren, Amos Streik and Robert Brady; the first two were court-martialled for desertion and the third for striking an officer. The other four men were civilians: Charles Williams had stolen a pistol and some clothing; John Jessop was guilty of 'larceny of anchor and chain'; and Jonathan Pellett and James Cornwell had committed highway robbery.[43]

The Pellett and Cornwell case, which took place at the same time as Reardon's, attracted public interest. Earlier the same year, on 26 February 1848, two Māori were found guilty of highway robbery and sentenced to six months' imprisonment. Resident Magistrate Thomas Beckham told the men while sentencing them that 'had they been Europeans, they would have been handed over to the Supreme Court, and transported for life'. This, according to the *Anglo-Maori Warder*, was an 'extraordinary admission' by Beckham. Pellett and Cornwell's sentences to 15 years' transportation demonstrably highlighted a gulf between sentences doled out to Māori and Pākehā in the civil courts in 1848 for what was, in essence, the same crime.[44] In reporting the presence of Pellett, Cornwell, Reardon and their fellow prisoners on the *Sisters*, the *Wellington Independent* could not resist taking a swipe at the township to its far north: it observed how 'our friends at Auckland appear to "turn out convicts" at an exceedingly rapid rate'. It also sniped at its Auckland-based counterpart, the *New Zealander*, claiming that it was likely to 'hold up the [then] "Capital" … as the most moral and best-behaved seaport town in the British Dominions'. This was despite a conviction rate of around 1000 in a population of 5000 people.[45]

The *Sisters* set sail for Hobart on 8 October after five days in port at Wellington, during which its agent secured a cargo of '36 casks of oil, 29 logs, 2 tons hides, 2 cases merchandize, 1 ton hides, 1 cask sperm oil, 23 casks oil'[46] – presumably some of these doubly listed goods were obtained from different exporters. Also on board were several other passengers.[47]

Reardon was not wholly unfamiliar with the Australian penal colonies. As young Margaret Lackey she travelled out to New South Wales from Ireland with her two older sisters on the *Duchess of Northumberland* in 1836. The women were accompanied by their older brother John and his wife and son. Another brother, William, was already in Sydney, having been transported on the *Sir Godfrey Webster* in 1826 for manslaughter. In Sydney Margaret married a much older man – emancipated convict Daniel Reardon (or Riordan). He was 66 years old at the time of the ceremony at St Mary's Catholic Church; Margaret was just 23. The marriage did not last. Soon after relocating to New Zealand in 1843 where her sister Sophia was living with her second husband William Aldwell, Reardon formed her ill-fated relationship with Burns.

In the aftermath of the Snow murders and the arrests that followed, Sophia took in William and James, Reardon's illegitimate children with Burns. She later emigrated to the United States in 1850 with her husband, their two children and her nephews. Carson has suggested that the family relocated in the late 1860s to the Australian colonies with at least one of Reardon and Burns' sons, meaning that a family reunion may have taken place after a decade apart.[48] Long-term separation from children, such as Reardon experienced in relation to her sons, was a feature of convict life for many transported women, although some were permitted to bring their children with them to the Australian penal colonies.

The *Sisters* arrived at Hobart on 20 October 1848 and, as per usual, Reardon was interviewed by the colonial authorities and asked to provide her particulars. She told them she was 26 years old and a Protestant, originally from County Longford in Ireland. She also claimed to be a dressmaker, although there is no surviving evidence of her having practised this trade in Auckland. Asked about her marital status, she responded 'widow' and said she had two children. She also said that she could 'read and write a little'. Questioned about her other relatives, Reardon stated that her two brothers, William and John, lived in Sydney, as did her sister, whom she referred to as 'Betsy'. She said that her other sister, Sophia, was in Auckland with Reardon's sons William and James. Their father, she told the authorities, was 'since executed for murder'. Reardon also told them that her brother was an 'under-sheriff' in Sydney – a description that tallies with a newspaper report from 1842 that mentions a man named Lackey being the sheriff's bailiff.[49]

Reardon would have been subject to the regulations governing female convicts during the probationary period in Van Diemen's Land. These regulations, issued on 1 July 1845, explained how:

in this first stage of probation [typically lasting six months] the attainment of two objectives is contemplated, 'punishment and reformation'. The first will be secured by the due application of coercive labour and restrictive discipline; the second, it is hoped, will be attained by means of religious and moral influences, and by the careful inculcation of industry and regularity.[50]

A combination of hard work, discipline, punishment and moral and religious instruction was the means by which women like Reardon were gradually to become reformed characters.

Stretching across the eastern seaboard of Australia was a series of establishments expressly for convict women. These sites were called female factories, houses of correction or penitentiaries. The southernmost was located at Cascades, South Hobart (replacing an earlier site at the Domain); and there were other Vandemonian female factories operating at Ross in the midlands and at Launceston and George Town in the north. In colonial New South Wales – which, at the time, included Queensland – two female factories operated at Parramatta in Sydney, and another two at Moreton Bay in Brisbane. There were similar institutions at Newcastle, Bathurst and Port Macquarie. Of the estimated 24,960 women transported to Australia, somewhere between 9000 and 10,000 spent time in these factories.[51] Reardon was among that number. Her conduct record does not specify where she was sent immediately on disembarkation from the *Sisters*: some women were sent immediately into service with a settler, while others were sent to serve their initial probationary period of six months on the convict hulk *Anson*, a converted transport that lay at anchor in Prince of Wales Bay near New Town on the outskirts of Hobart.

At the time of Reardon's arrival in Van Diemen's Land, the Cascades female factory was overcrowded with women. The *Anson* was repurposed to serve as a female probation station, and operated as such between 1844 and 1849. It held anywhere between 250 and 519 women at any given time.[52] These convict women were overseen by Dr and Mrs Bowden, and Reverend Giles visited to conduct religious services on board. Considerable attention was paid to hygiene – the female convicts were required to ensure that the *Anson* 'exhibited remarkable cleanliness'. During their probationary period the convicts completed essential domestic tasks such as cooking and laundering. They were taught a range of other domestic arts, including needlework, shoe manufacturing, straw-hat making and doormat making. Visitors remarked favourably on the 'subdued, respectful and … proper deportment of the women', and credited Mrs Bowden with achieving better results than those seen in similar establishments elsewhere in Australia.[53]

When they were exhibiting signs of becoming reformed, convict women were hired out into private service. Fiscal and moral responsibility for their care and upkeep was transferred from the state to their new master or mistress;[54] in return, the person or family to whom the convict was assigned demanded respect, compliance and hard work. This system was not without strong critics – some claimed that female convicts were 'so vice-ridden and morally repellent that "respectable" mistresses kept their distance from them' to avoid contamination.[55] Assigned women therefore did not necessarily receive the assumed benefits of an upstanding mistress's chastisements and encouragement towards reformation.

Just one month after her probationary period expired Reardon committed the first of two offences she was charged with while under sentence. She was found guilty of 'Dis[obedience] of orders and Insolence' – perhaps to her new master or mistress – and was sent to the Cascades female factory on 18 May 1849 to serve three months of hard labour. She served another two months there early the following year after being found 'Drunk'.[56]

The Cascades female factory served several purposes. It was a hiring depot from which convict women could be acquired as servants, and a place to which the women could be returned if they fell pregnant or otherwise did not meet their master or mistress's expectations. It was also a place where single men from the wider community could present themselves and their credentials – usually a character reference from their local clergyman or magistrate – to seek a wife. The matron would usher the man inside to wait while she visited the better class of prisoners to seek expressions of interest from any convict woman who wished to marry. The women were lined up for inspection and the colonial equivalent of speed dating would take place: the prospective husband would converse briefly with any women who appealed to him, and they in turn could ask him a question or two. Questions might range from information about any previous marriages through to occupation, status, property and religion. If a match was made, the matron was informed and a date was set for the wedding.[57]

It is hardly surprising, given the speed with which couples were wed, that men sometimes tired of their wives and returned them to the confines of the female factory; apparently some colonial women likewise tired of their convict husbands and disposed of them just as readily.[58] But convict women could not anticipate as many opportunities for betterment as their male counterparts in the penal colonies. As Kay Daniels explained, with an 'emphasis on female convicts as sexual partners, wives or mothers rather than workers' convict women had a 'slender chance … for achieving independence' at the expiration of their sentences. Women were seen as needing protection and this was usually afforded through their involvement in the domestic sphere where all was not equal between the sexes.[59]

The Cascades female factory site stands next to the Hobart rivulet and is surrounded by high stone walls. Its location adjacent to the foothills of Mount Wellington ensures that it remains a shady, windswept place for most of the year. Snow may fall in Tasmania at any time of the year, although it is more prevalent in the winter months. Once the wind is whistling down from the snow-capped mountain top, Cascades is a bitter place indeed. Conversely, in summer it can become unbearably hot.

Built in 1828 to plans designed by noted colonial architect John Lee Archer, the female factory was staffed by a superintendent, matron, crime-class overseer, crime-class task mistress, porter, gatekeeper, clerk and two constables. Visiting staff included a cleric and a medical attendant. Within the walls of the factory the convict women were organised into classes. Those who were considered better behaved and therefore further along the path of reformation were in the first class; and this class was also reserved for pregnant women or those incarcerated for minor crimes. The third-class or 'crime-class' prisoners were those whom Reardon would have joined when she was assigned to hard labour. Such labour might include working at the laundry tubs all day long – a chore that resulted in a woman's hands becoming red, raw and bleeding. In between these two classes were the second-class prisoners, those who were aspiring to the first class and eventual freedom. The different classes of prisoners were physically separated from one another into five yards, several of which also had sub-yards.[60]

The superintendent and the matron controlled the class to which women were consigned and their movement between classes. The regulations governing female convicts during the probation period allowed those women in the first and second classes within the factories to choose their own 'mess associates' – the women were formed into mess groups of 10. All women were expected to get up at sunrise and retire to their beds at 9pm on summer evenings and 8pm during the winter. They received daily rations that included four fifths of a pound of bread, half a pound each of meat and vegetables, a quarter ounce of salt and a quarter pint of oatmeal. Those in solitary confinement were restricted to a diet of bread and water: they received one and a half pounds of bread daily, and half an ounce of soap for hygiene purposes. To supplement the clothing they arrived in, every six months the inmates were issued with a maximum of a jacket, cap, apron, petticoat, shift and a handkerchief as well as one pair each of shoes and stockings. They were also issued with a hammock, a flock pillow and mattress, a blanket and a rug.[61]

Convicts who were illiterate received schooling. The incarcerated women were also expected to perform all of the tasks required to keep the establishment running smoothly, including cooking, cleaning, laundry work and scrubbing, on a weekly roster. Women who were passholders enjoyed tasks such as baking, nursing and being store attendants and servants. If there were too few passholders to perform these tasks, then those who had completed two thirds of their sentence and become first-class prisoners were given these roles. The higher-ranked female factory staff were allowed to take on convict servants at their own expense. Women at the female factory also engaged in a wide range of needlework – they created items ranging from gentlemen's shirts and collars to infants' shoes and women's petticoats and frocks. A scale of charges within government regulations established the price charged to members of the public for the items the women produced. Saturday afternoons were set aside for inspections to ensure the women's clothing, utensils, bedding and furniture were being kept in good order. Sunday was a holy day and a day of rest.[62]

Reardon's conduct record does not reveal her whereabouts outside of the confines of the Cascades female factory, but it is reasonable to assume that she was hired out as an assigned convict servant between and after her stints of hard labour. She received her only recorded indulgence, a ticket of leave, on 10 February 1852. This was rescinded later the same year, on 28 September, but no explanation for this was recorded.[63] While she was under sentence Reardon married William Redman – listed in the marriage register as a 'free' man – on 9 July 1850.[64] On 16 February 1851 Reardon gave birth to twin boys and named them William and John – the same names as her sons with Burns, boys since lost to her. These two new sons did not survive very long: baby William died on 21 February, and John died a little over a month later, on 31 March 1851. Reardon, now Redman, fell pregnant shortly after the birth of the twins, and gave birth to a daughter, Elizabeth, in Hobart in late 1851. Another daughter, Sarah, was born at Fryers Creek in Victoria in 1854.

William Redman was free to leave Van Diemen's Land, but Margaret was legally bound to stay within the district proscribed by her ticket of leave. She must have flouted the rules and either joined her husband – and many other Vandemonians – who were flocking across Bass Strait at the height of the goldrush; or else she illicitly joined him there later. After Redman died in 1860, Margaret lived another two decades before she died of 'old age and exhaustion' on 9 April 1890 at Castlemaine hospital in Victoria.[65]

CONCLUSION

An ideal society

I dealised as a new sort of colony to be populated by gentlefolk and free labour, New Zealand's early image of itself could only be realised through the brutal suppression of challenges to that idea. The complex realities of colonial life threatened that idyllic dream, and the threats were excised. Idle, dishonest or violent men were unwelcome, feared and censured. Some were imprisoned locally, and those considered to be the worst offenders were transported. Māori men were handed down exemplary punishments – several were hanged and others were exiled to demonstrate the empire's strength and reach.

This phenomenon was not so much about the individuals themselves as a wider and deep-seated societal concern that negative character traits and behaviours, if left unchecked, could spread and infect colonial society. Cleansing the colony by means of transportation was one response that was used until the early 1850s. Resisting the transportation of imperial convicts to New Zealand was a related measure. Quietly dropping all associations with convictism from the national story was yet another approach, and perhaps the most lasting.

The majority of the final 21 men who were shipped from New Zealand to Van Diemen's Land in the 1850s were civilians. Eight were currently serving or discharged soldiers. Many of the offenders were transported for crimes that echoed those committed by their 1840s counterparts, including larceny, burglary, robbery, cattle stealing and assault. Among their number were Joseph Massey, who counterfeited silver coin, and John O'Donnell, a colour sergeant (non-commissioned officer) who forged a cheque on his regimental bank. Unusually, two of the offenders transported in the 1850s were found guilty of manslaughter. Both arrived in Van Diemen's Land on the *Antares* on 29 May 1851 after their respective trials at the Supreme Court in Auckland. One was a corporal in the British Army, the other a labourer from Hawai`i. Corporal Francis Butcher was sentenced to transportation for life for the manslaughter of Francis McEwan of the 58th Regiment; Butcher explained that he 'stabbed him with a knife in the Barrack room. He lived 3 quarters of an hour.' The corporal received his ticket of leave on 9 March 1858, although this was revoked later the same year on 5 October when he was 'absent from muster'. The lack of any further annotations on his conduct record implies that, like countless others, he may have illicitly fled the penal colony.[1]

Heke, described as a 'Sandwich Islander but lately from the Bay of Islands', appeared before the Supreme Court in Auckland on Tuesday 4 March 1851 charged with 'the wilful murder of Jacky Maitara (also a native of the Sandwich Islands) at the Bay of Islands'. Heke supposedly understood te reo Māori after 'nearly four years residing among the natives at the Bay of Islands', so he was provided with a Māori-speaking interpreter. Through the interpreter Heke admitted killing 'the deceased by the blow', but pleaded that it had not been his intention to kill his compatriot. As the prisoner was destitute, an application was made to the court to provide him with counsel. The newly appointed barrister argued for a jury comprising at least some of Heke's peers but was told by Chief Justice Martin that 'our Colonial Law protects all who reside within the bounds of these shores, and that the Courts of the Colony were competent to take cognizance of all crimes committed against the peace of Her Majesty within the same limits'.[2] Heke was found guilty of manslaughter and sentenced to transportation for life.[3] His sentence was brief: his conduct record states that he was 'accidentally killed at Cascades 16th June 1851' – making him another demonstration of the broad reach of colonial justice in and beyond New Zealand.[4]

British-derived justice left peculiar inflections in each colonial society. Vandemonian society was dominated by its convict legacy. While it was demarcated by a class system similar to England's, Vandemonians further differentiated between convicts and emancipists – that is, between those who had become free by servitude and those who arrived free or were born free in the colony.

By the 1840s Vandemonians were debating the future of convict transportation. Central to this debate were ongoing concerns about the moral fibre of a colony built predominantly by convicts. Second to this were economic concerns. Maintaining the convict system was expensive, and the inflation triggered by a rush of Vandemonians to the goldfields of Victoria meant costs escalated. The switch from the earlier convict system of assignment to probation hastened the end of transportation. As Henry Reynolds has explained, probation with its 'concentration of prisoners in so many areas aroused fears of breakouts and bushranging and an often obsessive concern about homosexuality'.[5] Ultimately the anti-transportationists won the day. The last convict transport docked at Hobart on 26 May 1853. Vandemonians celebrated. They also changed the name of the island colony to Tasmania. The new name commemorated Abel Tasman who had 'discovered' the island. It carried connotations of a new beginning, and dissociated Tasmanians from the convict stain of the Vandemonian past.[6]

Despite the cessation of convict transportation to Van Diemen's Land, New Zealand judges continued to sentence prisoners to transportation until 1854. Justice Sidney Stephen sentenced five men to transportation in March 1853, including Ngāti Apa rangatira Panapa (Barnaby) Huru te Rangi, who was found guilty of robbing Mr W.H. Constable as well as stealing from Captain Daniell's station at Rangitikei. As Robert Burnett pointed out, when Panapa petitioned Governor George Grey to be allowed to remain in New Zealand the governor acceded to his request. Somewhat duplicitously, Grey failed to tell Panapa that convict transportation to Van Diemen's Land had ended and, moreover, that the British had in any case banned any more Māori from being sent there. Instead, he presented his decision as being based partly on Panapa's taking care of an insane person with whom he was lodged. Panapa finally received a pardon in May 1857.

In September 1853 three men who served in the 65th Regiment were sentenced to 10 years' transportation. With nowhere to send them, Stephens recommended their sentences be commuted to imprisonment with hard labour in New Zealand.[7]

Another Māori prisoner, Taraiwaru, died in custody in New Zealand in 1855 while he was under sentence to transportation. He was found guilty of murdering William Smally or Smalley, a man 'who so mysteriously disappeared while trading with the natives on the Thames'. Tellingly, Taraiwaru was described as 'a strong hale man when taken into custody a few months ago'. The *Maori Messenger: Te Karere Maori* went on to explain how 'a sense of his crimes, added to the loneliness of his situation, so affected him as to engender disease, and thus prematurely has he been ushered into the presence of the Great Judge'.[8] Taraiwaru's rapid decline in health and resulting death in custody accords with Burnett's explanation that imprisonment 'was something completely foreign to anything in their [Māori] customary law, an imported practice … certainly not fit for the free born'. The word 'prison', according to Burnett, became 'whare herehere' in te reo Māori.[9] The death of indigenous people in custody was a phenomenon across Britain's nineteenth-century empire wherever the rule of law was imposed by colonists.[10]

In the nineteenth century it was common for Britain and her colonies to transport their problems, including political prisoners, to the Australian penal colonies, where they were forced to perform hard labour both to punish and to reform them. At least 369 Irish rebels were sent to Van Diemen's Land after the failed uprising of 1798 and the rebellion of 1848, where they joined hundreds more Irish convicts whose crimes may well have been politically motivated. Other political prisoners in the Australian penal colonies included 96 rebels from America and Canada, as well as hundreds of rioters and rebels from England. Among the latter were 332 of those involved in the 'swing' riots in England in 1830, as well as 91 Chartists transported in the 1840s, and the Tolpuddle Martyrs, who tried to improve conditions for England's rural poor.[11] Constructed as rebels in their own times, the five Māori warriors transported as a result of the court martial at Porirua are an appropriate addition to this category.

What, then, of the other men transported from New Zealand to Van Diemen's Land? Simply put, many of those transported from the colony were at odds with the fledgling colony's image of itself. As Miles Fairburn has explained, early colonists embraced an 'idealised picture ... of their new society, a New Zealand with all kinds of marvellous features originating from naturally abundant resources and a minimal framework of associations'.[12] The colonists were adamantly in favour of the islands they were colonising being kept free of convicts. The proximity of the Australian penal colonies occasioned considerable agitation throughout the 1840s. In 1843 one Wellington newspaper claimed to have been told that 'a considerable number of those persons who have bolted from Melbourne, Sydney, and Van Diemen's Land, are now infesting parts of New Zealand'.[13] Another Wellington newspaper reported in the same year how some men recently transported from New Zealand to Van Diemen's Land had turned out to be convict absconders. 'This is satisfactory,' the newspaper told its readers, 'and bears out the opinion expressed by the Judge of the County Court that most of the vagabonds who have committed excesses in this place, do not belong to the emigrants sent out by the [New Zealand] Company, but are the refuse of neighbouring colonies.'[14] This was a reference to Judge Edmund Halswell's opening address to the county court earlier in the year, when he told those assembled that the prisoners committed for trial 'were all strangers; none of them could properly be called emigrants, or even settlers'.[15]

It is illuminating to note that the vast majority of convicts transported from New Zealand to Van Diemen's Land – 93 of the 110 prisoners, or 85 per cent – were young single men from a working-class background. Some were men without means. Others were – or had been – soldiers. Of the 13 who were married men, just six were recorded as having children. Two of the three widowers and the widow Margaret Reardon also had children. The third widower, a soldier of the 58th Regiment named John Fling, was aged just 23 when he was sentenced to transportation for life by the Auckland Supreme Court in December 1846 for the manslaughter of his wife Isabella, whom he had stabbed. There is no mention in his trial records nor in his convict records of the man having had any children with his late wife.[16] Fling's case was quite unusual. Most of those transported from New Zealand, whose average age was a little over 28, were transported for thefts and assaults or, in the case of the military, desertion; only two other men

(Butcher and Heke in the 1850s) were transported for manslaughter. By 1842, Wellingtonians were noticing an upsurge in 'the frequency of petty thefts in the streets of Wellington'. A key strategy in curbing crime was to round up alleged offenders, many of whom were viewed as vagrants, and put them on trial. It was hoped that 'the trials before the court, together with the punishment awarded in each case, will ... if not put a stop to, at least check the frequency of such proceedings'.[17]

Transportation to Van Diemen's Land was intended as a deterrent to others. It had the added advantage that many of those sent to the penal colony were unlikely, at least legally, to be able to return to New Zealand. There were of course some exceptions. White-collar criminal William Phelps Pickering is an obvious example: his case demonstrates how the convict stain did not necessarily attach itself to men from middle-class backgrounds. Individuals such as Pickering and medical doctor George Delvin Nugent were adept at reinventing themselves. Numerous convicts sought the governor's intercession – they presented formulaic petitions begging for pardon. Pickering was one of the few whose petitioning had a positive impact on his sentence.

Less evidence has survived in relation to working-class men, a few of whom managed to build materially successful lives for themselves once their sentence had expired. One example is former Parkhurst boy and Vandemonian convict Henry Butler Dowie, who built a successful family, business and political life in Tasmania. Some simply absconded from Van Diemen's Land and vanished without trace. Others changed their names after their sentence had expired. Most never saw their families again. A poignant remark survives on Jonathan Pellett's conduct record: the 24-year-old soldier from the 58th Regiment was found guilty in the Supreme Court at Auckland on 1 September 1848 of highway robbery along with fellow soldier James Cornwell. The two men, both of whom were single, were transported to Van Diemen's Land for 15 years.[18] Pellett's conduct record ends abruptly with an annotation indicating that he absconded without trace on 24 June 1852. Written diagonally in pencil across the lower left portion of this record is a note that reads: 'Enquiry made by Rachel Pellett, Foster Field, Billingham, Kent, 16 December 1869'. A note on Pellett's indent indicates that his father and mother lived at his 'native place', Kent. When he was transported Pellett had already served seven years with the 58th.[19]

Now, 17 years after he absconded from Van Diemen's Land and possibly 28 years after seeing him off in England, Pellett's mother desperately sought news of her absent son. But there was none to be had.

One striking statistic is that only one woman was transported from New Zealand: Margaret Reardon. This can be explained through the ways in which women's and men's actions were viewed and criminalised differently in colonial society – although the reasoning behind Reardon being charged with perjury and not with being at least an accessory to murder remains opaque. As Megan Simpson has observed, 'women were indicted for fewer serious crimes than men' in the early years of the colony. She has pointed out how only seven female defendants were brought before the Supreme Court in the 1840s, following 'a trend that can be observed in other jurisdictions in the British Empire'. This can be attributed at least in part to the fact that the Supreme Court heard cases of a more serious nature such as murder, fraud and so on, while 'cases which were more generally associated with female defendants, such as small theft, prostitution and drunkenness, were heard by the Resident Magistrate's Court'.[20] These types of crime were far less likely to result in a sentence to transportation from New Zealand.

By the end of January 1849, New Zealand colonists were aware that Van Diemen's Land was protesting vehemently to London against absorbing any more convicts. This raised the question within New Zealand as to 'whether it was intended that the present system of transportation to Van Diemen's Land should be only temporary, or that it should be continued'. Responding to these concerns, Grey said that he knew transportation was no longer going to continue as it once had. In future, 'the strictly penal part of the sentence' was to be carried out at the place where convicts were sentenced. 'Convicts were to be removed to the colonies,' said Grey, 'when they were likely to be really useful, and when they could be placed in a position which would enable them to earn their own sustenance by their labour.' The advantage of such people being 'prevented from returning to this country' would continue.[21]

Britain's policy shift to a system of exile as delineated by Grey echoed the former practice of shipping Parkhurst boys from the Isle of Wight to New Zealand when their sentences were partially or fully served. It was essentially the same scheme under which shipments of the so-called

Pentonville exiles (not all of whom were from Pentonville Prison) had been sent to the Australian colonies. This posed two distinct but interrelated problems for New Zealand. Colonists were concerned that New Zealand could be gazetted as a site to which exiles could be sent. At the same time, they were left with the problem of what to do with their own criminal class if they were no longer able to procure what was often a one-way passage for them to Van Diemen's Land.

Meetings were hastily convened across New Zealand, at which the possibility of the colony becoming a repository for British exiles was debated. At a meeting held at Nelson in October 1849 Francis Dillon Bell, who was chairing the session, claimed that 'among the great majority of settlers in every part of New Zealand, there was no difference of opinion whatever. Every one united to condemn, in unmistakable terms, any proposal that should, under any possible circumstances, introduce the criminal population of England into this colony.' The meeting's lengthy discussion concluded with a statement from Bell that 'he sincerely trusted that the straightforward declaration' of New Zealand settlers 'would be in time to arrest the evil with which they had been threatened, in the introduction of the proposed exiles'.[22]

New Zealand's Legislative Council believed that 'distinct pledges have been repeatedly given by the Home Government, that, whatever course might be pursued with regard to other colonies, New Zealand should not be made a receptacle for men banished by law from their own country on account of their crimes'. The Parkhurst boys were used as exemplars of the ways in which the criminal class almost inevitably 'relapsed into crime, and corrupted others'. Almost all of the magistrates across the colony were against the reception of exiles, as were 'the Natives', who had 'forwarded several earnest and touching petitions to the same effect'.[23] Māori and Pākehā agreed that neither stood to benefit from the introduction of English criminals into their midst. As this long debate in the Legislative Council neared its end, Grey introduced 'a new and striking feature of the subject' when he:

> suggested the feasibility and propriety of a plan by which New Zealand might take charge of its own convicts, carry out their punishment, and attempt their reformation, without casting the refuse of its population

on other colonies in the way in which it is feared lest England should
cast her criminals upon us.[24]

The *New Zealander* observed how under the present scheme Britain paid for
the punishment of criminals and provided places to where those convicted
in Britain or its colonies could be banished. There were strengths to be
gained by New Zealand adopting its own penal system – an eventuality that
would surely put the colony on a strong footing when it came to objecting
to receiving criminals from elsewhere.[25]

After the British Parliament passed legislation (16 & 17 Vic, c. 99) on
4 August 1853 that ended transportation from Britain for periods less
than 14 years, New Zealand's parliament formed a select committee to
consider how best to replace transportation as a punishment for criminals
convicted locally. Before this select committee could report its findings, a
bill to replace transportation with penal servitude was introduced into the
New Zealand parliament. On 16 September 1854, parliament passed 'An
Act to abolish the Punishment of Transportation, and to substitute Penal
Servitude within the Colony in lieu thereof'. Its first clause, which read 'On
and after the first day of January, one thousand eight hundred and fifty-
five, no person shall be sentenced to transportation', officially ended more
than a decade of convict transportation from New Zealand to Van Diemen's
Land.[26] New Zealand colonists were poised to experiment with new ways
of curbing crime and reforming people as part of their agenda to build an
ideal society.

Appendix

Convicts transported from New Zealand to Van Diemen's Land

SHIP	POLICE NUMBER	NAME	REGIMENT
John Pirie	173	Moses Booth	
Portenia	214	William Phelps Pickering	
Portenia	215	James Beckett	
Portenia	216	George Delvin Nugent	
Portenia	217	William Clarke	
Portenia	218	James Clarke (Thompson)	
Portenia	219	Patrick Mullins	
Portenia	220	William Root	
Portenia	221	Joseph Root	
Portenia	222	Francis (Daniel) McCarthy	
Portenia	223	William Jackson	
Portenia	224	Charles Rowley	
Portenia	225	John Coghlan	
Portenia	226	Henry Rogers	
Comet	303	William Ellis	
John Pirie	391	William Stewart	
John Pirie	392	Emmanuel Lewis	
John Pirie	393	Henry Butler Dowie	
Sisters	457	Margaret Reardon	
Victoria	484	John Green	
Victoria	485	John Clarence	
Victoria	486	Thomas Nowlans	
Victoria	487	Edward Hicks	
Cheerful	600	Timothy O'Meara	
Cheerful	601	George Bottomley	
Cheerful	602	Edwin Rose	
Waterlily	605	Richard Conway	
Bandicoot	634	Thomas Pilcher	
Castor	758	Richard Shea	99th
Castor	759	William Lane	99th
Castor	760	George Morris	99th
Castor	761	John Bailey	99th
Castor	762	George Langlands	
Castor	763	Joseph Davis	
Castor	764	Joseph Price	
Castor	765	Te Waretiti	
Castor	766	Hōhepa Te Umuroa	

DATE OF TRIAL	TRIAL	OFFENCE	SENTENCE
20 September 1844	Auckland SC	Stealing two guns	7 yrs
6 October 1841	Auckland QS	Obtaining valuable security under false pretences	7 yrs
16 August 1842	Wellington CC	Stealing in a dwelling house	7 yrs
17 January 1843	Wellington CC	Stealing in a dwelling house	7 yrs
21 February 1843	Wellington CC	Stealing in a dwelling house	7 yrs
21 February 1843	Wellington CC	Stealing in a dwelling house	7 yrs
7 April 1843	Wellington SC	Burglary	10 yrs
7 April 1843	Wellington SC	Burglary	10 yrs
7 April 1843	Wellington SC	Burglary	10 yrs
7 April 1843	Wellington SC	Burglary	10 yrs
7 April 1843	Wellington SC	Burglary	10 yrs
10 April 1843	Wellington SC	Burglary	10 yrs
10 April 1843	Wellington SC	Burglary	10 yrs
10 April 1843	Wellington SC	Burglary	10 yrs
11 March 1844	Auckland SC	Piracy	7 yrs
20 September 1844	Auckland SC	Stealing one sheep	10 yrs
20 September 1844	Auckland SC	Stealing one sheep	10 yrs
20 September 1844	Auckland SC	Burglary	7 yrs
1 September 1848	Auckland SC	Perjury	7 yrs
1 October 1844	Nelson SC	Killing a bullock	10 yrs
1 April 1845	Auckland SC	Burglary	10 yrs
1 April 1845	Auckland SC	Burglary	10 yrs
1 April 1845	Auckland SC	Burglary	10 yrs
2 June 1845	Wellington SC	Forging a government debenture	10 yrs
1 December 1845	Auckland SC	Stealing	7 yrs
1 December 1845	Auckland SC	Stealing	7 yrs
1 October 1845	Nelson SC	Assaulting a constable	15 yrs
2 December 1845	Wellington SC	Receiving stolen property	7 yrs
9 May 1846	Auckland CM	Striking an officer	Life
9 May 1846	Auckland CM	Desertion	Life
9 May 1846	Auckland CM	Desertion	Life
9 May 1846	Auckland CM	Desertion	Life
8 September 1846	Wellington SC	Burglary and putting in bodily fear	15 yrs
8 September 1846	Wellington SC	Burglary and putting in bodily fear	15 yrs
8 September 1846	Wellington SC	Burglary and putting in bodily fear	15 yrs
12 October 1846	Porirua CM	Rebellion	Life
12 October 1846	Porirua CM	Rebellion	Life

SHIP	POLICE NUMBER	NAME	REGIMENT
Castor	767	Te Kūmete	
Castor	768	~~Mataiumu~~ Matiu Tikiahi	
Castor	769	Te Rāhui	
Java	832	John Fling	58th
Julia	928	Henry Hodges	99th
Julia	929	William Johnson	
Julia	930	Patrick Shea	58th
Julia	931	Bernard McNally	99th
Julia	932	John Robinson	99th
Julia	933	James (Isaac) Brearley	99th
Julia	934	Michael Tobin	99th
Timbo	999	William Hughes	58th
Timbo	1000	Michael McGuire	58th
Timbo	1001	Charles Carson	58th
Julia	1026	William Spyke	96th
Julia	1128	Michael Farley	58th
Julia	1129	Thomas Ashe	58th
Julia	1130	Andrew Branagan	58th
Julia	1131	John Riches	58th
Julia	1132	Thomas Crutchley	58th
Julia	1133	Joseph Williams	
Sisters	1333	Charles Williams (William Davis)	
Sisters	1334	Jonathan Pellett	58th
Sisters	1335	James Cornwell	58th
Sisters	1336	Robert Brady	58th
Sisters	1337	Thomas Warren	58th
Sisters	1338	Amos Streik	58th
Sisters	1339	John Jessop	
Sisters	1439	William Wright	
Sisters	1440	James Lang	58th
Sisters	1441	William McGee	58th
Sisters	1442	David Fleur	58th
Sisters	1443	John Walker	58th
Perseverance	1467	Robert Young	65th
Perseverance	1468	John Jennings	65th
Perseverance	1469	Patrick Brady	65th

DATE OF TRIAL	TRIAL	OFFENCE	SENTENCE
12 October 1846	Porirua CM	Rebellion	Life
12 October 1846	Porirua CM	Rebellion	Life
12 October 1846	Porirua CM	Rebellion	Life
12 December 1846	Auckland SC	Manslaughter of his wife	Life
1 September 1846	Wellington SC	Rape	Life
1 March 1847	Auckland SC	Housebreaking	10 yrs
1 January 1847	Wellington CM	Drunkenness and firing at sergeant	Life
5 August 1846	Auckland CM	Desertion in vicinity of hostile natives	14 yrs
5 August 1846	Auckland CM	Desertion in vicinity of hostile natives	14 yrs
5 August 1846	Auckland CM	Desertion in vicinity of hostile natives	14 yrs
10 August 1846	Auckland CM	Desertion in vicinity of hostile natives and striking a captain	Life
1 September 1847	Auckland SC	Desertion and stealing in a dwelling house	17 yrs
1 September 1847	Auckland SC	Desertion and stealing in a dwelling house	17 yrs
1 September 1847	Auckland SC	Desertion and stealing in a dwelling house	10 yrs
1 October 1847	Nelson SC	Stealing a shirt; deserted from regiment	7 yrs
9 November 1847	Auckland CM	Striking sergeant	Life
18 December 1847	Auckland CM	Insubordinate conduct	7 yrs
2 December 1847	Auckland SC	Burglary	10 yrs
1 March 1848	Auckland SC	Larceny	7 yrs
2 December 1847	Auckland SC	Larceny	7 yrs
1 & 2 December 1847	Auckland SC	Larceny	10 yrs & 7 yrs
1 September 1848	Auckland SC	Felony; stealing a pistol and wearing apparel	15 yrs
1 September 1848	Auckland SC	Highway robbery	15 yrs
1 September 1848	Auckland SC	Highway robbery	15 yrs
20 December 1847	Auckland CM	Striking ensign	Life
21 February 1848	Auckland CM	Desertion and making away with his necessaries	7 yrs
11 April 1848	Auckland CM	Desertion and making away with his necessaries	9 yrs
2 June 1848	Auckland SC	Larceny; stealing a chain and anchor	7 yrs
1 December 1848	Wellington SC	Rape	Life
1 December 1848	Auckland SC	Stealing a watch	7 yrs
1 December 1848	Auckland SC	Stealing a watch	15 yrs
1 December 1848	Auckland SC	Stealing a watch	15 yrs
1 December 1848	Auckland SC	Stealing a watch	15 yrs
1 March 1849	Wellington SC	Highway robbery	15 yrs
1 March 1849	Wellington SC	Highway robbery	15 yrs
20 December 1848	Wellington CM	Striking adjutant	Life

SHIP	POLICE NUMBER	NAME	REGIMENT
Perseverance	1470	Alfred Dalton	65th
Adelaide	1510	Thomas Duck	58th
Adelaide	1523	John Glen	58th
Adelaide	1524	James Lappan	58th
Adelaide	1525	John Parker	58th
Adelaide	1526	John Donnelly Fox	
Fair Tasmanian	1549	William Brown	65th
Fair Tasmanian	1550	William (Richard) Whitehouse (Whitous)	
Fair Tasmanian	1551	John Ashley	
Fair Tasmanian	1552	Evan Lavendar	
Sisters	1573	Patrick Early	65th
Esperanza	1622	John Henry Brown	
Esperanza	1623	Edward Williams	
Perseverance	1639	David Cookman	65th
Perseverance	1640	John Connolly	65th
Sisters	1731	William Bannon	65th
Perseverance	1923	John Harris	
Perseverance	1924	William Thompson	
Perseverance	1925	John O'Donnell	65th
Perseverance	1926	Charles McDevitt	65th
Perseverance	1927	Christopher Martin	65th
Amicus	1980	Benjamin Campbell	
Amicus	1981	Joseph Massey	
Amicus	1982	Joseph Smith	
Amicus	1983	Samuel Bidwell	58th
Amicus	1984	John Lindy	58th
Eliza	2036	Edward Neil (Edward Read)	
Antares	2097	Francis Butcher	58th
Antares	2098	Heke	
Munford	2152	William Jones (William Adams)	96th
Munford	2205	Te Āhuru (Simon Peter)	
Exchange, then *Circassian*	2345	George Johnson	
Exchange, then *Circassian*	2346	James Woods	65th
Exchange, then *Circassian*	2349	Patrick Hayes	
Exchange, then *Circassian*	2374	Michael Morrissey	65th
Exchange, then *Circassian*	2375	George John Cartwright Goodwin (Godwin)	
Antares	2098x	John McGregor	

DATE OF TRIAL	TRIAL	OFFENCE	SENTENCE
20 December 1848	Wellington CM	Desertion; stealing a coat	14 yrs
30 October 1848	Auckland CM	Desertion	7 yrs
1 May 1849	Auckland CM	Desertion	7 yrs
16 May 1849	Auckland CM	Desertion	10 yrs
17 May 1849	Auckland CM	Firing at another soldier in the barracks	14 yrs
2 June 1849	Auckland SC	Stealing from his masters	7 yrs
8 June 1849	Wellington SC	Stealing money from the Treasury; I was on sentry duty at the time	15 yrs
8 June 1849	Wellington SC	Piracy	7 yrs
8 June 1849	Wellington SC	Wounding with intent to murder	Life
8 June 1849	Wellington SC	Wounding with intent to murder	Life
14 May 1849	Wellington CM	Larceny; striking a superior officer	Life
3 September 1849	Auckland SC	Cattle stealing	25 yrs
3 September 1849	Auckland SC	Cattle stealing	35 yrs
1 September 1849	Wellington CM	Burglary	10 yrs
1 September 1849	Wellington CM	Robbery with violence	15 yrs
1 December 1849	Wellington SC	Burglary	7 yrs
15 May 1850	Nelson SC	Stealing two old blankets	7 yrs
3 June 1850	Wellington SC	Robbery from the person with violence	7 yrs
18 March 1850	Wellington CM	Forging a cheque on regimental bank; I was colour sergeant	7 yrs
1 March 1850	Wellington SC	Robbery in a dwelling house	7 yrs
1 March 1850	Wellington SC	Robbery in a dwelling house	7 yrs
4 September 1850	Auckland SC	Larceny	7 yrs
3 September 1850	Auckland SC	Counterfeiting silver coin	14 yrs
4 September 1850	Auckland SC	Larceny	7 yrs
3 September 1850	Auckland SC	Larceny	7 yrs
3 September 1850	Auckland SC	Larceny	7 yrs
2 December 1850	Wellington SC	Larceny	7 yrs
10 December 1850	Auckland SC	Manslaughter	Life
4 March 1851	Auckland SC	Manslaughter of a native	Life
2 June 1851	Wellington SC	Stealing in a dwelling house	10 yrs
2 September 1851	Wellington SC	Larceny	7 yrs
9 November 1852	Lyttelton SC	Larceny	7 yrs
1 December 1852	Wellington SC	Robbery from the person with violence	15 yrs
1 December 1852	Wellington SC	Assault with intent to maim	7 yrs
1 December 1852	Wellington SC	Robbery from the person with violence	15 yrs
8 November 1852	Lyttelton SC	Stealing from his employer	7 yrs
10 December 1850; 1 March 1851	Auckland SC	Stealing wearing apparel	14 yrs (2 terms of 7 yrs)

NOTES

INTRODUCTION

1. Kristyn Harman, *Aboriginal Convicts: Australian, Khoisan, and Māori exiles* (Sydney: UNSW Press, 2012).
2. Verna Mossong referred to the first three prisoners being transported from New Zealand to Van Diemen's Land on the *Joseph Albino*, arriving in Hobart on 14 April 1844. This schooner carried three male intercolonial convicts but they were tried in Adelaide, South Australia, not in New Zealand. See Verna Mossong, 'Colonial chains: Convicts from New Zealand to Tasmania, Australia' in Garry Jeffery (ed.), *Landfall in Southern Seas: Proceedings of the 8th Australasian congress on genealogy and heraldry* (Christchurch: New Zealand Society of Genealogists, 1997), 125; 'Indents of convicts locally convicted or transported from other colonies', CON16/1/2, 90, Tasmanian Archive and Heritage Office, Hobart.
3. Heidi Huglin identified from archival records 125 prisoners sentenced in New Zealand to transportation. However, as Huglin noted, not all of these sentences were carried into effect. I identified 110 convicts transported from New Zealand to Van Diemen's Land by working methodically through all of the former penal colony's convict indents although, unusually, several convicts did not have surviving indents but instead were identified through their conduct register records. See Heidi Huglin, 'New Zealand's early convict history 1843–1853', *Legacy*, vol. 21, no. 1, 2009, 10–14.
4. Emmanuel Lewis, 'Conduct register of males arriving on non-convict ships or locally convicted', CON37/1/2, 392, Tasmanian Archive and Heritage Office, Hobart. Lewis was transported for stealing a sheep.
5. Robert Burnett, *Penal Transportation: An episode in New Zealand history* (Wellington: Victoria University of Wellington, 1978).
6. Mossong, 'Colonial chains', 125–37.
7. Huglin, 'New Zealand's early convict history', 10–14.
8. R v Thomas Larkins, from 'New Zealand's lost cases': www.victoria.ac.nz/law/nzlostcases/CaseDetails.aspx?casenumber=00487

CHAPTER 1

1. William Phelps Pickering, 'Indents of convicts locally convicted or transported from other colonies', CON16/1/2, 48, Tasmanian Archive and Heritage Office, Hobart.
2. *Launceston Advertiser*, 20 July 1837, 2.
3. *Hobart Town Courier*, 14 July 1837, 2.
4. Henry Reynolds, *The Other Side of the Frontier: Aboriginal resistance of the European invasion of Australia* (Victoria: Penguin, 1995), 21.

5.   Nicholas Clements, *The Black War: Fear, sex and resistance in Tasmania* (St Lucia: University of Queensland Press, 2014), 190.

6.   Penelope Edmonds, 'Collecting Looerryminer's "Testimony": Aboriginal women, sealers, and Quaker humanitarian anti-slavery thought and action in the Bass Strait Islands', *Australian Historical Studies*, vol. 45, no. 1, 2014, 18–22.

7.   Nick Brodie, *The Vandemonian War: The secret history of Britain's Tasmanian invasion* (Melbourne: Hardie Grant Books), 2017.

8.   Clements, *The Black War*, 1–3.

9.   *Colonial Times*, 15 October 1833, 2; *Colonial Times*, 11 January 1832, 2.

10. Hazel Petrie, *Outcasts of the Gods? The struggle over slavery in Māori New Zealand* (Auckland: Auckland University Press, 2015), 13.

11. See in particular N.J.B. Plomley (ed.), *Friendly Mission: The Tasmanian journals and papers of George Augustus Robinson 1829–1834*, 2nd edn (Launceston: Queen Victoria Museum and Art Gallery & Quintus Publishing, 2008).

12. See in particular N.J.B. Plomley (ed.), *Weep in Silence: A history of the Flinders Island Aboriginal settlement* (Hobart: Blubber Head Press, 1987).

13. Ian Brand, *The Convict Probation System: Van Diemen's Land 1839–1854* (Hobart: Blubber Head Press, 1990), 5.

14. Ibid., 1.

15. A.G.L. Shaw, *Convicts & the Colonies: A study of penal transportation from Great Britain & Ireland to Australia & other parts of the British Empire* (Melbourne: Melbourne University Press, 1966, 1998), 217–48.

16. Kathleen Fitzpatrick, 'Franklin, Sir John' from the Australian Dictionary of Biography: http://adb.anu.edu.au/biography/franklin-sir-john-2066/text2575

17. 'Hobart Town arrivals', *Sydney Monitor*, 13 November 1837, 2.

18. Pickering, 'Indent', CON16/1/2, 48; James Boyce, *1835: The founding of Melbourne and the conquest of Australia* (Melbourne: Black Inc., 2013), xiv.

19. *Perth Gazette and Western Australian Journal*, 8 March 1834, 246.

20. 'Dissolution of partnership', *Colonist*, 15 September 1838, 3.

21. *Hobart Town Courier*, 20 July 1838, 2.

22. Pickering, 'Indent', CON16/1/2, 48.

23. *Hobart Town Courier*, 15 March 1839, 3.

24. Rob White, 'Prisons', in Alison Alexander (ed.), *The Companion to Tasmanian History* (Hobart: Centre for Tasmanian Historical Studies, 2006), 289–90.

25. 'Launceston gaol', *Launceston Advertiser*, 10 May 1830, 3.

26. 'Original correspondence', *The Colonist and Van Diemen's Land Commercial and Agricultural Advertiser*, 1 April 1834, 4.

27. 'To P.A. Mulgrave Esq PM', *Cornwall Chronicle*, 26 September 1835, 2.

28. 'To the Editor', *Launceston Advertiser*, 21 January 1836, 3.

29. *Hobart Town Courier*, 15 March 1839, 3.

30. *Colonial Times*, 23 April 1839, 7; *Colonial Times*, 28 May 1839, 3; *Launceston Advertiser*, 6 June 1839, 4; *Colonial Times*, 3 September 1839, 3.

31. Pickering, 'Indent', CON16/1/2, 48; *Australasian Chronicle*, 20 March 1841, 3.

32. Alison Drummond & L.R. Drummond, *At Home in New Zealand: An illustrated*

history of everyday things before 1865 (Auckland: Blackwood & Janet Paul, 1967), 65–66; Anna Petersen, *New Zealanders at Home: A cultural history of domestic interiors, 1814–1914* (Dunedin: Otago University Press, 2001), 17.

33. Tony Ballantyne, *Entanglements of Empire: Missionaries, Māori, and the question of the body* (Auckland: Auckland University Press, 2015).

34. Ron Crosby, *The Musket Wars: A history of inter-iwi conflict 1806–45* (Auckland: Reed, 1999).

35. Trevor Bentley, *Tribal Guns and Tribal Gunners: The story of Māori artillery in 19th century New Zealand* (Christchurch: Willsonscott, 2013).

36. Crosby, *The Musket Wars*.

37. Claudia Orange, *The Treaty of Waitangi* (Wellington: Allen & Unwin, 1987).

38. K.A. Simpson, 'Hobson, William', from the Dictionary of New Zealand Biography: www.TeAra.govt.nz/en/biographies/1h29/hobson-william; 'Proclamation', *New Zealand Gazette and Wellington Spectator*, 28 August 1841, 2.

39. Margaret McClure, 'Auckland Region: The founding of Auckland: 1840–1869', Te Ara – The Encyclopedia of New Zealand: www.TeAra.govt.nz/en/auckland-region/page-7; Kristyn Harman, '"Some dozen raupo whares and a few tents": Remembering raupo houses in colonial New Zealand', *Journal of New Zealand Studies* no. 17, 2014, 39–57.

40. 'Auckland', *New Zealand Gazette and Wellington Spectator*, 28 August 1841, 3.

41. William Phelps Pickering, 'Conduct register of males arriving on non-convict ships or locally convicted', CON37/1/1, 214, Tasmanian Archive and Heritage Office, Hobart; Heidi Huglin, 'Penal transportation: New Zealand's early convict history 1843–1853, *Legacy*, vol. 21, no. 1, 2009, 11.

42. 'Neighbours: Early beginnings in Australasian Jewry' (Sydney: AM Rosenblum Jewish Museum): http://jewishonlinemuseum.org/neighbours-early beginnings-australasian-jewry

43. 'Sales by auction: Nathan & Joseph', *Daily Southern Cross*, 6 January 1844, 1; 'Notice', *New Zealand Gazette and Wellington Spectator*, 20 December 1843, 2; *New Zealand Gazette and Wellington Spectator*, 29 November 1843, 1; 'Neighbours: Early beginnings in Australasian Jewry'.

44. 'First sitting of the Legislative Council of New Zealand', *New Zealand Gazette and Wellington Spectator*, 30 July 1841, 1.

45. Ibid.

46. Robert Burnett, *Penal Transportation: An episode in New Zealand history* (Wellington: Victoria University of Wellington, 1978), 15.

47. 'VII Department of Public Works and Buildings', *New Zealand Gazette and Wellington Spectator*, 6 November 1841, 3.

48. 'Auckland', *Taranaki Herald*, 9 February 1853, 3.

49. R.C.J. Stone, 'Whitaker, Frederick', from the Dictionary of New Zealand Biography: www.TeAra.govt.nz/en/biographies/1w17/whitaker-frederick; 'Auckland', *New Zealand Gazette and Wellington Spectator*, 3 November 1841, 2.

50. Burnett, *Penal Transportation*, 11.

51. 'Auckland', *New Zealand Gazette and Wellington Spectator*, 3 November 1841, 2.

52. Robert Burnett, 'Hard Labour, Hard Fare and a Hard Bed': New Zealand's search for its own penal philosophy (Wellington: National Archives of New Zealand, 1995), 11.

53. Kristyn Harman, Aboriginal Convicts: Australian, Māori, and Khoisan exiles (Sydney: UNSW Press, 2012).

54. Burnett, Penal Transportation, 12.

55. Sheriff to Colonial Secretary, 20 December 1841, IA1 9, 1841/1613, Archives New Zealand, Wellington.

56. Harbour Master to Colonial Secretary, 20 December 1841, IA1 9, 1841/1613, Archives New Zealand, Wellington.

57. New Zealand Herald and Auckland Gazette, 25 December 1841, 4.

58. 'A convict's story: Transportation to Norfolk Island', Lyttelton Times, 25 April 1853, 4.

59. Burnett, Penal Transportation, 12.

60. Pickering, 'Conduct register', CON37/1/1, 214.

61. Burnett, Penal Transportation, 12.

62. Colonial Secretary of Van Diemen's Land to Colonial Secretary of New Zealand, 10 March 1842, IA1 11, 42/368, Archives New Zealand, Wellington.

63. John Johnson MD, Medical Report on William Phelps Pickering, 4 March 1842, IA1 11, 42/368, Archives New Zealand, Wellington.

64. Burnett, Penal Transportation, 12.

CHAPTER 2

1. André Brett, Acknowledge No Frontier: The creation and demise of New Zealand's provinces, 1853–76 (Dunedin: Otago University Press, 2016), 25–30.

2. New Zealand Gazette and Wellington Spectator, 26 March 1842, 2; Robert Burnett, Penal Transportation: An episode in New Zealand history (Wellington: Victoria University of Wellington, 1978), 15.

3. Miles Fairburn, 'Wakefield, Edward Gibbon', from the Dictionary of New Zealand Biography: www. TeAra.govt.nz/en/biographies/1w4/wakefield-edward-gibbon

4. New Zealand Gazette and Wellington Spectator, 6 February 1841, 2.

5. New Zealand Gazette and Wellington Spectator, 26 January 1842, 2. These replaced the earlier courts of requests and courts of petty sessions.

6. New Zealand Gazette and Wellington Spectator, 26 March 1842, 2; Robert Burnett, Penal Transportation: An episode in New Zealand history (Wellington: Victoria University of Wellington, 1978), 13.

7. New Zealand Gazette and Wellington Spectator, 23 April 1842, 2. The judge was assisted by a jury when called on to hear criminal cases.

8. New Zealand Gazette and Wellington Spectator, 20 April 1842, 2.

9. Ibid.

10. James Beckett, 'Conduct register of males arriving on non-convict ships or locally convicted', CON37/1/1, 215, Tasmanian Archive and Heritage Office, Hobart.

11. 'Government notice', *New Zealand Gazette and Wellington Spectator*, 16 August 1842, 4.

12. *New Zealand Gazette and Wellington Spectator*, 20 April 1842, 2.

13. Julie Bremner. 'Barrett, Richard', from the Dictionary of New Zealand Biography: www.TeAra.govt.nz/en/biographies/1b10/barrett-richard

14. 'County court', *New Zealand Colonist and Port Nicholson Advertiser*, 23 August 1842, 3.

15. Ibid.

16. Ibid.

17. Ibid.

18. Bruce Hardie, 'Table 28: Buildings in Wellington', *Statistics of New Zealand for the Crown Colony Period 1840–1852* (Auckland: Auckland University College, Department of Economics, 1955), 36.

19. 'Police office', *New Zealand Gazette and Wellington Spectator*, 14 January 1843, 2.

20. This was postponed until Saturday 21 January because of the weather conditions. See *New Zealand Gazette and Wellington Spectator*, 21 January 1843, 2.

21. Ian Wards, *The Shadow of the Land: A study of British policy and racial conflict in New Zealand 1832–1852* (Wellington: Department of Internal Affairs, 1968), 63.

22. *New Zealand Colonist and Port Nicholson Advertiser*, 17 January 1843, 4.

23. 'List of gentlemen presented to His Excellency', *New Zealand Colonist and Port Nicholson Advertiser*, 24 January 1843, 3.

24. George French Angas, *Savage Life and Scenes of Australia and New Zealand, Volume One* (Adelaide: Libraries Board of South Australia, 1969 facsimile edn), 234.

25. 'List of gentlemen presented to His Excellency', *New Zealand Colonist and Port Nicholson Advertiser*, 24 January 1843, 3.

26. 'Shipping intelligence', *New Zealand Gazette and Wellington Spectator*, 9 March 1842, 2.

27. 'County court', *New Zealand Gazette and Wellington Spectator*, 21 January 1843, 3.

28. George Delvin Nugent, 'Conduct register of males arriving on non-convict ships or locally convicted', CON37/1/1, 216, Tasmanian Archive and Heritage Office, Hobart.

29. 'Ten pounds reward', *New Zealand Colonist and Port Nicholson Advertiser*, 31 January 1843, 2.

30. Nugent, 'Conduct register', CON37/1/1, 216.

31. 'County court', *New Zealand Gazette and Wellington Spectator*, 21 January 1843, 3; Nugent, 'Conduct register', CON37/1/1, 216.

32. 'County court', *New Zealand Colonist and Port Nicholson Advertiser*, 24 March 1843, 2; 'County court', *New Zealand Gazette and Wellington Spectator*, 1 March 1843, 3.

33. William Clarke, 'Conduct register of males arriving on non-convict ships or locally convicted', CON37/1/1, 217, Tasmanian Archive and Heritage Office, Hobart; James Clarke, 'Conduct register of males arriving on non-convict ships or locally convicted', CON37/1/1, 218, Tasmanian Archive and Heritage Office, Hobart.

34. 'County court', *New Zealand Gazette and Wellington Spectator*, 1 March 1843, 3.

35. Ibid.

36. William Clarke and James Clarke, 'Indents of convicts locally convicted or transported from other colonies', CON16/1/2, 48, Tasmanian Archive and Heritage Office, Hobart.

37. *New Zealand Colonist and Port Nicholson Advertiser*, 22 April 1843, 2.

38. *New Zealand Colonist and Port Nicholson Advertiser*, 21 April 1843, 2.

39. *New Zealand Colonist and Port Nicholson Advertiser*, 22 April 1843, 2.

40. Burnett, *Penal Transportation*, 16.

41. See, for example, advertisements in *Te Karere o Nui Tireni* on 1 September 1842, 38; 1 July 1843, 28; 1 August 1843, 34; 2 October 1843, 2; 1 November 1843, 46; and 1 June 1844, 1–2. Thanks to Lachy Paterson for providing these references.

42. *New Zealand Gazette and Wellington Spectator*, 17 May 1843, 2; 'A list of ordinances relevant to the courts in New Zealand during the 1840s': www.victoria.ac.nz/law/nzlostcases/Ordinances_1840s.aspx

43. 'Public meeting', *New Zealand Gazette and Wellington Spectator*, 2 April 1842, 3.

44. G.P. Barton, 'Martin, William', from the Dictionary of New Zealand Biography: www.TeAra.govt.nz/en/biographies/1m21/martin-william

45. Steven Oliver, 'Maketu, Wirimu Kingi', from the Dictionary of New Zealand Biography: www.TeAra.govt.nz/en/biographies/1m5/maketu-wirimu-kingi

46. Barton, 'Martin, William'

47. Atholl Anderson, Judith Binney & Aroha Harris (eds), *Tangata Whenua: An illustrated history* (Wellington: Bridget Williams Books, 2014), 232.

48. 'Law intelligence: Supreme Court, April sittings', *New Zealand Colonist and Port Nicholson Advertiser*, 21 April 1843, 2.

49. Patrick Mullins, 'Conduct register of males arriving on non-convict ships or locally convicted', CON37/1/1, 219, Tasmanian Archives and Heritage Office, Hobart; Patrick Mullins, 'Indents of convicts locally convicted or transported from other colonies', CON16/1/2, 48, Tasmanian Archive and Heritage Office, Hobart.

50. Joseph Root, 'Conduct register of males arriving on non-convict ships or locally convicted', CON37/1/1, 221, Tasmanian Archive and Heritage Office, Hobart; William Root, 'Conduct register of males arriving on non-convict ships or locally convicted', CON37/1/1, 220, Tasmanian Archive and Heritage Office, Hobart.

51. Francis or Daniel McCarthy, 'Conduct register of males arriving on non-convict ships or locally convicted', CON37/1/1, 222, Tasmanian Archive and Heritage Office, Hobart.

52. 'Historical sketch of the colonization of New Zealand', *New Zealand Gazette and Wellington Spectator*, 21 August 1839, 4. The Ngāpuhi rangatira named as magistrates were Ruatara, his nephew Hongi Hika and Korokoro.

53. 'County court for the southern district of the colony', *New Zealand Gazette and Wellington Spectator*, 29 June 1842, 3; 'County court for the southern district of the colony, *New Zealand Gazette and Wellington Spectator*, 2 July 1842, 3.

54. Ibid.

55. John Pratt, *Punishment in a Perfect Society: The New Zealand penal system 1840–1939* (Wellington: Victoria University Press, 1992), 42.

56. 'Law intelligence, Supreme Court, April sittings', *New Zealand Colonist and Port Nicholson Advertiser*, 21 April 1843, 2.

57. 'Public meeting', *New Zealand Gazette and Wellington Spectator*, 12 November 1842, 2; *New Zealand Gazette and Wellington Spectator*, 4 May 1842, 2.

58. *New Zealand Colonist*, 5 August 1842, 2.

59. 'Married', *New Zealand Colonist and Port Nicholson Advertiser*, 13 January 1843, 2.

60. *New Zealand Gazette and Wellington Spectator*, 18 April 1840. 1.

61. McCarthy, 'Conduct register', CON37/1/1, 222.

62. 'Law intelligence, Supreme Court, April sittings', *New Zealand Colonist and Port Nicholson Advertiser*, 21 April 1843, 2.

63. 'County court', *New Zealand Colonist and Port Nicholson Advertiser*, 30 December 1842, 2. Constable James Futter was the author's great-grandmother's great-grandfather. He arrived in Wellington on 17 March 1841 from England on the *Lady Nugent* as a New Zealand Company settler.

64. Henry Rogers, 'Conduct register of males arriving on non-convict ships or locally convicted', CON37/1/1, 226, Tasmanian Archive and Heritage Office, Hobart; 'Law intelligence, Supreme Court, April sittings', *New Zealand Colonist and Port Nicholson Advertiser*, 21 April 1843, 2.

65. William Jackson, 'Conduct register of males arriving on non-convict ships or locally convicted', CON37/1/1, 223, Tasmanian Archive and Heritage Office, Hobart.

66. 'Law intelligence, Supreme Court, April sittings', *New Zealand Colonist and Port Nicholson Advertiser*, 21 April 1843, 2.

67. *New Zealand Gazette and Wellington Spectator*, 26 April 1843, 2.

68. 'Table of shipping', *New Zealand Gazette and Wellington Spectator*, 2 April 1842, 5.

69. S.A. Wood, *Daily Southern Cross*, 27 May 1843, 1.

70. 'To Agriculturalists', *Daily Southern Cross*, 27 May 1843, 1.

71. Burnett, *Penal Transportation*, 18; 'Table of shipping', *New Zealand Gazette and Wellington Spectator*, 2 April 1842, 5; 'Shipping intelligence: Port of Hobart Town', *Courier*, 30 June 1843, 2.

72. *Daily Southern Cross*, 13 January 1844, 3.

73. 'An ordinance for establishing a Supreme Court', *New Zealand Gazette and Wellington Spectator*, 17 February 1844, 4.

CHAPTER 3

1. Kristyn Harman, *Aboriginal Convicts: Australian, Khoisan, and Maori exiles* (Sydney: UNSW Press, 2012).

2. See, in particular, Hazel Petrie, *Chiefs of Industry: Māori tribal enterprise in early colonial New Zealand* (Auckland: Auckland University Press, 2007); Angela Wanhalla, *In/visible Sight: The mixed-descent families of southern New Zealand* (Wellington: Bridget Williams Books, 2009).

3. Simon Barnard, *Convict Tattoos: Marked men and women of Australia* (Melbourne: Text, 2016).

4. 'Movement of vessels', *Australasian Chronicle*, 20 July 1843, 3.

5. *Launceston Examiner*, 5 July 1843, 6.

6. 'Shipping intelligence: Port of Hobart Town', *Courier*, 30 June 1843, 2.

7. Ian Brand, *The Convict Probation System: Van Diemen's Land 1839–1854* (Hobart: Blubber Head Press, 1990), 13–23.

8. Ibid.

9. Ibid.

10. William Phelps Pickering, 'Indents of convicts locally convicted or transported from other colonies', CON16/1/2, 48, Tasmanian Archive and Heritage Office, Hobart; Robert Burnett, *Penal Transportation: An episode in New Zealand history* (Wellington: Victoria University of Wellington, 1978), 12.

11. E.J. Tapp, 'Hobson, William (1793–1842), from the Australian Dictionary of Biography: http://adb.anu.edu.au/biography/hobson-william-2189

12. Pickering, 'Indent', CON16/1/2, 48.

13. James Beckett, 'Indents of convicts locally convicted or transported from other colonies', CON16/1/2, 48, Tasmanian Archives and Heritage Office, Hobart.

14. Damaris Bairstow, *A Million Pounds, a Million Acres: The pioneer settlement of the Australian Agricultural Company* (Sydney: D. Bairstow, 2003); Mark Hannah, 'Aboriginal workers in the Australian Agricultural Company, 1824–1857', *Labour History* 82 (2002), 17–33.

15. Beckett, 'Indent', CON16/1/2, 48; James Beckett, Certificate of Freedom, 4/4320, Reel 992, T/L 32/376, State Archives & Records New South Wales, Sydney.

16. Beckett, 'Indent', CON16/1/2, 48.

17. George Delvin Nugent, 'Indents of convicts locally convicted or transported from other colonies', CON16/1/2, 48, Tasmanian Archive and Heritage Office, Hobart.

18. William Clarke, 'Indents of convicts locally convicted or transported from other colonies', CON16/1/2, 48, Tasmanian Archive and Heritage Office, Hobart; James Clarke, 'Indents of convicts locally convicted or transported from other colonies', CON16/1/2, 48, Tasmanian Archive and Heritage Office, Hobart.

19. James Clarke, 'Indent', CON16/1/2, 48.

20. Trial of James Thompson and John Jones, 6 January 1840, Old Bailey Online, (t18400106-504).

21. James Thompson, 'Conduct register of males arriving in the period of the probation system', CON33/1/5, Tasmanian Archive and Heritage Office, Hobart.

22. James Clarke, 'Indent', CON16/1/2, 48.

23. Patrick Mullen [Mullins], Annotated Printed Indenture, NRS 12189, X638, microfiche 716, State Archives & Records New South Wales, Sydney.

24. Patrick Mullins, 'Indents of convicts locally convicted or transported from other colonies', CON16/1/2, 48, Tasmanian Archive and Heritage Office, Hobart.

25. William Root, 'Indents of convicts locally convicted or transported from other colonies', CON16/1/2, 50, Tasmanian Archive and Heritage Office, Hobart; Joseph

Root, 'Indents of convicts locally convicted or transported from other colonies', CON16/1/2, 50, Tasmanian Archive and Heritage Office, Hobart.

26. Daniel (or Francis) McCarthy, 'Indents of convicts locally convicted or transported from other colonies', CON16/1/2, 50, Tasmanian Archive and Heritage Office, Hobart.

27. William Jackson, Bound Indentures, NRS 12188, 4/4005, Microfiche 636, State Archives & Records New South Wales, Sydney.

28. E. Flinn, 'Bowen, John (1780–1827)', from the Australian Dictionary of Biography: http://adb.anu.edu.au/biography/bowen-john-1811/text2065

29. Charles Rowley, 'Conduct register of males arriving on non-convict ships or locally convicted', CON37/1/1, 224, Tasmanian Archive and Heritage Office, Hobart.

30. Charles Rowley, 'Indents of convicts locally convicted or transported from other colonies', CON16/1/2, 50, Tasmanian Archive and Heritage Office, Hobart.

31. John Coghlan, 'Indents of convicts locally convicted or transported from other colonies', CON16/1/2, 50, Tasmanian Archive and Heritage Office, Hobart.

32. Henry Rogers, 'Indents of convicts locally convicted or transported from other colonies', CON16/1/2, 52, Tasmanian Archive and Heritage Office, Hobart.

33. 'Runaways', *Launceston Examiner*, 12 July 1843, 3.

34. Patrick Mullins, 'Conduct register of males arriving on non-convict ships or locally convicted', CON37/1/1, 219, Tasmanian Archive and Heritage Office, Hobart; William Jackson, 'Conduct register of males arriving on non-convict ships or locally convicted', CON37/1/1, 223, Tasmanian Archive and Heritage Office, Hobart.

35. John Coghlan, 'Conduct register of males arriving on non-convict ships or locally convicted', CON37/1/1, 225, Tasmanian Archive and Heritage Office, Hobart.

36. 'Runaways', *Launceston Examiner*, 12 July 1843, 3.

37. Brand, *The Convict Probation System*, 225–26.

CHAPTER 4

1. For Aboriginal segregation, see in particular Richard Broome, *Aboriginal Australians: Black responses to white dominance, 1788–2001* (New South Wales: Allen & Unwin, 2001).

2. James Semple Kerr, *Design for Convicts: An account of design for convict establishments in the Australian colonies during the transportation era* (Sydney: Library of Australian History, 1984), 146.

3. Rick Bullers, *Convict Probation and the Evolution of Jetties at Cascades, the Coal Mines, Impression Bay and Saltwater River, Tasman Peninsula, Tasmania: An historical perspective* (South Australia: Department of Archaeology, Flinders University, 2005), 3.

4. John Pratt, *Punishment in the Perfect Society: The New Zealand penal system 1840–1939* (Wellington: Victoria University Press, 1992), 15–17.

5. Ian Brand, *The Convict Probation System: Van Diemen's Land 1839–1854* (Hobart: Blubber Head Press, 1990), 182–84.
6. Ibid.
7. James Beckett, 'Conduct register of males arriving on non-convict ships or locally convicted', CON37/1/1, 215, Tasmanian Archive and Heritage Office, Hobart.
8. 'Police court: Larceny', *Tasmanian Daily News*, 25 September 1855, 4.
9. Patrick Mullins, 'Conduct register of males arriving on non-convict ships or locally convicted', CON37/1/1, 219, Tasmanian Archive and Heritage Office, Hobart.
10. Patrick Mullins, 'Register of applications for permission to marry', CON52/1/4, Tasmanian Archive and Heritage Office, Hobart.
11. Margaret Mannion, 'Indents of female convicts', CON15/1/6, Tasmanian Archive and Heritage Office, Hobart; Margaret Mannion, 'Description list', CON19/1/9, Tasmanian Archive and Heritage Office, Hobart.
12. Mullins and Mannion, 'Register of applications for permission to marry', CON52/1/3, 318, Tasmanian Archive and Heritage Office, Hobart.
13. Mullins, 'Conduct register', CON37/1/1, 219.
14. Thomas Larkin and Margaret Mannion, 'Register of applications for permission to marry', CON52/1/7, 260, Tasmanian Archive and Heritage Office, Hobart.
15. Margaret Mannion, 'Conduct register of female convicts', CON41/1/28, Tasmanian Archive and Heritage Office, Hobart.
16. 'Police court', *Launceston Examiner*, 9 September 1871, 3.
17. James Thompson, 'Conduct register of males arriving in the period of the probation system', CON33/1/5, Tasmanian Archive and Heritage Office, Hobart.
18. Brand, *The Convict Probation System*, 197–98.
19. Thompson, 'Conduct register', CON33/1/5.
20. Brand, *The Convict Probation System*, 191.
21. Ibid., 192.
22. Henry Rogers, 'Conduct register of males arriving on non-convict ships or locally convicted', CON37/1/1, 226, Tasmanian Archive and Heritage Office, Hobart.
23. Rogers, 'Conduct register', CON37/1/1, 226.
24. John Coghlan, 'Conduct register of males arriving on non-convict ships or locally convicted', CON37/1/1, 225, Tasmanian Archive and Heritage Office, Hobart.
25. Joseph Root, 'Conduct register of males arriving on non-convict ships or locally convicted', CON37/1/1, 221, Tasmanian Archive and Heritage Office, Hobart.
26. Brand, *The Convict Probation System*, 184–85.
27. Joseph Root, 'Conduct register', CON37/1/1, 221.
28. Daniel or Francis McCarthy, 'Conduct register of males arriving on non-convict ships or locally convicted', CON37/1/1, 222, Tasmanian Archive and Heritage Office, Hobart.
29. Ibid.
30. Brand, *The Convict Probation System*, 185–86.
31. William Derrincourt, ed. Louis Becke, *Old Convict Days* (Harmondsworth, UK: Penguin, 1975 [1899]), 53–57.

32. William Clarke, 'Conduct register of males arriving on non-convict ships or locally convicted', CON37/1/1, 217, Tasmanian Archive and Heritage Office, Hobart.

33. Richard Whithous, 'Conduct register of males arriving on non-convict ships or locally convicted', CON37/1/5, 1550, Tasmanian Archive and Heritage Office, Hobart.

34. Robert Burnett, *Penal Transportation: An episode in New Zealand history* (Wellington: Victoria University of Wellington, 1978), 18–19.

35. William Ellis, 'Conduct register of males arriving on non-convict ships or locally convicted', CON37/1/1, 303, Tasmanian Archive and Heritage Office, Hobart.

36. William Jackson, 'Conduct register of males arriving on non-convict ships or locally convicted', CON37/1/1, 223, Tasmanian Archive and Heritage Office, Hobart.

37. Charles Rowley, 'Conduct register of males arriving on non-convict ships or locally convicted', CON37/1/1, 224, Tasmanian Archive and Heritage Office, Hobart.

38. Ancestry.com, *Tasmania, Australia, Convict Court and Selected Records, 1800–1899* [database online]. Provo, UT, USA: Ancestry.com Operations, Inc., 2015. Original data: Tasmanian Colonial Convict, Passenger and Land Records. Various collections (30 series). Tasmanian Archive and Heritage Office, Hobart.

39. 'Government Order No. 35', Colonial Secretary's Office, *Hobart Town Courier*, 14 June 1828, 1.

40. Brand, *The Convict Probation System*, 175–77.

41. Ibid.

42. Charles Rowley, 'Conduct register', CON37/1/1, 224.

43. William Root, 'Conduct register of males arriving on non-convict ships or locally convicted', CON37/1/1, 220, Tasmanian Archive and Heritage Office, Hobart.

44. Ibid.

45. N.J.B. (Brian) Plomley (ed.), *Friendly Mission: The Tasmanian journals and papers of George Augustus Robinson 1829–1834*, 2nd edn (Launceston: Queen Victoria Museum and Art Gallery and Quintus Publishing, 2008), 49–140.

46. William Root, 'Conduct register', CON37/1/1, 220.

47. George Delvin Nugent, 'Conduct register of males arriving on non-convict ships or locally convicted', CON37/1/1, 216, Tasmanian Archive and Heritage Office, Hobart.

48. 'Coroner's inquest', *Colonial Times*, 2 June 1848, 3.

49. *Hobarton Guardian, or, True Friend of Tasmania*, 19 August 1848, 2.

50. Nugent, 'Conduct register', CON37/1/1, 216.

51. Ibid.

52. 'Museum of Natural History', *Banner*, 30 June 1854, 7–8.

53. L.K. Paszkowski, 'Blandowski, William (1822–1878)', from the Australian Dictionary of Biography: http://adb.anu.edu.au/biography/blandowski-william-3014/text4413

54. 'Museum of Natural History', *Banner*, 30 June 1854, 7–8.

55. 'Death from lock-jaw', *Sydney Morning Herald*, 17 August 1857, 5.

56. William Phelps Pickering, 'Conduct register of males arriving on non-convict ships or locally convicted', CON37/1/1, 214, Tasmanian Archive and Heritage Office, Hobart.

57. Reverend John F. Churton, transmitting petition from convict W.P. Pickering, 29 March 1844, IA1 Box 30, 1844/763, 39, Archives New Zealand, Wellington.

58. Ibid.

59. This quotation is from *Aeneid* 1.574 with the standard version reading 'Tros Tyriusque mihi nullo discrimine agetur'. Fifth-century author Nonius Marcellus (in *De compendiosa doctrina*) concluded this quotation with 'habetur', indicating that FitzGerald may have had access to that edition. Thanks to Graeme Miles for a fruitful discussion on this topic.

60. Reverend John F. Churton, transmitting petition from convict W.P. Pickering, 29 March 1844, IA1 Box 30, 1844/763, 39, Archives New Zealand, Wellington.

61. Pickering, 'Conduct register', CON37/1/1, 214.

62. 'Convict department', *Colonial Times*, 11 February 1845, 2.

63. Marriage Certificate of William Phelps Pickering and Jane Lightfoot Dodsworth, 82/1846 V184682 31C Registrar of Births, Deaths, and Marriages, Sydney, New South Wales.

64. William Phelps Pickering to Colonial Secretary, letter dated 10 February 1847 and marginalia, IA1 54, 1847/261, Archives New Zealand, Wellington.

65. William Phelps Pickering, Application for Bush Licence at Port Cooper dated 27 June 1849, NM8 37, 1849/751, 10, Archives New Zealand, Wellington.

66. William Phelps Pickering, Applying for Employment, 24 March 1849, NM8 36, 1849/300, 7, Archives New Zealand, Wellington; William Phelps Pickering to Colonial Secretary New Munster, Application for Employment, 12 July 1850, NM8 41, 1850/576, 15, Archives New Zealand, Wellington.

67. Salmon v. Pickering, from New Zealand's Lost Cases: www.victoria.ac.nz/law/nzlostcases/CaseDetails.aspx?casenumber=00212

68. *Wellington Independent*, 12 June 1858, 4.

69. Margery Renwick, 'The Karori Hotel', *Stockade* 43, 2011, 11–16.

70. *Wellington Independent*, 10 November 1863, 3.

71. *Wellington Independent*, 22 May 1871, 2.

72. N.A.C. McMillan, 'Tempsky, Gustavus Ferninand von', from the Dictionary of New Zealand Biography: www.teara.govt.nz/en/biographies/1t90/tempsky-gustavus-ferdinand-von

73. Peter Cobham to Kristyn Harman, email dated 16 July 2016.

74. Marriage Certificate of William Phelps Pickering and Grace Martha Palmer, 29 August 1873, 1873, 3595, Registrar of Births, Deaths, and Marriages, Melbourne, Victoria.

75. *Evening Post*, 27 August 1877, 2; Will of William Phelps Pickering, died 26 August 1877, Series 6029, 23/1096, Item R22205362, Archives New Zealand, Wellington.

CHAPTER 5

1. Ron Palenski, *The Making of New Zealanders* (Auckland: Auckland University Press, 2012), 129.

2. 'Z', Letter to the Editor, *New Zealand Journal*, cited in Paul Buddee, *Fate of the Artful Dodger: Parkhurst boys transported to Australia and New Zealand, 1842–1852* (Perth: St George Books, 1984), 58.

3. Buddee, *Fate of the Artful Dodger*, 5, 24.

4. Roderick Floud and Kenneth Wachter, 'Poverty and physical stature: Evidence on the standard of living of London boys 1770–1870', *Social Science History*, vol. 6, no. 4, 1982, 424.

5. Edwin Rose, 'Register of prisoners', Gloucestershire Archives, Q/Gc/5/6, Gloucestershire Prison Collections, Gloucester, England.

6. Edwin Rose, 'Register of prisoners', Q/Gc/5/6.

7. Buddee, *Fate of the Artful Dodger*, 33–34, 167.

8. Ensign A.D. Best, journal entry for 25 October 1842, cited in Buddee, *Fate of the Artful Dodger*, 59.

9. Buddee, *Fate of the Artful Dodger*, 63.

10. 'The Parkhurst boys', *New Zealand Gazette and Wellington Spectator*, 10 December 1842, 3.

11. *New Zealand Gazette and Wellington Spectator*, 14 December 1842, 2.

12. *New Zealand Colonist and Port Nicholson Advertiser*, 13 January 1843, 2.

13. David Rough, Guardian of Boys, Auckland, to the Secretary of State for the Colonies, letter dated 30 March 1843, IA1 Box 19, 1843/274, Item 22, Archives New Zealand, Wellington.

14. Felton Mathew, Chief Police Magistrate, Police Office, Auckland, to the Chief Colonial Magistrate, letter dated 3 April 1843, IA1 Box 20, 1843/521, Item 11, Archives New Zealand, Wellington.

15. 'Auckland', *New Zealand Colonist and Port Nicholson Advertiser*, 2 June 1843, 3.

16. 'Auckland', *Nelson Examiner and New Zealand Chronicle*, 17 June 1843, 267; Buddee, *Fate of the Artful Dodger*, 72–73.

17. Thomas Jordan, '"Stay and starve, or go and prosper!" Juvenile emigration from Great Britain in the nineteenth century, *Social Science History*, vol. 9, no. 2, 1985, 150.

18. Buddee, *Fate of the Artful Dodger*, 69–72.

19. Ibid., 74.

20. 'The *Mandarin*', *Nelson Examiner and New Zealand Chronicle*, 4 November 1843, 346.

21. Trial of George Bottomley, 16 December 1839, Old Bailey Online (t18391216-314).

22. Buddee, *Fate of the Artful Dodger*, 168.

23. Thomas F. McGauran, *Mandarin* ship, letter dated 17 November 1843 to Governor Willoughby Shortland, IA1 Box 26, 1843/2139, Item 32, Archives New Zealand, Wellington.

24. Felton Mathew, Chief Police Magistrate, Police Office, Auckland, to the Colonial Secretary, letter dated 14 November 1843, IA1 Box 26, 1843/2128, Item 30, Archives New Zealand, Wellington.

25. Greg Jackman, 'Get thee to church: Hard work, godliness and tourism at Australia's first rural reformatory', *Australasian Historical Archaeology*, vol. 19, 2001, 9.

26. Felton Mathew, Chief Police Magistrate, Police Office, Auckland, to the Colonial Secretary, letter dated 14 November 1843, IA1 Box 26, 1843/2128, Item 30, Archives New Zealand, Wellington.

27. Heather Shore, 'Transportation, penal ideology and the experience of juvenile offenders in England and Australia in the nineteenth century', *Crime, History & Societies*, vol. 6, no. 2, 2002, 7.

28. David Rough, Guardian of Boys, Auckland, to the Governor, letter dated 22 November 1843, IA1 Box 30, 1843/2156, Item 28, Archives New Zealand, Wellington.

29. Ibid.

30. Felton Mathew, Chief Police Magistrate, Police Office, Auckland, to the Colonial Secretary, letter dated 21 March 1844, IA1 Box 30, 1844/710, Item 28, Archives New Zealand, Wellington.

31. 'Supreme Court criminal sittings', *New Zealander*, 4 September 1850, 3.

32. Felton Mathew, Chief Police Magistrate, Police Office, Auckland, to the Colonial Secretary, letter dated 21 March 1844, IA1 Box 30, 1844/710, Item 28, Archives New Zealand, Wellington.

33. Felton Mathew, Chief Police Magistrate, Police Office, Auckland, to the Colonial Secretary, letter dated 18 March 1844, IA1 Box 30, 1844/710, Item 28, including annotations, Archives New Zealand, Wellington.

34. Ibid.

35. Felton Mathew, Chief Police Magistrate, Police Office, Auckland, to the Colonial Secretary, letter dated 28 June 1844, IA1 Box 34, 1844/1507, Item 23, including annotations, Archives New Zealand, Wellington.

36. Dowie's name was misspelt as Henry Bulbe Dowie. 'Domestic intelligence', *Daily Southern Cross*, 7 September 1844, 4.

37. Trial of Henry Butler Dowie, 18 June 1838, Old Bailey Online (t18380618-1486); Verna Mossong, 'Colonial chains: Convicts from New Zealand to Tasmania, Australia', in Garry Jeffery (ed.), *Landfall in Southern Seas: Proceedings of the 8th Australasian congress on genealogy and heraldry* (Christchurch: New Zealand Society of Genealogists, 1997), 128.

38. 'Domestic intelligence', *Daily Southern Cross*, 7 September 1844, 4.

39. Henry Butler Dowie, 'Conduct register of males arriving on non-convict ships or locally convicted', CON37/1/2, 393, Tasmanian Archive and Heritage Office, Hobart; Ian Brand, *The Convict Probation System: Van Diemen's Land 1839-1854* (Hobart: Blubberhead Press, 1990), 188–89.

40. Henry Butler Dowie and Barbara Angus, 'Register of applications for permission to marry', CON52/1/4, RDG37/9: 1850/757, Tasmanian Archive and Heritage Office, Hobart.

41. 'Rural municipality of Evandale', *Launceston Examiner*, 30 December 1865, 5.
42. 'Notices of births, marriages and deaths', *Launceston Examiner*, 15 August 1889. See Alison Alexander, *Tasmania's Convicts: How felons build a free society* (Crows Nest, New South Wales: Allen & Unwin, 2014) for a pertinent book-length discussion about the long-term impacts of convictism on Tasmanian society and convicts' varied life outcomes.
43. 'Police court', *New Zealander*, 27 September 1845, 2.
44. 'Supreme Court', *New Zealander*, 6 December 1845, 3.
45. Ibid.
46. 'Shipping intelligence', *New Zealander*, 13 December 1845, 2.
47. 'Shipping intelligence', *New Zealander*, 7 February 1846, 2.
48. Timothy O'Meara, 'Indents of convicts locally convicted or transported from other colonies', CON16/1/3, 224, Tasmanian Archive and Heritage Office, Hobart; Timothy O'Meara, 'Conduct register of males arriving on non-convict ships or locally convicted', CON37/1/2, 600, Tasmanian Archive and Heritage Office, Hobart.
49. Joseph Massey, 'Conduct register of males arriving on non-convict ships or locally convicted', CON37/1/6, 1981, Tasmanian Archive and Heritage Office, Hobart; 'Supreme Court, criminal session', *Daily Southern Cross*, 6 September 1850, 3.
50. 'Resident magistrate's court', *Daily Southern Cross*, 26 July 1850, 3; 'Supreme Court, criminal session', *Daily Southern Cross*, 6 September 1850, 3.
51. Massey, 'Conduct register', CON37/1/6, 1981t.
52. Edwin Rose, 'Indents of convicts locally convicted or transported from other colonies', CON16/1/3, 224, Tasmanian Archive and Heritage Office, Hobart; George Bottomley, 'Indents of convicts locally convicted or transported from other colonies', CON16/1/3, 224, Tasmanian Archive and Heritage Office, Hobart.
53. Edwin Rose, 'Conduct register of males arriving on non-convict ships or locally convicted', CON37/1/2, 602, Tasmanian Archive and Heritage Office, Hobart.
54. Brand, *The Convict Probation System*, 181–82.
55. Rose, 'Conduct register', CON37/1/2, 602.
56. 'Marks of seton' implies that Bottomley had received treatment for inflammation of the eyes through a seton having been inserted through his brain and spinal cord; the resulting inflammation was thought to enable the eyes to return to their natural state. See the review of Martyn Payne, *The Institutes of Medicine*, (New York: Harper & Brothers, 1858) in *Dublin Quarterly Journal of Medical Science*, vol. 28, 1859, 444.
57. For a discussion of the Cotton legacy in Tasmania, including a summary of the debate over whether the Cottons secretly harboured Aboriginal people in their garden, see Nicholas Brodie, 'Quaker dreaming: The "lost" archive and the Aborigines of Van Diemen's Land', *Journal of Religious History*, vol. 40, no. 3, September 2016, 303–25.
58. George Bottomley, 'Conduct register of males arriving on non-convict ships or locally convicted', CON37/1/2, 601, Tasmanian Archive and Heritage Office, Hobart.

59. George Williams alias Bottomley, Victoria Police Gazette, series 10958, reels 3129–3143, 3594–3606, 8 July 1858, 281, State Archives & Records New South Wales, Sydney.

60. George Williams alias Bottomly, Victoria Police Gazette, series 10958, reels 3129–3143, 3594–3606, 19 May 1859, 357, State Archives & Records New South Wales, Sydney.

61. *Star*, 4 September 1863, 2.

62. 'The late fatal affray with the police at Lockwood', *Bendigo Advertiser*, 3 September 1863, 2.

CHAPTER 6

1. 'The 65th Regiment', *New Zealand Spectator and Cook's Strait Guardian*, 13 November 1847, 2.

2. 'Colonial news', *New Zealand Gazette and Wellington Spectator*, 13 June 1840, 2.

3. Vincent O'Malley, *Beyond the Imperial Frontier: The contest for colonial New Zealand* (Wellington: Bridget Williams Books, 2014), 73.

4. 'Colonial news', *New Zealand Gazette and Wellington Spectator*, 13 June 1840, 2.

5. James Belich, *The New Zealand Wars* (Auckland: Penguin Books, 1998), 21.

6. Ibid., 29, 36, 41, 48, 58.

7. 'Wanganui petty sessions', *New Zealand Gazette and Wellington Spectator*, 14 February 1844, 4.

8. 'Supreme Court', *New Zealand Spectator and Cook's Strait Guardian*, 21 June 1845, 2.

9. Robert Burnett, *Penal Transportation: An episode in New Zealand history* (Wellington: Victoria University of Wellington, 1978), 27, 59.

10. William Spyke, 'Conduct register of males arriving on non-convict ships or locally convicted', CON37/1/4, 1026, Tasmanian Archive and Heritage Office, Hobart.

11. John Green, 'Conduct register of males arriving on non-convict ships or locally convicted', CON37/1/2, 484, Tasmanian Archive and Heritage Office, Hobart; Richard Conway, 'Conduct register of males arriving on non-convict ships or locally convicted', CON37/1/3, 605, Tasmanian Archive and Heritage Office, Hobart.

12. Unattributed, 'O'Connell, Sir Maurice Charles', from the Australian Dictionary of Biography: http://adb.anu.edu.au/biography/oconnell-sir-maurice-charles-2517/text3405

13. 'Courts martial', *New Zealander*, 11 October 1845, 4.

14. Burnett, *Penal Transportation*, 4–5.

15. John O'Donnell, 'Conduct register of males arriving on non-convict ships or locally convicted', CON37/1/6, 1925, Tasmanian Archive and Heritage Office, Hobart; William Brown, 'Conduct register of males arriving on non-convict ships or locally convicted', CON37/1/5, 1549, Tasmanian Archive and Heritage Office, Hobart.

16. William Lane, 'Indents of convicts locally convicted or transported from other colonies', CON16/1/3, 314, Tasmanian Archive and Heritage Office, Hobart; George Morris, 'Indents of convicts locally convicted or transported from other colonies', CON16/1/3, 314, Tasmanian Archive and Heritage Office, Hobart; John Bailey, 'Indents of convicts locally convicted or transported from other colonies', CON16/1/3, 314, Tasmanian Archive and Heritage Office, Hobart.
17. *New Zealand Spectator and Cook's Strait Guardian*, 10 June 1846, 2.
18. Trevor Bentley, *Pakeha Maori: The extraordinary story of the Europeans who lived as Maori in early New Zealand* (Auckland: Penguin Books, 1999), 76.
19. Phillip Hilton, 'Branded D on the left side': A study of former soldiers and marines transported to Van Diemen's Land, 1804–1854', PhD thesis, University of Tasmania, Hobart, 2010, 8, 140.
20. 'Auckland. Court martial', *New Zealand Spectator and Cook's Strait Guardian*, 14 October 1846, 3.
21. Unattributed, 'O'Connell, Sir Maurice Charles', from the Australian Dictionary of Biography.
22. 'Colonial governors, their qualifications and duties', *New Zealand Gazette and Wellington Spectator*, 3 July 1841, 3.
23. 'Auckland. Court martial', *New Zealand Spectator and Cook's Strait Guardian*, 14 October 1846, 3.
24. *New Zealander*, 1 June 1850, 2.
25. D.G. Edwards, 'Chapman, Henry Samuel', from the Dictionary of New Zealand Biography: www.TeAra.govt.nz/en/biographies/1c14/chapman-henry-samuel
26. 'Resident magistrate's court', *New Zealander*, 6 February 1847, 3.
27. Patrick Brady, 'Conduct register of males arriving on non-convict ships or locally convicted', CON37/1/5, 1469, Tasmanian Archive and Heritage Office, Hobart.
28. Hilton, 'Branded D on the left side', 174–76.
29. Lane, 'Indent', CON16/1/3, 314; Morris, 'Indent', CON16/1/3, 314; Bailey, 'Indent', CON16/1/3, 314.
30. Richard Shea, 'Indents of convicts locally convicted or transported from other colonies', CON16/1/3, 314, Tasmanian Archive and Heritage Office, Hobart.
31. 'Garrison court martial', *Sydney Morning Herald*, 6 January 1845, 2.
32. Timothy Causer, '"Only a place fit for angels and eagles": The Norfolk Island penal settlement, 1825–1855', PhD thesis, Menzies Centre for Australian Studies, King's College, London, 2009, 84.
33. Ibid., 18–19.
34. George Gipps to Lord Stanley, 23 February 1844, *Historical Records of Australia: Governors' despatches to and from England*, series I, vol. XXIII (Sydney: Library Committee of the Commonwealth Parliament, 1878), 417–18.
35. Godfrey Charles Mundy, *Our Antipodes; Or residence and rambles in the Australian colonies: with a glimpse of the gold fields.* (London: Richard Bentley, 1852), 112.
36. Causer, '"Only a place fit for angels and eagles"', 315.
37. Ibid., 316.

38. William Lane, 'Conduct register of males arriving on non-convict ships or locally convicted', CON37/1/3, 759, Tasmanian Archive and Heritage Office, Hobart.

39. George Morris, 'Conduct register of males arriving on non-convict ships or locally convicted', CON37/1/3, 760, Tasmanian Archive and Heritage Office, Hobart.

40. John Bailey, 'Conduct register of males arriving on non-convict ships or locally convicted', CON37/1/3, 761, Tasmanian Archive and Heritage Office, Hobart.

41. Richard Shea, 'Conduct register of males arriving on non-convict ships or locally convicted', CON37/1/3, 758, Tasmanian Archive and Heritage Office, Hobart.

42. Ibid.

43. Lane, 'Conduct register', CON37/1/3, 759.

44. William Lane and Rosina Morgan, 'Register of applications for permission to marry', CON52/1/6, RDG37/12, 292, Tasmanian Archive and Heritage Office, Hobart.

45. Rosina Morgan, 'Conduct registers of female convicts arriving in the period of the probation system', CON41/1/21, Tasmanian Archive and Heritage Office, Hobart.

46. Lane, 'Conduct register', CON37/1/3, 759.

47. Bailey, 'Conduct register', CON37/1/3, 761.

48. Morris, 'Conduct register', CON37/1/3, 760.

49. George Morris and Mary Ann Jackson, 'Register of applications for permission to marry', CON52/1/7, 298, Tasmanian Archive and Heritage Office, Hobart; Mary Ann Jackson, 'Conduct register of female convicts arriving in the period of the probation system', CON41/1/37, Tasmanian Archive and Heritage Office, Hobart.

50. Jackson, 'Conduct register', CON41/1/37.

51. *New Zealander*, 16 August 1849, 2.

52. Michael Tobin, 'Indents of convicts locally convicted or transported from other colonies', CON16/1/3, 390, Tasmanian Archive and Heritage Office, Hobart.

53. John Robinson, 'Indents of convicts locally convicted or transported from other colonies', CON16/1/3, 388, Tasmanian Archive and Heritage Office, Hobart.

54. Bernard McNally, 'Indents of convicts locally convicted or transported from other colonies', CON16/1/3, 388, Tasmanian Archive and Heritage Office, Hobart.

55. James (Isaac) Brearly, 'Indents of convicts locally convicted or transported from other colonies', CON16/1/3, 388, Tasmanian Archive and Heritage Office, Hobart.

56. Ron Crosby, *Kūpapa: The bitter legacy of Māori alliances with the Crown* (New Zealand: Penguin Random House, 2015), 8.

57. Vertrees Malherbe, 'How the Khoekhoen were drawn into the Dutch and British defensive systems, to c. 1809', *Military History Journal*, Vol. 12, No. 3, 2002, 96.

58. See in particular Henry Reynolds, *With the White People* (Ringwood, Victoria, Australia: Penguin, 1990); Shino Konishi, Maria Nugent and Tiffany Shellam (eds), *Indigenous Intermediaries: New perspectives on exploration archives*

(Canberra: ANU Press, 2015); Tiffany Shellam, Maria Nugent, Shino Konishi and Allison Cadzow (eds), *Brokers & Boundaries: Colonial expansion in indigenous territory* (Canberra: ANU Press, 2016); and Victoria Haskins, 'On the doorstep: Aboriginal domestic service as a "Contact Zone"', *Australian Feminist Studies*, vol. 16, no. 34, 2001, 13–25.

59. Ian Brand, *The Convict Probation System: Van Diemen's Land 1839–1854* (Hobart: Blubberhead Press, 1990), 170–71.

60. Bernard McNally, 'Conduct register of males arriving on non-convict ships or locally convicted', CON37/1/3, 931, Tasmanian Archive and Heritage Office, Hobart.

61. Bernard McNally and Ann Currie, 'Register of applications for permission to marry', CON52/1/7, 298, Tasmanian Archive and Heritage Office, Hobart.

62. Ann Currie, 'Conduct registers of female convicts arriving in the period of the probation system', CON41/1/37, Tasmanian Archive and Heritage Office, Hobart.

63. McNally, 'Conduct register', CON37/1/3, 931.

64. Bernard McNally, 'Deaths in the district of Hobart', RGD35/1/8, number 1742, Tasmanian Archive and Heritage Office, Hobart.

65. Michael Tobin, 'Conduct register of males arriving on non-convict ships or locally convicted', CON37/1/3, 934, Tasmanian Archive and Heritage Office, Hobart.

66. Michael Tobin and Elizabeth Bracken, 'Marriages in the district of Launceston', RGD37/1/17, number 536, Tasmanian Archive and Heritage Office, Hobart.

67. John Robinson, 'Conduct register of males arriving on non-convict ships or locally convicted', CON37/1/3, 932, Tasmanian Archive and Heritage Office, Hobart.

68. James (Isaac) Brearly, 'Conduct register of males arriving on non-convict ships or locally convicted', CON37/1/3, 932, Tasmanian Archive and Heritage Office, Hobart.

69. Patrick Shea, 'Conduct register of males arriving on non-convict ships or locally convicted', CON37/1/3, 930, Tasmanian Archive and Heritage Office, Hobart.

70. 'The captured bushrangers', *Hobarton Guardian, or, True Friend of Tasmania*, 22 March 1848, 5.

71. 'Oatlands criminal sessions', *Colonial Times*, 14 April 1848, 3.

72. 'Oatlands criminal sessions', *Colonial Times*, 18 April 1848, 3.

73. Shea, 'Conduct register', CON37/1/3, 930.

74. 'Supreme Court sittings', *New Zealand Spectator and Cook's Strait Guardian*, 5 September 1846, 3.

75. Henry Hodges, 'Conduct register of males arriving on non-convict ships or locally convicted', CON37/1/3, 928, Tasmanian Archive and Heritage Office, Hobart.

76. William Wright, 'Indents of convicts locally convicted or transported from other colonies', CON16/1/3, 516, Tasmanian Archive and Heritage Office, Hobart.

77. William Wright, 'Conduct register of males arriving on non-convict ships or locally convicted', CON37/1/5, 1439, Tasmanian Archive and Heritage Office, Hobart.

78. William Wright to the Colonial Secretary seeking remission of his sentence, 7 March 1853, and associated papers, IA1 133, 1854/1709, 53/13, Archives New Zealand, Wellington.

79. Register of Convicts Transported to Van Diemen's Land 25 November 1847–22 February 1853, NM11 1, Archives New Zealand, Wellington.

80. Wright, 'Conduct register', CON37/1/5, 1439.

81. 'Supreme Court, criminal sittings', *New Zealand Spectator and Cook's Strait Guardian*, 4 December 1852, 2.

82. James Woods, 'Conduct register of males arriving on non-convict ships or locally convicted', CON37/1/7, 2346, Tasmanian Archive and Heritage Office, Hobart.

83. Michael Morrissey, 'Conduct register of males arriving on non-convict ships or locally convicted', CON37/1/7, 2374, Tasmanian Archive and Heritage Office, Hobart.

CHAPTER 7

1. Robert Burnett, *Penal Transportation: An episode in New Zealand history* (Wellington: Victoria University of Wellington, 1978), 2. Also see *New Zealand Gazette and Wellington Spectator*, 6 June 1840, 2.

2. John Pratt, *Punishment in a Perfect Society: The New Zealand penal system 1840–1939* (Wellington: Victoria University Press, 1992), 38.

3. 'Court of quarter sessions', *New Zealand Gazette and Wellington Spectator*, 9 October 1841, 3.

4. Ibid.

5. Ibid.

6. Ibid. No trial record seems to have survived in relation to the defendant named as E'Wara.

7. 'Court of quarter sessions', *New Zealand Gazette and Wellington Spectator*, 8 January 1842, 3.

8. *New Zealand Gazette and Wellington Spectator*, 20 April 1842, 2.

9. 'Police court', *New Zealand Gazette and Wellington Spectator*, 24 May 1843, 2.

10. *Wellington Independent*, 7 May 1845, 3.

11. Ron Crosby, *The Musket Wars: A history of inter-iwi conflict 1806–45* (Auckland: Reed, 1999), 94.

12. Ibid., 95.

13. 'Public meeting at the Hutt', *New Zealand Spectator and Cook's Strait Guardian*, 12 October 1844, 4.

14. 'Militia ordinance', *Wellington Independent*, 9 April 1845, 3.

15. Justice Chapman, 'Notebook: Criminal trials No. 3', 1846, MS-0411/011, Hocken Collections, University of Otago, Dunedin, 2–57.

16. 'Supreme Court', *Wellington Independent*, 1 April 1846, 3.

17. 'An Epitome of Official Documents Relevant to Native Affairs and Land Purchases in the North Island of New Zealand', No. 2 H.T. Kemp, Esq., to the Chief

Protector, Report of Visit to Kaipara, Auckland, 24 March 1841, *New Zealand Electronic Text Collection/Te Pūhikotuhi o Aotearoa*: http://nzetc.victoria.ac.nz/tm/scholarly/tei-TurEpit-t1-g1-t2-g1-t2.html

18. 'Supreme Court', *Wellington Independent*, 1 April 1846, 3.

19. 'Supreme Court sittings, special commission', *New Zealand Spectator and Cook's Strait Guardian*, 4 April 1846, 3.

20. 'Supreme Court', *Wellington Independent*, 1 April 1846, 3.

21. 'Port Nicholson', *Nelson Examiner and New Zealand Chronicle*, 16 May 1846, 42.

22. Danny Keenan, *Wars Without End: The land wars in nineteenth-century New Zealand* (Auckland: Penguin, 2009), 154; James Belich, *The New Zealand Wars*, (Auckland: Penguin, 1998 [1986]), 73–74.

23. Crosby, *The Musket Wars*, 105–06.

24. Major Last to Governor Grey, 16 August 1846, *Wellington Independent*, 7 October 1846, 3; Edward Jerningham Wakefield, *Adventure in New Zealand* (Auckland: Golden Press, 1975), 97.

25. Ruth Wilkie, 'Te Umuroa, Hohepa: Biography', from the Dictionary of New Zealand Biography: www.TeAra.govt.nz/en/biographies/1t80/1; Major Last to Governor Grey, 16 August 1846, *Wellington Independent*, 7 October 1846, 3; 'Wellington', *New Zealander*, 10 April 1847, 3.

26. John Tattersall, *Maoris on Maria Island* (Napier: Hawke's Bay Museum & Art Gallery, 1973), 7; 'Execution of one of the rebels', *New Zealander*, 10 October 1846, 2; George Rusden, *History of New Zealand: Volume One* (Melbourne: Melville, Mullen & Sboye,1895), 411.

27. Tattersall, *Maoris on Maria Island*, 5.

28. *Wellington Independent*, 7 October 1846, 2. The correspondent's identity is unknown; however, it has been suggested that the argumentation in the letter emulates an earlier example of Bishop Selwyn's work. See E. Ellis, Turnbull Library, New Zealand, to T. Hume, 18 September 1972, NS 776/3/3, Archives New Zealand, Wellington.

29. *Wellington Independent*, 16 September 1846, 2; *Wellington Independent*, 14 October 1846, 2; 'Proceedings of Court Martial Maori Prisoners Captured at Pari Pari', IA1, NM 46/494, Archives New Zealand, Wellington.

30. 'Proceedings of Court Martial Maori Prisoners Captured at Pari Pari', IA1, NM 46/494, Archives New Zealand, Wellington.

31. 'Wanganui' (from our correspondent), *Wellington Independent*, 8 May 1847, 2.

32. Burnett, *Penal Transportation*, 4.

33. 'Proceedings of Court Martial'.

34. 'Proceedings of Court Martial'. Under the provisions of the Unsworn Testimony Ordinance, non-Christian Māori were allowed to make an affirmation before tendering legal evidence rather than being required to swear an oath on the Bible. See Robert Burnett, *'Hard Labour, Hard Fare and a Hard Bed': New Zealand's search for its own penal philosophy* (Wellington: National Archives of New Zealand, 1995), 33.

35. Tattersall, *Maoris on Maria Island*, 10–11.

Chapter 8

1. Kristyn Harman, *Aboriginal Convicts: Australian, Khoisan and Maori exiles* (Sydney: UNSW Press, 2012), 2, 66–67.

2. *Britannia and Trades' Advocate*, 19 November 1846, 2; 'Conduct register of males arriving on non-convict ships or locally convicted', CON37/1/7, 765–69, Tasmanian Archive and Heritage Office, Hobart; 'Indents of convicts locally convicted or transported from other colonies', CON 16/1/3, 312–15, Tasmanian Archive and Heritage Office, Hobart.

3. Governor George Grey to His Excellency, the Officer Administering the Government of Van Diemen's Land, 31 October 1846, enclosed with Despatch 34, 30 November 1846, CO280/197, Australian Joint Copying Project, Reels 545 & 546, 408–11, Tasmanian Archive and Heritage Office, Hobart.

4. 'Justice', 'To the Editor of the New Zealander', *New Zealander*, 7 November 1846, 2.

5. *Colonial Times and Tasmanian*, 13 November 1846, 4.

6. *Britannia and Trades' Advocate*, 19 November 1846, 2; *Colonial Times and Tasmanian*, 24 November 1846, 3.

7. 'New Zealand prisoners', *Hobart Town Courier and Government Gazette*, 25 November 1846, 2.

8. 'New Zealand prisoners', *Hobart Town Courier and Government Gazette*, 18 November 1846, 2.

9. 'Supreme Court sittings: Special Commission', *New Zealand Spectator and Cook's Strait Guardian*, 4 April 1846, 3.

10. James Brodie, 'Mason, Thomas: Biography', from the Dictionary of New Zealand Biography: www.TeAra.govt.nz/biographies/2m38/1; Mary Trott, 'Walker, George Washington (1800–1859)', from the Australian Dictionary of Biography: http://adb.anu.edu.au/biography/walker-george-washington-2764/text3923

11. *Colonial Times*, 27 November 1846, 3; 'New Zealand prisoners', *Hobart Town Courier and Government Gazette*, 25 November 1846, 2.

12. E. Simmons, *A Brief History of the Catholic Church in New Zealand* (Auckland: Catholic Publications Centre, 1978), 27.

13. Ngahuia Te Awekotuku with Linda Waimarie Nikora, *Mau Moko: The world of Māori tattoo* (Auckland: Penguin, 2007), 56.

14. Thomas Mason to Comptroller General of Convicts Hampton, 25 November 1846, and C.J. La Trobe to Earl Grey, 30 November 1846, Correspondence Files: Maoris, Tasmanian Archive and Heritage Office, Hobart.

15. Ibid.

16. Administrator La Trobe to Earl Grey, 30 November 1846, NS 776/1/4, Archives New Zealand, Wellington; 'The New Zealanders', *Hobart Town Courier and Government Gazette*, 28 November 1846, 2.

17. Colonial Office to Administrator La Trobe, 21 May 1847, NS 776/1/7, Archives New Zealand, Wellington.

18. Ian Brand, *The Convict Probation System: Van Diemen's Land 1839–1854* (Hobart: Blubber Head Press, 1990), 177–78.

19. Harman, *Aboriginal Convicts*, 178; 'The New Zealanders', *Hobart Town Courier and Government Gazette*, 28 November 1846, 2.
20. 'An old colonist', *Queenslander*, 25 May 1901, 1019.
21. Dawn Smith, 'The Strange Case of Dr J.J. Imrie', *Journal of the Nelson and Marlborough Historical Societies*, vol. 1, no. 5, October 1985: www.nzetc.org/tm/scholarly/tei-NHSJ04_05-t1-body1-d9.html
22. 'Family Group Sheet' supplied to the author by Greg Carlill, an Imrie descendant based in Brisbane, Australia.
23. Brand, *The Convict Probation System*, 133, 177, 236.
24. Transcript of the diary of J.J. Imrie while he was in charge of the Maori Exiles on Maria Island, 20 December 1846–25 March 1848 (Imrie Diary), NS 1093/1, Tasmanian Archive and Heritage Office, Hobart.
25. Ibid.
26. Imrie Diary.
27. Colonial Office to Governor George Grey, 7–8 May 1847, NS 776/1/5, Archives New Zealand, Wellington; Colonial Office to Administrator La Trobe, 31 May 1847, NS 776/1/6, Archives New Zealand, Wellington.
28. *Colonial Times*, 25 February 1848, 3; Imrie Diary.
29. *New Zealand Spectator and Cook's Strait Guardian*, 8 August 1849, 2.
30. Te Ahuru, 'Indents of convicts locally convicted or transported from other colonies', Hobart: Tasmanian Archive and Heritage Office, CON16/1/4, 246.
31. R v Te Ahuru, from 'New Zealand's lost cases', Victoria University of Wellington: www.victoria.ac.nz/law/nzlostcases/CaseDetails.aspx?casenumber=00717; Te Ahuru, 'Conduct register of males arriving on non-convict ships or locally convicted', CON37/1/7, 2205, Tasmanian Archive and Heritage Office, Hobart; Te Ahuru 'Indent', CON16/1/4, 246; Robert Burnett, *Penal Transportation: An episode in New Zealand history* (Wellington: Victoria University of Wellington, 1978), 25–26; Lieutenant-Governor Denison to Earl Grey, letter dated 15 January 1852 and enclosures, GO33/1/73, Tasmanian Archive and Heritage Office, Hobart.
32. John Tattersall, *Maoris on Maria Island* (Napier: Hawke's Bay Museum & Art Gallery, 1973).
33. Chris Heald, 'The lost son of Wanganui', *Listener*, 10 September 1988, 33–34.
34. David Creswell, 'Report on the repatriation of the remains of Hohepa Te Umuroa', ABHM 6097, W4678, Box 10, Archives New Zealand, Wellington.
35. Heald, 'The lost son of Wanganui', 34; Karen Sinclair, *Maori Times, Maori Places: Prophetic histories* (Wellington: Bridget Williams Books, 2002), 186.
36. Sinclair, '*Maori Times, Maori Places*, 185–87; Heald, 'The lost son of Wanganui', 34.
37. Andrew Darby, 'A warrior's people return for his spirit', *Age*, 2 August 1988, 1.
38. Heald, 'The lost son of Wanganui', 34.
39. Max Mariu, 'Te Awhitu, Wiremu Hakopa Toa: Biography', from the Dictionary of New Zealand Biography: www.TeAra.govt.nz/en/biographies/5t6/1; 'Maori warrior in final resting place', *Wanganui Chronicle*, 9 August 1988.
40. Sinclair, '*Maori Times, Maori Places*, 193, 256.

CHAPTER 9

1. *New Zealander*, 27 October 1847, 2.
2. Ibid.; Kristyn Harman, '"Some dozen raupo whares, and a few tents": Remembering raupo houses in colonial New Zealand', *Journal of New Zealand Studies*, vol. 17, 2014, 39–57.
3. *New Zealander*, 27 October 1847, 2; 'Horrible murders at Auckland', *Nelson Examiner and New Zealand Chronicle*, 4 December 1847, 155; Terry Carson, *The Axeman's Accomplice: The true story of Margaret Reardon and the Snow family murders* (Auckland: Alibi Press, 2016).
4. *New Zealander*, 27 October 1847, 2.
5. 'Horrible murders at Auckland', *Nelson Examiner and New Zealand Chronicle*, 4 December 1847, 155.
6. 'Coroner's inquest', *New Zealander*, 27 October 1847, 2.
7. Ibid.
8. 'Auckland extracts: The late murders', *Nelson Examiner and New Zealand Chronicle*, 11 December 1847, 1.
9. 'Auckland', *New Zealand Spectator and Cook's Strait Guardian*, 15 January 1848, 3.
10. John Pratt, *Punishment in a Perfect Society: The New Zealand penal system 1840–1939* (Wellington: Victoria University Press, 1992), 43.
11. 'Supreme Court', *New Zealander*, 4 March 1848, 3; Carson, *The Axeman's Accomplice*, 33.
12. 'Supreme Court', *New Zealander*, 4 March 1848, 3.
13. Ibid.
14. *New Zealander*, 11 March 1848, 2.
15. *New Zealander*, 4 March 1848, 2.
16. 'Resident magistrates' court', *New Zealander*, 8 March 1848, 2; 'Auckland', *Wellington Independent*, 19 April 1848, 2.
17. Ibid.
18. Ibid.
19. Kristyn Harman, 'Making Shift: Mary Ann Hodgkinson and hybrid domesticity in early colonial New Zealand', *New Zealand Journal of History*, vol. 48, no. 1, 2014, 30–50.
20. Janice Mogford, 'Joseph Burns, 1805–06?–1848', Te Ara – the Encylopedia of New Zealand: www.teara.govt.nz/en/biographies/1b51/burns-joseph
21. 'Resident magistrates' court', *New Zealander*, 8 March 1848, 2; 'Auckland', *Wellington Independent*, 19 April 1848, 2.
22. Ibid.
23. Carson, *The Axeman's Accomplice*, 52.
24. Ibid., 53.
25. Ibid.
26. 'Supreme Court', *New Zealander*, 3 June 1848, 2; *Anglo-Maori Warder*, 6 June 1848, 2; *New Zealand Spectator and Cook's Strait Guardian*, 15 July 1848, 2.
27. 'A murder by law', *Daily Southern Cross*, 17 June 1848, 2.

28. Carson, *The Axeman's Accomplice*, 95–97.

29. 'Execution of Joseph Burns', *New Zealander*, 21 June 1848, 2.

30. 'A murder by law', *Daily Southern Cross*, 17 June 1848, 2.

31. 'Execution of Joseph Burns', *New Zealander*, 21 June 1848, 2. Maketū was the first man hanged in the colony.

32. 'Exhumation of bodies in the old gaol', *New Zealand Herald*, 19 November 1866, 4. The author thanks David Verran for drawing this newspaper article to her attention.

33. 'Cemetery Records: Symonds Street and St Stephens', *Auckland City Library*: www. aucklandcity.govt.nz/dbtw-wpd/exec/dbtwpub.dll

34. Thomas Beckham, Resident Magistrate, Auckland, to the Colonial Secretary, letter dated 10 March 1848, IA1 66, 1848/502, Archives New Zealand, Wellington.

35. 'Supreme Court', *New Zealander*, 1 September 1848, 2.

36. *New Zealander*, 6 September 1848, 3.

37. *Anglo-Maori Warder*, 7 September 1848, 2.

38. Megan Simpson, 'R v Margaret Reardon, Supreme Court Auckland, 1 September 1848', *Victoria University of Wellington Law Review*, vol. 41, 2010, 103.

39. Carson, *The Axeman's Accomplice*, 90.

40. *Daily Southern Cross*, 14 October 1848, 1.

41. 'Casualty at sea', *Wellington Independent*, 7 October 1848, 3.

42. 'Narrow escape', *Nelson Examiner and New Zealand Chronicle*, 14 October 1848, 132.

43. 'Indents of convicts transported locally or from other colonies', CON16/1/3, 502–505, Tasmanian Archive and Heritage Office, Hobart.

44. *Anglo-Maori Warder*, 7 September 1848, 2.

45. *Wellington Independent*, 4 October 1848, 3.

46. *Wellington Independent*, 11 October 1848, 2.

47. 'Shipping intelligence: Departures', *New Zealand Spectator and Cook's Strait Guardian*, 11 October 1848, 2.

48. Liz Rushen, 'Margaret Reardon (1820?–1890)', Edges of Empire Biographical Dictionary: www.eoe.convictwomenspress.com.au/index.php/biographical-dictionary/22-r/144-reardon-margaret; Carson, *The Axeman's Accomplice*, 82.

49. Margaret Reardon, 'Indents of convicts locally convicted or transported from other colonies', CON16/1/5, 46, Tasmanian Archive and Heritage Office, Hobart; 'Law intelligence', *Sydney Morning Herald*, 2 September 1842, 2.

50. Ian Brand, Appendix V: 'Regulations of the probationary establishment for female convicts in Van Diemen's Land, *The Convict Probation System: Van Dieman's Land 1839–1854* (Hobart: Blubber Head Press, 1991), 242–51.

51. Gay Hendriksen, 'Women transported: Myth and reality', in Gay Hendriksen, Trudy Cowley & Carol Liston (eds), *Women Transported: Life in Australia's convict female factories* (Sydney: Parramatta Heritage Centre, 2012), 7.

52. Brad Williams, 'The archaeological potential of colonial prison hulks: The Tasmanian case study', *Bulletin for the Australasian Institute for Maritime Archaeology*, vol. 29, 2005, 80.

53. 'The *Anson*', *Cornwall Chronicle*, 6 November 1844, 2.
54. 'The "Anson"', *Launceston Examiner*, 22 September 1847, 3.
55. Kirsty Reid, *Gender, Crime and Empire: Convicts, settlers and the state in early colonial Australia* (Manchester: Manchester University Press, 2007), 179.
56. Margaret Reardon, 'Conduct registers of female convicts arriving in the period of the assignment system', CON40/1/8, 292, Tasmanian Archive and Heritage Office, Hobart.
57. J.C. Byrne, *Twelve Years Wandering in the British Colonies, from 1835 to 1847, vol. 1* (London: R. Bentley, 1848), 230–31.
58. *Sydney Herald*, 13 May 1839, 2.
59. Kay Daniels, *Convict Women* (St Leonards: Allen & Unwin, 1998), ix.
60. Trudy Cowley, 'Female factories of Van Diemen's Land', in Hendriksen, Cowley & Liston (eds), *Women Transported*, 54, 59–63.
61. Brand, Appendix V, 242–51.
62. Ibid.
63. Reardon, 'Conduct register', CON40/1/8, 292.
64. Margaret Reardon and William Redman, 'Register of applications for permission to marry', CON52/1/3, 381, Tasmanian Archive and Heritage Office, Hobart.
65. Rushen, 'Margaret Reardon'.

CONCLUSION

1. Francis Butcher, 'Conduct register of males arriving on non-convict ships or locally convicted', CON37/1/6, 2097, Tasmanian Archive and Heritage Office, Hobart.
2. 'Supreme Court', *New Zealander*, 5 March 1851, 3.
3. 'Supreme Court', *Daily Southern Cross*, 7 March 1851, 2.
4. Heke, 'Conduct register of males arriving on non-convict ships or locally convicted', CON37/1/6, 2098, Tasmanian Archive and Heritage Office, Hobart.
5. Henry Reynolds, *A History of Tasmania* (Cambridge: Cambridge University Press, 2011), 143–45.
6. Lloyd Robson, *A Short History of Tasmania* (Oxford: Oxford University Press, 1985), 33.
7. Robert Burnett, *Penal Transportation: An episode in New Zealand history* (Wellington: Victoria University of Wellington, 1978), 37; 'Supreme Court', *Wellington Independent*, 12 March 1853, 3.
8. *Maori Messenger: Te Karere Maori*, 1 January 1855, 10.
9. Robert Burnett, *"Hard Labour, Hard Fare and a Hard Bed": New Zealand's search for its own penal philosophy* (Wellington: National Archives of New Zealand, 1995), 32.
10. Kristyn Harman and Hamish Maxwell-Stewart, 'Aboriginal deaths in custody in colonial Australia, 1805–1860s', *Journal of Colonialism & Colonial History*, vol. 13, no. 2, 2012. DOI: 10.1353/cch.2012.0023.

11. Henry Reynolds, *A History of Tasmania* (Cambridge: Cambridge University Press, 2011), 140.

12. Miles Fairburn, *The Ideal Society and Its Enemies: Foundations of modern New Zealand society, 1850–1900* (Auckland: Auckland University Press, 2013), 38.

13. *New Zealand Colonist and Port Nicholson Advertiser*, 12 May 1843, 3.

14. 'Runaways', *New Zealand Gazette and Wellington Spectator*, 14 October 1843, 2.

15. 'County court', *New Zealand Gazette and Wellington Spectator*, 1 March 1843, 3. This is the session at which the two Clarke 'brothers' appeared who were transported to Van Diemen's Land on the *Portenia* and were found on their arrival at Hobart to be convict absconders.

16. R v John Fling, from New Zealand's Lost Cases: www.victoria.ac.nz/law/nzlostcases/CaseDetails.aspx?casenumber=00086; John Fling, 'Conduct register of males arriving on non-convict ships or locally convicted', CON37/1/3, 832, Tasmanian Archive and Heritage Office, Hobart.

17. 'Port Nicholson', *Nelson Examiner and New Zealand Chronicle*, 20 August 1842, 95.

18. 'Supreme Court', *Daily Southern Cross*, 9 September 1848, 3.

19. Jonathan Pellett, 'Conduct register of males arriving on non-convict ships or locally convicted', CON37/1/4, 1334, Tasmanian Archive and Heritage Office, Hobart; Jonathan Pellett, 'Indents of convicts locally convicted or transported from other colonies', CON16/1/3, 502, Tasmanian Archive and Heritage Office, Hobart.

20. Megan Simpson, 'R v Margaret Reardon, Supreme Court Auckland, 1 September 1848', *Victoria University of Wellington Law Review*, vol. 41, 2010, 99.

21. 'Transportation to Van Diemen's Land', *New Zealander*, 31 January 1849, 3.

22. 'Meeting to oppose convictism in New Zealand', *Nelson Examiner and New Zealand Chronicle*, 20 October 1849, 130.

23. *New Zealander*, 16 August 1849, 2.

24. Ibid.

25. Ibid.

26. Burnett, *Penal Transportation*, 43–44, Appendix B.

Bibliography

Primary

Archival and manuscripts

Archives New Zealand
ABHM Political papers
IA1 Central filing system
NM8 Colonial Secretary's inwards correspondence
NM11 Colonial Treasurer general outwards correspondence
Series 6029 Wellington probate files

New Zealand's Lost Cases, Victoria University of Wellington
R v John Fling: www.victoria.ac.nz/law/nzlostcases/CaseDetails.
    aspx?casenumber=00086
R v Te Ahuru: www.victoria.ac.nz/law/nzlostcases/CaseDetails.
    aspx?casenumber=00717
R v Thomas Larkins: www.victoria.ac.nz/law/nzlostcases/CaseDetails.
    aspx?casenumber=00487
Salmon v. Pickering: www.victoria.ac.nz/law/nzlostcases/CaseDetails.
    aspx?casenumber=00212

Old Bailey Online
Trial of James Thompson and John Jones, 6 January 1840 (t18400106-504)
Trial of George Bottomley, 16 December 1839 (t18391216-314)
Trial of Henry Butler Dowie, 18 June 1838 (t18380618-1486)

State Archives & Records New South Wales
4/4320 Certificates of Freedom
10958 Victoria Police Gazette
NRS 12188 Bound Indentures
NRS 12189 Annotated Printed Indentures

Tasmanian Archive and Heritage Office
CO280 Colonial Office
CON15 Indents of female convicts
CON16 Indents of convicts locally convicted or transported from other colonies
CON19 Description lists
CON33 Conduct registers of male convicts arriving in the period of the probation
    system
CON37 Conduct registers of males arriving on non-convict ships or locally convicted

CON40 Conduct registers of female convicts arriving in the period of the assignment
    system
CON41 Conduct registers of female convicts arriving in the period of the probation
    system
CON52 Registers of applications for permission to marry
Correspondence files: Maoris
GO33 Governor's duplicate despatches received by the Colonial Office
NS776 Material relating to Maoris transported to Van Diemen's Land, 1846
NS1093 Copy of the diary of Dr Imrie while he was in charge of the Maori exiles on
    Maria Island
RGD35 Deaths in the district of Hobart
RGD37 Marriages in the district of Launceston

Others

3595, Marriage Certificates, Registrar of Births, Deaths, and Marriages, Melbourne,
    Victoria
MS-0411/011, Chapman, Justice. 'Notebook: Criminal trials No. 3', 1846, Hocken
    Collections, University of Otago, Dunedin
Q/Gc/5/6, Register of Prisoners, Gloucestershire Archives, Gloucestershire Prison
    Collections, Gloucester, England
V184682 31C, Marriage Certificates, Registrar of Births, Deaths, and Marriages,
    Sydney, New South Wales

OFFICIAL

'A List of Ordinances Relevant to the Courts in New Zealand During the 1840s': www.
    victoria.ac.nz/law/nzlostcases/Ordinances_1840s.aspx
'Cemetery Records: Symonds Street and St Stephens', *Auckland City Library*: www.
    aucklandcity.govt.nz/dbtw-wpd/exec/dbtwpub.dll
Hardie, Bruce, *Statistics of New Zealand for the Crown Colony Period 1840–1852*,
    Auckland: Auckland University College, Department of Economics, 1955

NEWSPAPERS

Australian newspapers
Age, 1988
Australasian Chronicle, 1841–43
Banner, 1854
Bendigo Advertiser, 1863
Colonial Times, 1832–48
Colonist, 1838
Cornwall Chronicle, 1835–44
Hobart Town Courier, 1828–43
Hobart Town Courier and Government Gazette, 1846

Hobarton Guardian, or, True Friend of Tasmania, 1848
Launceston Advertiser, 1830–39
Launceston Examiner, 1843–89
Perth Gazette and Western Australian Journal, 1834
Queenslander, 1901
Star, 1863
Sydney Herald, 1839
Sydney Monitor, 1837
Sydney Morning Herald, 1842–57
Tasmanian Daily News, 1855
The Colonist and Van Diemen's Land Commercial and Agricultural Advertiser, 1834

New Zealand newspapers
Anglo-Maori Warder, 1848
Britannia and Trades' Advocate, 1846
Daily Southern Cross, 1843–51
Evening Post, 1877
Lyttelton Times, 1853
Maori Messenger: Te Karere Maori, 1855
Nelson Examiner and New Zealand Chronicle, 1842–49
New Zealand Colonist and Port Nicholson Advertiser, 1842–43
New Zealand Gazette and Wellington Spectator, 1839–44
New Zealand Herald, 1866
New Zealand Herald and Auckland Gazette, 1841
New Zealand Spectator and Cook's Strait Guardian, 1844–52
New Zealander, 1845–51
Taranaki Herald, 1853
Te Karere o Nui Tireni 1842–44
Wanganui Chronicle, 1988
Wellington Independent, 1845–71

OTHER PUBLICATIONS
'An Epitome of Official Documents Relevant to Native Affairs and Land Purchases in the North Island of New Zealand', no. 2, H.T. Kemp, Esq., to the Chief Protector, Report of Visit to Kaipara, Auckland, 24 March 1841, *New Zealand Electronic Text Collection/Te Pūhikotuhi o Aotearoa*: http://nzetc.victoria.ac.nz/tm/scholarly/tei-TurEpit-t1-g1-t2-g1-t2.html
Ancestry.com, *Tasmania, Australia, Convict Court and Selected Records, 1800–1899* [database online]. Provo, UT, USA: Ancestry.com Operations, Inc., 2015. Original data: Tasmanian Colonial Convict, Passenger and Land Records. Various collections (30 series). Tasmanian Archive and Heritage Office, Hobart.
Angas, George French, *Savage Life and Scenes of Australia and New Zealand, vol. 1* (Adelaide: Libraries Board of South Australia, 1969 facsimile edn).

Bullers, Rick, *Convict Probation and the Evolution of Jetties at Cascades, the Coal Mines, Impression Bay and Saltwater River, Tasman Peninsula, Tasmania: An historical perspective* (South Australia: Department of Archaeology, Flinders University, 2005).

Byrne, J.C., *Twelve Years Wandering in the British Colonies, from 1835 to 1847, vol. 1* (London: R. Bentley, 1848).

Derrincourt, William, edited by Louis Becke, *Old Convict Days* (Harmondsworth, UK: Penguin, 1975 [1899]).

Heald, Chris, 'The lost son of Wanganui', *Listener*, 10 September 1988, 33–34.

Historical Records of Australia: Governors' despatches to and from England, series I, vol. XXIII (Sydney: Library Committee of the Commonwealth Parliament, 1878).

McClure, Margaret, 'Auckland Region – The Founding of Auckland: 1840–1869', Te Ara – the Encyclopedia of New Zealand: www.TeAra.govt.nz/en/auckland-region/page-7

Mundy, Godfrey Charles, *Our Antipodes; Or residence and rambles in the Australian colonies: with a glimpse of the gold fields* (London: Richard Bentley, 1852).

Review of Martyn Payne, *The Institutes of Medicine* (New York: Harper & Brothers, 1858) in *Dublin Quarterly Journal of Medical Science* 28, 1859, 444.

Rusden, George, *History of New Zealand, vol. 1* (Melbourne: Melville, Mullen & Sboye, 1895).

Unattributed, 'Neighbours: Early beginnings in Australasian Jewry' (Sydney: AM Rosenblum Jewish Museum): http://jewishonlinemuseum.org/neighbours-early beginnings-australasian-jewry

Wakefield, Edward Jerningham, *Adventure in New Zealand* (Auckland: Golden Press, 1975).

Secondary

Books

Alexander, Alison, *Tasmania's Convicts: How felons build a free society* (Crows Nest, NSW: Allen & Unwin, 2014).

Anderson, Atholl, Judith Binney & Aroha Harris (eds), *Tangata Whenua: An illustrated history* (Wellington: Bridget Williams Books, 2014).

Bairstow, Damaris, *A Million Pounds, a Million Acres: The pioneer settlement of the Australian Agricultural Company* (Sydney: D. Bairstow, 2003).

Ballantyne, Tony, *Entanglements of Empire: Missionaries, Māori, and the question of the body* (Auckland: Auckland University Press, 2015).

Barnard, Simon, *Convict Tattoos: Marked men and women of Australia* (Melbourne: Text, 2016).

Belich, James, *The New Zealand Wars* (Auckland: Penguin Books, 1998).

Bentley, Trevor, *Pakeha Maori: The extraordinary story of the Europeans who lived as Maori in early New Zealand* (Auckland: Penguin Books, 1999).

——, *Tribal Guns and Tribal Gunners: The story of Māori artillery in 19th century New Zealand* (Christchurch: Willsonscott, 2013).

Boyce, James, *1835: The founding of Melbourne and the conquest of Australia* (Melbourne: Black Inc., 2013).

Brand, Ian, *The Convict Probation System: Van Diemen's Land 1839–1854* (Hobart: Blubber Head Press, 1990).

Brett, André, *Acknowledge No Frontier: The creation and demise of New Zealand's provinces, 1853–76* (Dunedin: Otago University Press, 2016).

Brodie, Nick, *The Vandemonian War: The secret history of Britain's Tasmanian invasion* (Melbourne: Hardie Grant Books, 2017).

Broome, Richard, *Aboriginal Australians: Black responses to white dominance, 1788–2001* (New South Wales: Allen & Unwin, 2001).

Buddee, Paul, *Fate of the Artful Dodger: Parkhurst boys transported to Australia and New Zealand, 1842–1852* (Perth: St George Books, 1984).

Burnett, Robert, *Penal Transportation: An episode in New Zealand history* (Wellington: Victoria University of Wellington, 1978).

——, *'Hard Labour, Hard Fare and a Hard Bed': New Zealand's search for its own penal philosophy* (Wellington: National Archives of New Zealand, 1995).

Carson, Terry, *The Axeman's Accomplice: The true story of Margaret Reardon and the Snow family murders* (Auckland: Alibi Press, 2016).

Clements, Nicholas, *The Black War: Fear, sex and resistance in Tasmania* (St Lucia: University of Queensland Press, 2014).

Crosby, Ron, *The Musket Wars: A history of inter-iwi conflict 1806–45* (Auckland: Reed, 1999).

——, *Kūpapa: The bitter legacy of Māori alliances with the Crown* (New Zealand: Penguin Random House, 2015).

Daniels, Kay, *Convict Women* (St Leonards: Allen & Unwin, 1998).

Drummond Alison & L.R. Drummond, *At Home in New Zealand: An illustrated history of everyday things before 1865* (Auckland: Blackwood & Janet Paul, 1967).

Fairburn, Miles, *The Ideal Society and its Enemies: Foundations of modern New Zealand society, 1850–1900* (Auckland: Auckland University Press, 2013).

Harman, Kristyn, *Aboriginal Convicts: Australian, Khoisan, and Māori exiles* (Sydney: University of New South Wales Press, 2012).

Keenan, Danny, *Wars Without End: The land wars in nineteenth-century New Zealand* (Auckland: Penguin, 2009).

Kerr, James Semple, *Design for Convicts: An account of design for convict establishments in the Australian colonies during the transportation era* (Sydney: Library of Australian History, 1984).

Konishi, Shino, Maria Nugent & Tiffany Shellam (eds), *Indigenous Intermediaries: New perspectives on exploration archives* (Canberra: Australian National University Press, 2015).

O'Malley, Vincent, *Beyond the Imperial Frontier: The contest for colonial New Zealand* (Wellington: Bridget Williams Books, 2014).

Orange, Claudia, *The Treaty of Waitangi* (Wellington: Allen & Unwin, 1987).

Palenski, Ron, *The Making of New Zealanders* (Auckland: Auckland University Press, 2012).

Petersen, Anna, *New Zealanders at Home: A cultural history of domestic interiors, 1814–1914* (Dunedin: Otago University Press, 2001).

Petrie, Hazel, *Chiefs of Industry: Māori tribal enterprise in early colonial New Zealand* (Auckland: Auckland University Press, 2007).

——, *Outcasts of the Gods? The struggle over slavery in Māori New Zealand* (Auckland: Auckland University Press, 2015).

Plomley, Brian (ed.), *Weep in Silence: A history of the Flinders Island Aboriginal settlement* (Hobart: Blubber Head Press, 1987).

——, *Friendly Mission: The Tasmanian journals and papers of George Augustus Robinson 1829–1834*, 2nd edn (Launceston: Queen Victoria Museum and Art Gallery & Quintus Publishing, 2008).

Pratt, John, *Punishment in a Perfect Society: The New Zealand penal system 1840–1939* (Wellington: Victoria University Press, 1992).

Reid, Kirsty, *Gender, Crime and Empire: Convicts, settlers and the state in early colonial Australia* (Manchester: Manchester University Press, 2007).

Reynolds, Henry, *With the White People* (Ringwood, Victoria, Australia: Penguin, 1990).

——, *The Other Side of the Frontier: Aboriginal resistance of the European invasion of Australia* (Victoria: Penguin, 1995).

——, *A History of Tasmania* (Cambridge: Cambridge University Press, 2011).

Robson, Lloyd, *A Short History of Tasmania* (Oxford: Oxford University Press, 1985).

Shaw, Alan, *Convicts & the Colonies: A study of penal transportation from Great Britain & Ireland to Australia & other parts of the British Empire* (Melbourne: Melbourne University Press, 1966, 1998).

Shellam, Tiffany, Maria Nugent, Shino Konishi & Allison Cadzow (eds), *Brokers & Boundaries: Colonial expansion in indigenous territory* (Canberra: Australian National University Press, 2016).

Simmons, E., *A Brief History of the Catholic Church in New Zealand* (Auckland: Catholic Publications Centre, 1978).

Sinclair, Karen, *Maori Times, Maori Places: Prophetic histories* (Wellington: Bridget Williams Books, 2002).

Tattersall, John, *Maoris on Maria Island* (Napier: Hawke's Bay Museum & Art Gallery, 1973).

Te Awekotuku, Ngahuia with Linda Waimarie Nikora, *Mau Moko: The world of Māori tattoo* (Auckland: Penguin, 2007).

Wanhalla, Angela, *In/visible Sight: The mixed-descent families of Southern New Zealand* (Wellington: Bridget Williams Books, 2009).

Wards, Ian, *The Shadow of the Land: A study of British policy and racial conflict in New Zealand 1832–1852* (Wellington: Department of Internal Affairs, 1968).

ARTICLES AND BOOK CHAPTERS

Brodie, Nicholas, 'Quaker dreaming: The "lost" archive and the Aborigines of Van Diemen's Land', *Journal of Religious History*, vol. 40, no. 3, 2016, 303–25.

Cowley, Trudy, 'Female factories of Van Diemen's Land', in *Women Transported: Life in Australia's convict female factories*, Gay Hendriksen, Trudy Cowley & Carol Liston (eds) (Sydney: Parramatta Heritage Centre, 2012), 53–68.

Edmonds, Penelope, 'Collecting Looerryminer's "testimony": Aboriginal women, sealers, and Quaker humanitarian anti-slavery thought and action in the Bass Strait Islands', *Australian Historical Studies*, vol. 45, no. 1, 2014, 18–22.

Floud, Roderick & Kenneth Wachter, 'Poverty and physical stature: Evidence on the standard of living of London boys 1770–1870', *Social Science History*, vol. 6, no. 4, 1982, 424.

Hannah, Mark, 'Aboriginal workers in the Australian Agricultural Company, 1824–1857', *Labour History* 82, 2002, 17–33.

Harman, Kristyn, '"Some dozen raupo whares and a few tents": Remembering raupo houses in colonial New Zealand', *Journal of New Zealand Studies*, vol. 17, 2014, 39–57.

——, 'Making shift: Mary Ann Hodgkinson and hybrid domesticity in early colonial New Zealand', *New Zealand Journal of History*, vol. 48, no. 1, 2014, 30–50.

Harman, Kristyn & Hamish Maxwell-Stewart, 'Aboriginal deaths in custody in colonial Australia, 1805–1860s', *Journal of Colonialism & Colonial History*, vol. 13, no. 2, 2012, DOI: 10.1353/cch.2012.0023.

Haskins, Victoria, 'On the doorstep: Aboriginal domestic service as a "contact zone"', *Australian Feminist Studies*, vol. 16, no. 34, 2001, 13–25.

Hendriksen, Gay, 'Women transported: Myth and reality', in Gay Hendriksen, Trudy Cowley & Carol Liston (eds), *Women Transported: Life in Australia's convict female factories* (Sydney: Parramatta Heritage Centre, 2012).

Huglin, Heidi, 'New Zealand's early convict history 1843–1853', *Legacy*, vol. 21, no.1, 2009, 10–14.

Jackman, Greg, 'Get thee to church: Hard work, godliness and tourism at Australia's first rural reformatory', *Australasian Historical Archaeology*, 19, 2001, 6–13.

Jordan, Thomas, '"Stay and starve, or go and prosper!" Juvenile emigration from Great Britain in the nineteenth century', *Social Science History*, vol. 9, no. 2, 1985, 145–66.

Malherbe, Vertrees, 'How the Khoekhoen were drawn into the Dutch and British defensive systems, to c. 1809', *Military History Journal*, vol. 12, no. 3, 2002, 94–99.

Mossong, Verna, 'Colonial chains: Convicts from New Zealand to Tasmania, Australia', in Garry Jeffery (ed.), *Landfall in Southern Seas: Proceedings of the 8th Australasian congress on genealogy and heraldry* (Christchurch: New Zealand Society of Genealogists, 1997), 125–37.

Renwick, Margery, 'The Karori Hotel', *Stockade* 43, 2011, 11–16.

Shore, Heather, 'Transportation, penal ideology and the experience of juvenile offenders in England and Australia in the nineteenth century', *Crime, History & Societies*, vol. 6, no. 2, 2002, 81–102.

Simpson, Megan, 'R v Margaret Reardon, Supreme Court Auckland, 1 September 1848', *Victoria University of Wellington Law Review* 41, 2010, 99–106.

Smith, Dawn, 'The strange case of Dr J.J. Imrie', *Journal of the Nelson and Marlborough Historical Societies*, vol. 1, no. 5, 1985: www.nzetc.org/tm/scholarly/tei-NHSJ04_05-t1-body1-d9.html

White, Rob, 'Prisons', in Alison Alexander (ed.), *The Companion to Tasmanian History* (Hobart: Centre for Tasmanian Historical Studies, 2006), 289–90.

Williams, Brad, 'The archaeological potential of colonial prison hulks: The Tasmanian case study', *Bulletin for the Australasian Institute for Maritime Archaeology* 29, 2005, 77–86.

UNPUBLISHED THESES

Causer, Timothy, '"Only a place fit for angels and eagles": The Norfolk Island penal settlement, 1825–1855', PhD thesis, Menzies Centre for Australian Studies, King's College, London, 2009.

Hilton, Phillip, 'Branded D on the left side: A study of former soldiers and marines transported to Van Diemen's Land, 1804–1854', PhD thesis, University of Tasmania, Hobart, 2010.

DICTIONARIES OF BIOGRAPHY

Barton, G.P., 'Martin, William', from the Dictionary of New Zealand Biography: www.TeAra.govt.nz/en/biographies/1m21/martin-william

Bremner, Julie, 'Barrett, Richard', from the Dictionary of New Zealand Biography: www.TeAra.govt.nz/en/biographies/1b10/barrett-richard

Brodie, James, 'Mason, Thomas: Biography', from the Dictionary of New Zealand Biography: http://www.TeAra.govt.nz/biographies/2m38/1

Edwards, D.G., 'Chapman, Henry Samuel', from the Dictionary of New Zealand Biography: www.TeAra.govt.nz/en/biographies/1c14/chapman-henry-samuel

Fairburn, Miles, 'Wakefield, Edward Gibbon', from the Dictionary of New Zealand Biography: www. TeAra.govt.nz/en/biographies/1w4/wakefield-edward-gibbon

Fitzpatrick, Kathleen, 'Franklin, Sir John' from the Australian Dictionary of Biography: http://adb.anu.edu.au/biography/franklin-sir-john-2066/text2575

Flinn, E., 'Bowen, John (1780–1827)', from the Australian Dictionary of Biography: http://adb.anu.edu.au/biography/bowen-john-1811/text2065

Mariu, Max, 'Te Awhitu, Wiremu Hakopa Toa: Biography', from the Dictionary of New Zealand Biography: www.TeAra.govt.nz/en/biographies/5t6/1

McMillan, N.A.C., 'Tempsky, Gustavus Ferninand von', from the Dictionary of New Zealand Biography: www.teara.govt.nz/en/biographies/1t90/tempsky-gustavus-ferdinand-von

Mogford, Janice, 'Joseph Burns, 1805–06?–1848', Te Ara – the Encylopedia of New Zealand: www.teara.govt.nz/en/biographies/1b51/burns-joseph

Oliver, Steven, 'Maketu, Wirimu Kingi', from the Dictionary of New Zealand
    Biography: www.TeAra.govt.nz/en/biographies/1m5/maketu-wirimu-kingi
Paszkowski, L.K., 'Blandowski, William (1822–1878)', from the Australian Dictionary
    of Biography: http://adb.anu.edu.au/biography/blandowski-william-3014/
    text4413
Rushen, Liz, 'Margaret Reardon (1820?–1890), from the Edges of Empire Biographical
    Dictionary: www.eoe.convictwomenspress.com.au/index.php/biographical-
    dictionary/22-r/144-reardon-margaret
Simpson, K.A., 'Hobson, William', from the Dictionary of New Zealand Biography:
    www.TeAra.govt.nz/en/biographies/1h29/hobson-william
Stone, R.C.J., 'Whitaker, Frederick', from the Dictionary of New Zealand Biography:
    www.TeAra.govt.nz/en/biographies/1w17/whitaker-frederick
Tapp, E.J., 'Hobson, William (1793–1842)', from the Australian Dictionary of
    Biography: http://adb.anu.edu.au/biography/hobson-william-2189
Trott, Mary, 'Walker, George Washington (1800–1859)', from the Australian Dictionary
    of Biography: http://adb.anu.edu.au/biography/walker-george-washington-2764/
    text3923
Unattributed, 'O'Connell, Sir Maurice Charles', from the Australian Dictionary of
    Biography: http://adb.anu.edu.au/biography/oconnell-sir-maurice-charles-2517/
    text3405
Wilkie, Ruth, 'Te Umuroa, Hōhepa: Biography', from the Dictionary of New Zealand
    Biography: www.TeAra.govt.nz/en/biographies/1t80/1

INDEX

Page numbers in **bold** refer to illustrations.